THE WORD MADE FLESH

AN OVERVIEW OF THE CATHOLIC FAITH

Anthony Marinelli

Paulist Press ▪ *New York/Mahwah, N.J.*

Artwork by Larry Nolte.

Nihil obstat: Rev. Francis J. Schneider
Censor librorum
May 8th, 1992

Imprimatur: Most Reverend John R. McGann, D.D.
Bishop of Rockville Centre
May 12th 1992

Library of Congress Cataloging-in-Publication Data

Marinelli, Anthony J.
    The Word made flesh : an overview of the Catholic Faith / by Anthony Marinelli.
        p.   cm.
    ISBN 0-8091-3391-1 (pbk.)
    1. Catholic Church—Doctrines.   I. Title.
BX1751.2.M335   1993
282—dc20
                                                    92-45629
                                                    CIP

Published by Paulist Press
997 Macarthur Boulevard
Mahwah, NJ 07430

Printed and bound in the
United States of America

Contents

*This book is dedicated to
Charlie Biss and Jack McHale,
in gratitude for a lifetime of friendship.*

Introduction

This book is an attempt to summarize the essentials of Catholic Christian faith for those without any sophisticated background in theology. It is written specifically for young adults, older teens and those who are young at heart.

The text of the book is meant to explain as clearly as possible the meaning of Christian faith. The questions for personal reflection and discussion hope to help the reader to make connections between the faith of the church and his or her own personal experience. They are an essential ingredient in the book and should not always be skipped over to get to the "meat" of the matter.

This book has certain accents or emphases. First and foremost, the book is unabashedly christocentric. Whenever and wherever possible, the book tries to connect the various topics to the person of Jesus Christ and to understand them in relation to him.

Second, the book places heavy emphasis on scripture as a foundation for contemporary faith. Yet it treats the word of God as a living word which must come alive for every age and generation.

Third, this book seeks to take seriously the historical dimension of faith, and tries to locate the church and sacraments in an historical perspective.

Finally, the book tries to maintain a healthy and creative tension between faith as "belief" and as lived experience.

I would like to thank a special group of people who helped give me the freedom to write this book. First, my wife Pat, who changed many diapers without my help; next, my daughters Christine and Caitlin, who gave up a large part of their usual summer fare so daddy could work on his book. I would also like

1

to thank my friend and colleague, Jack Lannig, who was nice enough to go on vacation and leave me his house as a workplace. I thank my mother Julia who proofread a good deal of the text and corrected my grammar and offered some valuable ideas. Finally, I thank my students at Holy Trinity High School who provide the laboratory for trying out these ideas and who continually challenge me to be a better teacher.

It is my hope that this book may offer its readers a tiny glimpse into a profoundly beautiful mystery: God's love for them in Jesus Christ.

1

Religion and the Art
of Being Fully Human

"CHURCH IS BORING"

This book is all about Catholic Christian faith. If your first impulse is to yawn, I would like to ask why. Why is it that many young people find religion boring? Here are the top three answers that I have received from my students concerning this question:

1. *"It's boring because you go to church every week and hear the same thing being said.*
2. *"It's boring because it really has nothing to do with my **real** life.*
3. *"It's boring because it's just not for teenagers. Maybe when I get older I'll be more interested, but now I've got other things to worry about."*

Now I can't promise you to make sermons better in your parish, but this book is written with the conviction that religion is very much for teenagers. However, it is very often a different notion of religion than most accept. First, let's begin by admitting that **religion can indeed be boring and lifeless. In fact, this was one of the main problems that Jesus faced when he was on this earth.** Some of the religious leaders of the time had turned the faith of Israel into a system of laws and rules and lost its heart and soul. It was a lifeless religion lived only by a certain elite group. But for the common, everyday person, it was a system that

3

often asked for more than they could possibly deliver. Jesus was born and raised as a Jew. He read the Hebrew scriptures and found in them a God who called his people to live their lives with passion, joy, mercy, courage and love. **For Jesus, religion was all about life and how it was meant to be lived with an open heart and a giving soul.**

For Personal Reflection and Discussion

Of course, not all young people find religion boring, but many do. Where do you fit into the debate? Is your faith boring? Why or why not? What can you do to make it less boring? If you could give your local pastor one piece of advice on how to make faith appeal to young adults, what would you tell him?

RELIGION AS A "SYSTEM"

Sometimes religious leaders take the heart out of religion and turn it into a "system" of rules and obligations. There is nothing wrong with many of these rules. In fact they can be very important, but they are not at the heart of religious faith. **Too many Catholics have been taught that their religion is really a system that eventually will get them to heaven.** All you have to do is learn how to play the game. Here's a short outline of how the game is played:

1. Get baptized.
2. Receive first penance (get sins removed for first communion).
3. Receive first communion.
4. Go to mass on Sundays and penance from time to time.
5. Receive confirmation (something about an adult commitment to the faith; for many it simply means the end of religion classes).
6. Get married in a church before a priest.
7. Keep going to church.
8. Follow the ten commandments.

9. Get anointed when sick.
10. Die and go to heaven.

In this system, religion is basically a ticket to heaven. Play the game correctly and in the end, you win!

Jesus had a very different formula for getting into heaven. When a man asked him how to gain eternal life, he wound up telling a story about the good Samaritan. The Samaritan pulls a beaten man from a ditch, takes him to an inn and pays for his expenses. Another time he told a story about the end of the world and the final judgment, and he said that in the end we will be invited to live with God forever because "I was hungry and you gave me to eat, I was thirsty and you gave me to drink; I was naked and you clothed me." In both cases the bottom line was not whether persons went to church, but whether or not they loved and cared about their fellow human beings.

A word of caution here: there is nothing wrong with going to church or receiving the sacraments. In fact, they are extremely important elements in helping us grow in our relationship with God. But if they are only religious obligations and never make their way into our hearts or change the way we live and relate to others, then they are almost a waste of time. In the end, God is not going to say to us, "Come on in to heaven. You earned it with all those times you went to mass." God's final judgment will more likely involve the way we lived and, perhaps, even more than that, God's infinite love and mercy. **Catholicism, as an organized religion, has as its goal the creation of more loving, compassionate people who will help transform the world by their love.**

Unless our religion has something to do with who we are, how we live, act, relate to ourselves and other people, it will be virtually irrelevant and almost inevitably boring.

For Personal Reflection and Discussion

Which better reflects your understanding of your faith: Catholicism—the system to get you to heaven—or Jesus' teaching on caring for others? Is your faith connected to your everyday life and the way that you live? How?

ADOLESCENT DEVELOPMENT:
PHYSICAL, SEXUAL, EMOTIONAL, INTELLECTUAL,
PSYCHOLOGICAL, SPIRITUAL

Many people assume that the connection between teens and religion is like the connection between a fish and a bicycle. There is none. But this is only true if you are dealing with religion as a lifeless system. If you understand religion the way that Christ did, you might be surprised at the connections between teens and faith.

Let's take a quick look at what it means to be a young adult. This book is generally intended for people between sixteen and twenty. What makes you tick as a group?

Physical Development. The turmoils of puberty are behind you, and you are moving into a second stage of adolescence. The rapid and confusing changes of early adolescence are probably no longer treating you like a human yo-yo. The growth process is still continuing for most of you (especially the males), but it has reached a certain stage of balance if not calm. Early teen years are often spent in reaction to these rapid changes. This is no longer the case. The challenges now are more emotional, psychological and social. **How are you to make sense of yourself now that you have the body of a man (not a boy) or the body of a woman (not a girl)?**

You may think that our bodies have nothing to do with religion or faith. In fact, they do. **Faith is about our whole selves in relation to God, not just some invisible soul.** Christians believe that the Son of God became flesh (John 1:14). Jesus did not join us as some ghost but shared our humanity fully and completely. Our body is one of God's greatest gifts to us, and we have a responsibility to care for it and develop it just as we do our minds and spirits.

For Personal Reflection and Discussion

There seems to be a temptation to either give our bodies too much importance (being pre-occupied with the way we look, obssessed with losing weight, depressed because we are not better looking) or not giving them enough importance (overeating, not exercising, abusing alcohol or drugs). In which direction do you tend to go? How might you change that?

Sexual Development. One of the most dramatic changes that takes place in teen years is related to sexuality. These changes have a physical basis, but they are more than physical. Equally important is the ability to answer the question in your own life: **What does it mean for me to be a young man or a young woman?** How can I relate maturely and intimately with others? How can I develop relationships with the opposite sex that are meaningful? What will it mean for me to develop a capacity for intimacy and commitment? If sex were only about the physical drives of our sexuality, it would be much less complex. But for human beings, sexuality involves our entire selves as male or female. **One of the single most important tasks of adolesence is to develop a maturing sense of our sexuality—to learn to share ourselves with others and ultimately with one other.**

What does your sexuality have to do with faith? More than you might imagine. For humans, sexuality is not just for reproducing. Our sexuality is at the core of our selves and our self-understanding. It is the basis for our capacity to relate intimately with others. **It is through our sexuality that God invites us into the mystery of love and into the process of creation itself.** (This will be discussed in greater depth later in the book in the chapter on the sacrament of marriage.)

For Personal Reflection and Discussion

This is a hard question but an important one. How has your ability to relate to the opposite sex grown and developed in the past two years? What has helped bring about that growth?

Emotional Development. If we have developed in a healthy fashion, we have usually achieved a certain self-confidence by the time we are eleven or twelve years old. When puberty arrives, much of that confidence is temporarily shaken. Early adolescence often deals with this loss of confidence and confusion. By mid to late adolescence, self-confidence and esteem should be getting reestablished once again. It is a time in which one is gradually becoming more comfortable with one's own strengths and limits. The key to such self-esteem seems to be rooted in self-knowledge and self-acceptance. The way that we feel about ourselves is tremendously important. Self-esteem, however, is not something that we simply decide to have. In some ways it is earned by developing the gifts and talents that we have. In another way, it is a gift given to us by those who love us unconditionally. **In any case, without a healthy level of self-esteem, people tend to develop an unhealthy level of self-doubt which paralyzes them from making choices, or they develop a false confidence which is more of a cover for their insecurities.**

Christian faith relies on emotional maturity. Christian faith calls for a person who is capable of loving other people. You cannot give what you haven't got.

For Personal Reflection and Discussion

On a scale of one to ten, how would you rate your own self-confidence? How would you have rated it two years ago? In what situations do you tend to be most confident? When are you least confident?

Intellectual Development. It is possible for the intellectual changes of this time in life to be ignored because of all the other radical changes that are occurring, yet the intellectual changes can be equally profound. **The biggest change is in the ability to do abstract thinking.** When this type of thinking is applied to religion, it may leave you with the sense that you have not been told the truth in the past. There is a new-found capacity to see the larger picture and ask new questions. These questions can sometimes be unsettling for you and the adults in your life. Some adults see these questions as a challenge to their authority. For young people, there is the recognition that the world is a more complex place than childhood might have realized.

In the sphere of religion, the ability to think abstractly often leads to questions concerning the faith. What was once "taken on faith" might now be questioned. This is by no means the end of belief. It may indeed be the end of some of childhood's beliefs or understanding. These changes can be troubling, but they are also essential. Faith must grow with a person's capacity to think. **Faith does not exclude our capacity to question, but, to the contrary, is based on our capacity to question and seek deeper answers to life's questions.**

For Personal Reflection and Discussion

Make a list of the questions you have about your faith that you have begun to ask since becoming a teenager. Which of these questions is still most in need of a satisfying answer? (If this book is being read as part of a class, maybe the whole group could brainstorm some answers to these questions.)

Psychological Development. Adolescence is identified as a period in our life in which we **should develop a sense of identity.** You are no longer a child, yet you are not yet an adult. Developing a sense of identity is a task for each individual. You must answer the question: Who am I? What makes me tick? At the heart of this psychological task is your ability to decide on what is truly valuable—to establish your own personal value system. Very often throughout adolescence, we "try on" different personalities and identities. What may have seemed "cool" when we were freshmen is now downright embarrassing. This process of identity usually continues well into our twenties, but in late adolescence we should have formed some of the foundations for the basis of our values.

Religiously, this aspect of adolescence is extremely important. Ultimately, **faith must be freely chosen.** We must decide if we want to be Christians, if we want to follow in the footsteps and values of Jesus. We must learn to take a stand on what is important in life and what is not. From this perspective, adolescent development and growth is essential to develop the foundations for an adult faith.

For Personal Reflection and Discussion

Our identities are often shaped by people around us whom we respect. Name two people who have had great influence on

MATURING FAITH

It is probably helpful to view faith not as a "thing" that we either "have" or "don't have." Faith is more deeply who we are in relation to God and, for Christians, in relation to Christ. But, like ourselves, faith is a living, growing entity. We may know all the answers to all the questions in this book, but that does not mean that we are people of deep faith. Faith must grow or mature as we do. Theologian James Fowler has done a great deal of work studying various "stages of faith." In his work, faith is not necessarily Christian faith, but the human response to God and the quest for ultimate meaning in life.

Stage One: At first (ages four to seven), faith comes from an intuitive understanding of the values and attitudes of significant persons in life (usually parents). Faith is largely emotional and imitative of others.

Stage Two: As the child's intellectual abilities expand, he/she becomes more aware of being part of a broader faith community and begins to learn the stories of faith and the language of faith (for Catholics, learning biblical stories and entering into the sacraments). These stories are accepted on a very literal level. (Thus, it is common for us to think of God as an old man with a white beard or to think of Adam and Eve as historical figures.)

Stage Three: As persons enter pre-adolescence, they seek direction from sources outside themselves. There is a tendency to accept the authority of others and to be pleasing to them. However, one's peers, teachers, parents, church, social groups all begin to make demands for allegiance, and there is a tendency for persons to be different in different circumstances.

Stage Four: During later adolescence (and beyond), it becomes essential to distinguish a deeper sense of self, to establish what I really think and believe. Choices and values become a more personal commitment. Commitment to a church truly becomes one's own. This is an important stage but can lack the flexibility needed to deal with life's paradoxes and contradictions.

Stage Five: A deeply mature and adult faith (which is rather rare) learns to deal with the fact that life is not black and white but many shades of gray. It can remain committed to institutions or churches even in the face of their inadequacies and weaknesses without giving up its principles.

Stage Six: Most rare of all, people's faith may develop to the point that their very lives become absorbed into the mystery of God's love. Less self-seeking, they become visible signs of the meaning of life and God's love on earth.

you and in what ways they have affected who you are today.
How would you like to be more like these people?

Spiritual Development. Contrary to many adult stereotypes, teenagers are often very spiritual people. Many have a hunger to find answers to life's questions; many possess a desire for creating a better world; the overwhelming majority claim that they pray on a regular basis. Yet some of the most spiritual teens have no idea that they are spiritual. When they think of spiritual, they are often thinking of a priest or the pope or a nun. They do not realize that their questions and searching have a spiritual basis; their friendships are spiritual; even the pain and anguish they suffer is related to the spiritual life. This is another important change that can take place in adolescence. It is time to begin to recognize that **a spiritual life is not a life "up in the clouds"; it is not an escape from this world.** A real Christian spiritual life is a relationship with God in the here and now. Adolescence is a time when your spiritual life must expand or it will almost certainly die or at least go into hibernation. An important shift is one that gets God down from the clouds and into the real world. The God that may have been good enough for you in grammar school simply will not suffice any longer. It is important for you to know how God is involved in your thoughts, feelings, hopes, dreams and disappointments.

For Personal Reflection and Discussion

How has your understanding of God changed throughout your life?

BECOMING FULLY HUMAN

Adolescence can be a very difficult time because changes are occurring at such a rapid pace. In fact, however, we never stop growing or changing. That is the great wonder of being a human being. But with all this change, we must ask a question: Why? Why change? Why grow? Is it so that we can get smarter in order that we may some day get rich and powerful? Sad to say, that is the answer for some people. But maybe there is another direction to this growth. **Maybe we are supposed to be getting not only bigger but better as well.** Perhaps this is the whole point of life, **to become more** than we were: more insightful, more forgiving, more loving, more understanding, more honest, more caring, more open-minded, more reasonable, more intelligent, more human.

How can a person become more human? Isn't a human being a human being? Yes and no. Biologically, yes. A human is a human. But on a different level, **some people are more human than others.** Persons who constantly put other people down, are verbally and physically abusive, use people, cannot be trusted and hate everyone not of their ethnic background are not much of a human being. This doesn't mean they are beyond hope. But for whatever reason, they have not progressed much in the art of being human. **Being human also means becoming human.** And this is indeed an art. Like any art, it is not mastered overnight. It is a process. Likewise some people seem to be more naturally gifted at it. (There is no doubt that while people all deserve equal dignity, they do not start off life with equal opportunities. Some are exposed to people and situations that help make them more open to becoming more fully human. Others are not. This is one reason why it is never possible to judge other human beings. They may not be acting very humanly, and we can reject their values, but we never know for sure what goes into those choices.)

As a high school teacher I have had the wonderful privilege of watching hundreds of students grow before my very eyes. Many, in the course of four years, become people that I would be proud to call friends. Some, however, just seem to get bigger. They may have learned a few things about math, science, history, and English, but there has not been much noticeable change in them. Their attitudes and values haven't grown with the rest of them. For whatever reason, they have not progressed much in the art of becoming fully human. (Many "catch up" later in life; others never do.)

This book is written with the belief that our faith in God and in Christ makes us more fully human, more fully alive. It is my hope that in understanding the basis for Christian faith, you will constantly be asking yourself: "What does this mean for me today? How should this affect the way I live my attitudes and values? How is it challenging me to be more fully human?"

For Personal Reflection and Discussion

List what you would consider ten characteristics of being fully human.

JESUS AS THE MODEL FOR HUMANITY

As we will see later in this book, the church teaches that Jesus is truly God and truly human. It seems that many people have a hard time believing the second part of this. If Jesus is God, they think he can't be human. The two contradict each other. Maybe it would help if we started from the other side: Jesus is truly human. This means that Jesus had to grow and develop just as any human being would. As a baby he was totally dependent on his parents. As a boy he learned a craft from his father (carpentry). As a teen he had to grow and mature into adulthood just as all teens do. But Jesus is not only truly human: he is fully human. By that I mean that Jesus not only reveals who God is but also reveals who we are meant to be as human beings. In Jesus we see the qualities that make us fully human: love, compassion, gentleness, passion for justice and truth, intelligence, goodness, commitment and a total and profound trust in his heavenly Father. In the New Testament Jesus is referred to as a new creation, a new Adam. Just as Adam turned away from God's love and betrayed his humanity, Jesus represents the true meaning of our humanity. He is the model of our humanity.

Every aspect of Catholic Christian faith is intended to somehow draw our lives more deeply into a relationship with God the Father and Jesus. It is by living in their Spirit that we not only come to know Jesus better, but come to know ourselves better as well.

For Personal Reflection and Discussion

What quality of Jesus' personality would you like to develop more within yourself? Why do you choose that one?

Questions for Review

1. What is the difference between religion as a "system for heaven" and religion as Jesus understood it?
2. What were Jesus' standards for gaining eternal life?
3. What is one of the important emotional needs of older teens?
4. What psychological task is associated with later adolescence?
5. In what way is sexuality more than physical actions or drives?
6. What intellectual change occurs in adolescence and how might this change affect a person's faith?
7. What important spiritual development often takes place in adolescence?
8. What is meant by becoming fully human? How is this related to faith?
9. In what sense is Jesus the model for being human?

2

Faith: Our Relationship with God

What does it mean to be a person of faith? Does it mean going to church every Sunday? Does it mean praying? How about having statues of Mary and the saints? These are all certainly outward signs that a person is a believer. But faith is really something that lives in the heart and it is not easily defined. In this chapter we will look at different aspects of being a believer and try to recognize that faith means a variety of attitudes in our relationship to God.

For Personal Reflection and Discussion

Whom do you know that you would call a person of deep faith? What is there about the person that makes you say this?

FAITH AS TRUST

I was eight years old when my father died. I remember taking the school bus home and seeing an ambulance in the driveway as we approached. I was steered to a neighbor's house and about an hour later told by my mother that my father was dead. I remember sitting with my brothers and sister as my mother told us that somehow everything would be O.K. It seemed to me that the world had come crashing down around me, and I'm sure it felt much worse for my mother. Yet we were to trust.

This is perhaps the most powerful notion of faith that I learned as a child. In the face of what looks like the worst possible thing, we can still somehow trust in God. This is really the notion of faith that is contained in the children's song: "He's got the whole world in his hands." The idea behind the song is that we are not alone in the world. God has not created the world and

then abandoned it. **Our lives are ultimately in God's hands.** This may seem like a very simple and naive faith, but it is at the core of Christian faith. We are to live with a childlike trust in God. This does not mean that we should avoid responsibility, but rather we are to live and love as deeply as we can and put the rest in God's hands. **The classic example of this in the Old Testament was Abraham.** He trusted in the promises of God that he would be the father of a great people in the face of all odds.

This attitude of trust filled the life and message of Jesus as well. He taught his followers:

> Look at the birds in the sky. They do not sow or reap, they gather nothing into barns; yet your heavenly Father feeds them. Are you not more important than they? Which one of you by worrying can add a moment to his lifespan. . . . Stop worrying, then, over questions like "What are we to eat, or what are we to drink, or what are we to wear?" . . . Your heavenly Father knows all you need. Seek first his kingship over you, his way of holiness, and all these things will be given you besides (Matthew 6:26–27. 31–33).

Jesus did more than preach about faith as trust in God; he lived it as well. He was rejected by most of his listeners, one of his closest disciples betrayed him, and ultimately he had to face being killed for his message. On the night before his death, we are told that he prayed intensely that another path be found for him to take. In the end, however, he placed his trust in God even in the face of a brutal death by crucifixion.

The anonymous prayer "Footprints" is all about this type of faith.

FOOTPRINTS

One night a man had a dream. He dreamed he was walking along the beach with the Lord. Across the sky flashed scenes from his life. For each scene he noticed two sets of footprints in the sand, one belonging to him and the other to the Lord. When the last scene of his life flashed before him, he looked back at the footprints in the sand. He noticed that many times along the path of his life there was only one set of footprints. He also noticed that this happened at the very lowest and saddest times in his life. This really bothered him and he questioned the Lord about it. "Lord, you said that once I decided to follow you, you'd walk with me all the way. But I have noticed that during the most troublesome times in my life, there is only one set of footprints. I don't understand why when I needed you most you would leave me." The Lord replied, "My precious, precious child, I love you and I would never leave you. During your times of trial and suffering, when you see only one set of footprints, it was then that I carried you."

For Personal Reflection and Discussion

Whom do you trust more than anyone in life? Has there ever been a time when you had to place your trust in God? What was the situation?

FAITH AS KNOWLEDGE AND LOVE OF GOD

Faith is more than trust in God. It is a relationship with God that we are born into. As such it is a gift from God. Faith is the name of our relationship with God. Human beings sometimes discover within themselves a yearning for God—a desire to know and love God more fully. This desire can never be fully satisfied in this life. Because we are not God we can never possibly know him completely. But this does not stop us from seeking to know who God is and what God desires from us. In the Old Testament the author of Psalm 42 describes this longing:

> As the deer longs for running waters,
> so my soul longs for you, O God.
> Athirst is my soul for God, the living God.
> When shall I go and behold the face of God?

Jesus speaks of this longing as well when he says, "Ask and you will receive. Seek and you will find. Knock and it will be opened to you" (Matthew 7:7). He is not talking about requests that we make to God ("Please help me pass this math test!"), but a lifetime of seeking after God. If we stay on track, ultimately we will reach our goal.

This longing for God is at the very heart of our being. All of our dreams and hopes for happiness and fulfillment are a way of longing for God who is the final and true fulfillment of our lives. This hunger within us, however, can be easily led astray. It is not uncommon for people to seek their fulfillment in things that simply are incapable of providing it. St. Augustine was a man whose searching led him into a study of philosophy and a relationship with a woman who bore his child. But, ultimately, neither his philosophy nor his mistress could satisfy his deepest needs. When he became a Christian, he at last realized that he was created for God's love and glory. In looking back over his life, he wrote: "You have made us for yourself, O Lord, and our hearts are restless until they rest in you."

For Personal Reflection and Discussion

What do you think are some of the "dead ends" that people pursue in looking for happiness?

FAITH AS A WAY OF LIFE

For the Jewish people, the best way to know and love God was through fidelity to the Torah (the teaching or "law"). **Faith was not simply a set of ideas—it was a way of life.** The Torah was a sure guide to walk in the ways of the Lord. Thus the author of the first psalm writes:

> Happy the man who follows not
> the counsel of the wicked
> Nor walks in the way of sinners,
> nor sits in the company of the insolent,
> But delights in the law of the Lord
> and meditates on his law day and night. . . .
> For the Lord watches over the way of the just
> but the way of the wicked vanishes.

What is important here is the recognition that **faith has everything to do with the way we live.** (It is the "way of the just.") There was the temptation among some of the Jewish people to reduce faith to religious rituals. This mentality was roundly condemned by the prophets. They insisted that true faith was concerned with real life and the real needs of others. Listen to the prophet Amos condemn the false faith of his time which tried to substitute feasts and sacrifices for justice and compassion as he proclaims the Lord's message:

> I hate, I spurn your feasts,
>   I take no pleasure in your solemnities. . . .
> But if you would offer me holocausts,
>   then let justice surge like water,
>   and goodness like an unfailing stream (Amos 5:21–24).

This problem also existed in the early church (and throughout the history of the church). Apparently there was a problem in one of the communities about some of the believers who were not living their faith. Here is what James writes to them in his epistle:

> My brothers, what good is it to profess faith, without practicing it. Such faith has no power to save one, has it? If a brother or sister has nothing to wear and no food for the day, and you say to them, "Good-bye and good luck! Keep warm and well fed," but do not meet their bodily needs, what good is that? So it is with the faith that does nothing in practice. It is thoroughly lifeless (James 2:14–17).

Today, there seems to be a terrible tendency to associate faith with one hour per week on Sunday. There is no doubt that the eucharist is extremely important, but it is not the entirety of faith. Christians come together on Sunday to celebrate a faith that they are called to live daily, hourly. It is important to remember that Christianity was originally called "the way" and that the mark of the Christian was always to be love for God and others. Jesus himself insisted on this consistently. He said,

> Anyone who hears my words and **puts them into practice** is like the wise man who built his house on rock. When the rainy season set in, the torrents came and the winds blew and buffeted his house. It did not collapse; it had been solidly set on rock. Anyone who hears my words but does not put them

into practice is like the foolish man who built his house on sandy ground. The rains fell, the torrents came, the winds blew and lashed against his house. It collapsed under all this and was completely ruined (Matthew 7:24–27).

For Personal Reflection and Discussion

How could you apply the message of the prophet Amos to our time in history?

FAITH FROM THE HEART

The most important relationships in our lives are ones that are deeply rooted in our hearts. There exists a bond of love in close relationships, so much so that people literally become parts of each other. The same should be true with our relationship with God. The more our relationship with God grows, the more deeply it becomes a part of who we are. Like a deep friendship or family relationship, we cannot imagine what we would be like without it. Yet such a faith is not easily achieved, and for many people it does not grow to such a depth until well into adulthood (if at all). There is a story in the gospel of Mark which illustrates three different ways of understanding faith, only one of which is the genuine article. The story takes place while Jesus is in the temple area in Jerusalem.

> In the course of his teaching, [Jesus] said, "Be on guard against the scribes who love to parade around in their robes and accept signs of respect in public, front seats in the synagogues, and places of honor at banquets. These men devour the savings of widows and recite long prayers for appearance' sake; it is they who will receive the severest sentence."
>
> Taking a seat opposite the treasury, he observed the crowd putting money into the collection box. Many of the wealthy put in sizable amounts; but one poor widow came and put in two small copper coins worth a few cents. He called his disciples over and told them, "I want you to observe that this poor widow contributed more than all the others who donated to the treasury. They gave from their surplus wealth, but she gave from her want, all that she had to live on" (Mark 12:38–44).

This story illustrates three different ways of understanding the meaning of faith. For the scribes described, faith is a matter of pious externals which win them respect from people. There is no distinction between being a religious person and a person of faith. The scribes, however, are really interested in their own status and position. They use the faith of Israel for their own glorification. This type of faith is the kind that will be a temptation for people who are professionally "religious" (like the author of this book).

The second view of faith is represented by the wealthy who make great contributions to the temple. Jesus is not trying to comment on how much money people should give. He is using their donations as a symbol for their faith. The wealthy in the story only give a part of themselves. Faith is a part of their lives, but it is not at the core of their selves. Just as they have their families, friends, business, and hobbies, so too they have their religious responsibilities. They are faithful to them, but God only gets a piece of who they are.

The widow, on the other hand, represents the true believer. She gives of her very self. She personifies the commandment that Jesus chooses as the greatest of all the commandments:

> Hear, O Israel! The Lord our God is Lord alone. Therefore you shall love the Lord your God with all your heart, with all your soul, with all your mind, and with all your strength (Mark 12:29–30).

FAITH AS PERSONAL COMMITMENT

The sad truth is that countless Christians are Christian in name only. Their "faith" is little more than an accident of birth. They were baptized as infants, brought into the church, and were thus "Christians" or "Catholics." This is about as far removed from Jesus' understanding of faith as is possible. For Jesus, faith meant a personal conversion. The key to faith is that people choose it for themselves. Their faith reflects who they are and what they believe is important.

In the Catholic Church, the sacrament of confirmation is often associated with making a personal choice to be a Christian.

Arianism - the doctrine of Arius, an Alexandrian of the 4th century, who taught that Jesus was not the same substance as God, but only the best of created beings.

24   THE WORD MADE FLESH

THE GREAT RELIGIONS OF THE WORLD

HINDUISM

Origins: Beginning some 2,500 years before Christ, Hinduism is not a highly structured religion with a clear set of beliefs for all its members. It seems to have begun in northern India with the worship of mother-goddesses and expanded and adapted in contact with Arian religions.

Central Ideas: The great force in the universe is Brahman which is the really real. Brahman is all-pervading and present within all. All else is illusion (maya). According to the law of karma those who do good and perform spiritual exercises of asceticism are reborn (samsara) into a higher form. Salvation is found in release from illusion through rebirth and total absorption (moksha) into Brahman.

Writings: The three different periods of Hinduism are marked by their three great texts: the Vedas, the Upanishads and the Bhagavad-Gita.

Followers Today: Approximately 700 million, mostly in India.

BUDDHISM

Origins: An offshoot of Hinduism begun by Siddhartha Gautama (born 560 BCE), who was the original Buddha (meaning "the enlightened one").

Central Ideas: Rejected the asceticism of Hinduism and opted for the "Middle Path" between pleasure seeking and asceticism. Focus is on meditation leading to enlightenment. The Buddha discovered the four noble truths of enlightenment:
1. All life involves suffering.
2. Suffering results from desire or greed.
3. Suffering ends when greed ends.
4. Enlightenment comes from knowing these truths and following the eightfold path: right understanding, right thoughts, right speech, right action, right means of livelihood, right effort, right mindfulness, right concentration.

Writings: Two branches of Buddhism following different writings: The Theravadins accept only the Pali scriptures which

(*continued*)

THE GREAT RELIGIONS OF THE WORLD (*continued*)

deal with the teaching of the Buddha. The Mahayanas accept the sutra scriptures as well.
Followers Today: Approximately 310 million.

CONFUCIANISM

Origins: Began with the teaching of K'ung Fu-tzu (Confucius, born ca. 570 BCE) who was more interested in people than in gods.
Central Ideas: Living in a time of political chaos, he taught a doctrine which sought the good of the community through a series of social duties. At the heart of his teaching was the concept of "jen," which is the attitude of humaneness or care for others, and "li," which is proper conduct toward others. It is a very practical religious tradition which gave great respect to elders and thus fit into China's ancient practice of ancestor worship.
Writings: The Confucian classics: The Book of History (Shu-Ching), the Book of Poetry (Shih Ching), the Book of Rites (Li-Ching), the Book of Changes (I-Ching) and the Annals of Spring and Autumn (Ch'un Ch'iu). These works were more likely edited by Confucius than written by him.
Followers Today: Approximately 6 million; many have abandoned their beliefs due to the cultural revolution of Mao Tse-tung in the 1960s.

TAOISM

Origins: Begun in China, by Lao-tzu, born ca. 600 BCE.
Central Ideas: It is considered by some more a philosophy than a religion. Unlike Confucianism, it focuses not on society but the individual. The Tao is the way of life in accord with the harmony of nature (which is comprised of the opposing yet complementary forces of the yin and the yang). It stresses a life of non-political simplicity and the vanity of human achievement.
Writings: Main source is the Tao Te Ching.
Followers Today: Approximately 20 million.

(*continued*)

THE GREAT RELIGIONS OF THE WORLD (*continued*)

JUDAISM

Origins: Abram and Sara are promised that they will become the parents of a great nation (ca. 1800 BCE). Moses later leads the Hebrews from slavery in Egypt and forms them into a people (ca. 1250 BCE).

Central Ideas: A religion in which God is actively involved in the history of his people, Judaism is based on the covenant made with Abraham and Moses and David. The heart of the covenant is the Torah (the teaching or the law) which is the path of righteousness that leads to God. The Jewish people await the coming of the messiah, the "anointed one" who will bring God's final victory over evil.

Writings: The Hebrew scriptures (the Old Testament; see chart in Chapter 4).

Followers Today: Approximately 17 million.

ISLAM

Origins: Begun by the prophet Muhammed (born ca. 570 AD), who wrote down revelation from the angel Gabriel in what was to become the Koran.

Central Ideas: Islam is based on total surrender in faith to Allah who spoke through the prophet Muhammed. There is a deep connection between religion and state (Muhammed assumed both religious and political leadership). It accepts five great prophets: Abraham, Moses, Noah, Jesus and Muhammed, and is based on five pillars: the creed, prayer, fasting, the poor-due and the pilgrimage to Mecca.

Writings: The Koran plays such an important role that Muslims believe it should be read in its original Arabic, because it contains the pure divine revelation.

Followers Today: Divided into two groups, Shiites and Sunnis; there are approximately 900 million.

But is this really the case for most of the people who receive the sacrament? Or is it not an example of faith as a "system"? Get on line and receive the sacraments. Sometimes young adults have a very difficult time making a commitment to their faith. This is not surprising. Our ability to make commitments is just beginning in adolescence. There is so much confusion that goes with the age that faith can also be confusing. Perhaps the important question in adolescence is whether or not I am trying to grow in my faith as much as I can. Am I trying to live the values of my faith? Am I seeking time to pray? Am I seeking answers to my questions? For many this is the time to prepare the foundation for a future commitment. For others the commitment is already present.

For Personal Reflection and Discussion

On a scale of one to ten, how much of your faith is your own choice and commitment? What are you doing to help make that faith grow?

MANY FAITHS; ONE FAITH

If faith is the human relationship with God, we must admit from the beginning that faith is broader than Christianity. Many people who are not Christians have a deep and real faith in God. The various religions of the world are the expressions of the faith of many and diverse people. Moslems, Jews, Hindus, Buddhists, and Christians represent some of the "major" world religions. But there are also many other religious traditions among various groups and cultures throughout the world. **Is one of them the true religion while all the others are false religions? The Catholic Church rejects such an interpretation of other faiths.** In one sense, there can be only one faith because God is one. However, the expressions of that one faith can be diverse depending on the culture and traditions of a people. It is also possible that some "faiths" or religions express the one faith more fully, deeply and richly.

⌐ The Catholic Church teaches that faith in Jesus Christ is not the only way to God but it is unique among all religions⌐ The reason for this is not because Christians are unique and special people, but rather because **Christ is unique in all history.** Jesus Christ is the full and total revelation of the Father in a way that no other person is or ever will be. (On an individual level it is possible for a devout Hindu, Moslem, Jew, etc., to be holier or closer to God than a particular Christian. Likewise, it is very possible for Christians to learn from other religions and non-Christians about prayer, ritual and living the life of faith. But none of this replaces the uniqueness of Christ and his role in salvation history.)

For Personal Reflection and Discussion

Christians seem to be in a bind. On the one hand, they must avoid the arrogance of seeing themselves as the only ones with the true or real faith. On the other hand, they continue to maintain the special uniqueness of Jesus. Given this problem, what do you think should be the mission of the church in countries that are predominantly non-Christian in their religious traditions? Should we actively seek to convert them to Christianity? If so, why?

CHRISTIAN FAITH: ACCEPTING JESUS AS LORD

We spoke of faith originally as a trust in God. This is a basic, fundamental faith. But this faith also transcends Christianity. A Jew, Moslem, Hindu, Buddhist, or any human being may possess that first type of faith. Christian faith is a unique way of believing. Christians believe that the God whom they trust and seek has been revealed to us in and through Jesus Christ. **Faith becomes Christian faith when a person and community accepts Jesus as God's revelation in history.** This is the primary notion of faith that can be found in the New Testament. In the gospels, people come to faith in Jesus because they recognize and accept the power of God at work in him.

> As Jesus approached Capernaum, a centurion approached him with this request: "Sir, my serving boy is at home in bed paralyzed, suffering painfully." He said to him, "I will come

and cure him." "Sir," the centurion said in reply, "I am not worthy to have you under my roof. Just give an order and my servant will get better. I am a man under authority myself and I have troops assigned to me. If I give one man the order, 'Dismissed,' off he goes. If I say to another, 'Come here,' he comes. If I tell my slave, 'Do this,' he does it." Jesus showed amazement on hearing this and remarked to his followers, "I assure you, I have never found this much faith in Israel" (Matthew 8:5–10).

During the life of Jesus, faith was understood as the recognition that God was at work in Jesus. Many, of course, rejected such a claim. Some of the religious leaders saw Jesus as a threat to the true faith of Israel. They were scandalized by his association with sinners, and they saw his miraculous powers as signs of the presence of Satan.

After the death and resurrection of Jesus, faith in Jesus meant accepting his death and resurrection as God's saving power. The focus moved away from his words and deeds to his death and resurrection. Christian faith now focused on Christ himself as Messiah and Lord.

Today, there are many varieties of Christian faith, but they all have at least one thing in common. They all accept Jesus as the way to God's salvation.

FAITH AND REVELATION

One of the big problems that crept into the early church was that of "false teachers." Many of the books in the New Testament make reference to such people and warn the believers to beware of them. In other words, faith now had certain "beliefs" which were truly revealed by God. These make up the content of faith. They are **what** believers believe. Until now we have emphasized **whom** believers believe in: God. But there is another element to faith as well which we see in the creeds of the church. Faith has a content. Catholic faith has a certain content which is different than Judaism or Islam or Buddhism, etc. These are the teachings of the faith.

One of the biggest differences between Catholic Christian faith and Protestant Christian faith has been the Catholic Church's insistence that faith includes "intellectual assent to divinely revealed truths." This does not negate the notion of faith as trust in God, but it adds a different dimension. It does not eliminate the need to live the faith in deeds, but it emphasizes that faith is not only confidence in God and following his "way"; it is the truth as well. Faith is our relationship with God which allows us to understand the truth as God has revealed it to us. These truths are known as dogmas. They are essential beliefs of the faith (such as the resurrection of Jesus, his divinity and humanity, the Trinity etc.). In the past this aspect of faith has sometimes lost sight of the need to live faith and to have a personal relationship with God. This was evident in some of the education that was given to Catholics before the Second Vatican Council (1962–1965). One learned about the faith usually by memorizing questions and answers concerning the teaching of the church. There was very little emphasis placed on the teaching and person of Jesus, and the Bible was almost never opened. In the years since the council, the church has tried to rediscover the more biblical notions of faith, while maintaining the importance of faith as knowledge of revealed truth.

For Personal Reflection and Discussion

Ask your parents and teachers about their religious education as children. Depending on their age, see if it reflects this notion of faith as memorizing the dogmas of the church.

THE CONTENT OF FAITH

Catholic faith is not reinvented in each generation. There are, at the core of this faith, certain beliefs which make up the heart of Catholicism. These beliefs are not intended to be dry ideas isolated from life. **What** we believe should have implications for **how** we live. For example, our beliefs about God will affect our lives a great deal. If we believe that God is a God of wrath and vengeance, we might live our lives in fear and obedience but probably not in love. If we believe that the Catholic Church is the only way to salvation, then we might spend our lives trying to convince others that they are wrong and we are right. The table of contents to this book will reveal a great deal about the "content" of faith. Catholics have specific beliefs about God, salvation, Jesus, the church, the sacraments and morality. This book will attempt to examine those beliefs. But it is very important that we keep asking ourselves the question: How does this belief affect me and the way I live and relate to others?

It may be helpful to explain various elements within the contents of faith:

1. *Dogmas:* These are **essential teachings** of the church. They are the beliefs that are at the core of our faith. For example, Jesus is truly God and truly human. Dogmas cannot change without changing the faith itself. However, our understanding of a dogma can change and develop.
2. *Doctrines:* These are official teachings of the church. In theory, some of these could possibly change. For example, women cannot become priests in the Catholic Church. Although this teaching may never change, in theory most theologians believe that it could since it is not a dogma of faith. (All dogmas are doctrines, but not all doctrines are dogmas.)
3. *Canon Law:* These are the official laws that govern the running of the church. They cover a wide variety of topics.
4. *Theology:* This is the attempt to understand and explain the teaching of the church. Theologies can vary from one teacher to the next as they seek ways that are best to explain the meaning of Christian faith.

CATHOLIC CHRISTIAN FAITH

What is unique about **Catholic** Christian faith? How is it distinct from other forms of Christian faith? This is an extremely difficult question to answer, but it may be possible to reveal some characteristics of Catholic Christian faith that, when put together, give it a unique perspective. In addition to its "dogmatic" elements, some other characteristics of Catholic Christian faith would include the following:

1. **The word "Catholic" means universal.** Catholic faith is open to the universal experience of what it means to be a human being. It is intended for all and includes all. Catholicism is never to be exclusive. Within the Catholic Church there have always been competing ideas, thoughts, and cultures. It is big enough for everyone.

2. **Catholic faith is deeply "sacramental."** This simply means that it accepts the world as the place in which the presence of God can be found. The world is not God, but it reflects his presence. The world and human experience are sacramental: they are a sign of the presence of God; they believe that God is to be found in the ordinary experiences of living.

3. **Catholic faith is profoundly "traditional."** It has a long and sacred history that it takes seriously. Yet its notion of tradition is not tied to the past. New traditions are always in the process of being created and handed down. The purpose of this tradition is not to make the church live in the past, but rather to help keep the faith alive for each new generation. Thus the eucharist is an ancient and revered tradition in the church, but it can be celebrated in different ways that seek to make it come alive for people of the twentieth century and for people of different cultures.

4. **Catholic faith is communal.** Catholicism is a faith of a people. We will see more of this in the chapter on the church. The journey of faith is one that each individual must make, but he or she never makes it alone. We do so in relationship with others. To be a Catholic is to be part of a faith community which enriches the lives of all its members.

5. **Catholic faith takes sin seriously, but it takes grace even more seriously.** Catholicism sees human beings as flawed, wounded, in need of healing. But even more profoundly, it understands people as loved by God and capable of loving and

caring. There is always a tension between these two elements of our personalities, and neither can be ignored. But Catholicism has always emphasized God's grace over human sinfulness.

6. **Catholic faith accepts the pope as the successor of Peter and the head of the bishops who are the successors of the apostles.** It takes seriously the role of authority in the church while at the same time recognizing the importance of individual conscience.

In this chapter we have tried to examine the meaning of faith, recognizing that faith eludes any attempts at simple description. Rather than settling on any one notion of faith, we have tried to examine a number of ways of understanding faith. These different ways do not exclude each other. They all make up part of the panorama of faith.

In fact there are two distinct elements of faith that are present. The first emphasizes the attitudes of faith that should be present in the community of believers: trust, personal relationship, commitment, living the faith. The second focuses on the content of faith. It refers to "the faith" as a body of beliefs. Both of these elements must be maintained. Faith cannot simply be doctrines written on a piece of paper. On the other hand, faith is more than a subjective feeling. The doctrines of the faith should ideally help a person deepen and direct his or her personal relationship with God.

Both of these elements also come together in the person of Jesus Christ. Jesus is the model of our faith in his trust, commitment and relationship with God the Father. He is also at the center of the content of faith. It is belief in Jesus that makes Christian faith Christian.

Questions for Review

1. What person in the Hebrew scriptures is portrayed as the model of faith? Why?
2. What was the message of the prophet Amos? What does it tell us about faith?
3. What does the epistle of James say about faith without good works?

4. In the story of the widow in the temple, compare the attitude of the scribes, the wealthy and the widow.
5. What does it mean to say that faith is a commitment?
6. Is Christian faith the only true faith? How are other faiths related to it?
7. How was faith in Jesus different before and after the resurrection?
8. What is meant by the content of faith?
9. What is one of the biggest differences between Catholic Christian faith and Protestant Christian faith?
10. Define: dogma, doctrine, canon law and theology.
11. What does the word "Catholic" mean?
12. What does it mean to say that Catholic faith is "sacramental"?
13. What is the role of tradition in the Catholic faith?
14. How do Catholics understand the relationship between sin and grace?
15. How is Jesus both the content and the model of faith?

3

Sin and Salvation

A fire had broken out in the middle of the night. The smoke detectors went off and the family managed to escape except for a four year old girl trapped in her bedroom on the third floor of the house. The father of the girl raced outside beneath her window. He called her to the window and told her to jump. "Daddy," she called out, "I can't see you." "That's all right," he answered. "I can see you. Jump!" She jumped and the father made the catch of his life. She had escaped the flames around her and been reunited with the family that she loved.

This story is a parable for the human quest and need for salvation. Like the little girl in the story, humans find themselves living in a situation of destruction and peril. We cannot make it on our own. But also, like the little girl, we are offered a way out, a way to life and love. Salvation is the religious term which describes this situation and the way to freedom and hope.

THE HUMAN QUEST FOR MEANING

If you examine your reading list for English this year, it is almost certain that the books and plays you will be reading will have much to do with the theme of salvation. They may not even mention God or Jesus, but many are about the struggle between good and evil and the search for meaning in life. These are the great themes of literature because they are the great themes of life.

The questions concerning salvation are those that humans have been asking for thousands of years:

- "Why were the world and people created in the first place?"
- "Why was I born? What is the purpose and goal of my life?"
- "Why is there so much evil in the world? Are people basically evil?"
- "Is there any hope for improvement on planet earth?"
- "Does God care about the human situation? If so, why doesn't he do something about it?"
- "Why do the innocent suffer?"
- "What happens to us when we die?"
- "Does it really matter whether we have lived morally or not?"

All religions deal in one way or another with these questions. Religion is concerned primarily with life's meaning. What's the point? Why are we here? Religions try to offer some solution to these questions. There are a number of different ways of trying to answer these questions. One way is through philosophy. History is filled with great thinkers who have grappled with the question of life's meaning. A second way of dealing with these questions is not through philosophy but through stories, art and poetry. These often deal with the same issues but in different ways. **Philosophy speaks to the logical side of the mind. Stories and art speak more to the whole person, including our feelings and intuitions.**

In the Bible we can find both stories and theology which seek to understand the meaning of salvation. The classic stories in the Old Testament are found in the first eleven chapters of Genesis. In these chapters we find the stories of creation, Adam and Eve, the fall and expulsion from Eden, Cain and Abel, Noah and the flood, and the tower of Babel. These stories are not meant to be exact, literal descriptions of events. Rather they are the Jewish people's way of grappling with the questions of good and evil and life's meaning. These stories represent a long history of storytelling among the Hebrew people finally compiled and brought together by a single scribe. But more than that, these stories are part of God's inspired revelation. Our main concern is to see what they tell us about the meaning of salvation.

The first story of creation in the book of Genesis (1:1—2:4) is the description of God creating the world in six days and resting on' the seventh. In order to understand this story, it is important to distinguish between two categories: the scientific explanation and the religious meaning. The author of the story in the Bible knew little about the origins of the universe from a scientific viewpoint. (Today we know a great deal more, but we are still only scratching the surface.) **The important point is the religious meaning of the story.** What is that meaning? There are three key points:

1. **The universe is the result of God's creative power.** In this creation account, the author emphasizes the great power of God. God speaks and his word has power: "God said, 'Let there be light,' and there was light." Religiously, it is unimportant whether God created the world in seven days or through a process of creative evolution. Either way, it is God who is the source of the creative power.

2. **God's creation is good.** I have met people who believe that this world is hell. The author of the creation story wants to make it clear that the world is intended to be a good place. God's creation is good. This is reiterated throughout the story. After each day, God looks upon his creation and declares it to be good, and after the sixth and final day of creation, "God looked upon everything that he had made, and he found it **very** good."

3. **Human beings are God's masterpiece and are given responsibility over creation.** "God created man in his image: in the divine image he created him; male and female he created them. God blessed them, saying 'Be fertile and multiply, fill the earth and subdue it. Have dominion over the fish of the sea, the birds of the air, and all living things that move on earth'" (Genesis 1:27–28). Human beings have a unique place in the creation. They alone are created "in God's image." What does this mean? It is clear from the passage that humanity shares in the image of God by being given responsibility to share in the work of creation. They are to multiply and care for the earth. It is important to note here that the word "man" here refers to both male and female. Males alone are not created in the image of God. People are.

For Personal Reflection and Discussion

History reveals that humans have exploited the earth as well as cared for it. We cannot forget that the passage says that people are part of the creation. They are not God. In what ways have you become more sensitive to environmental concerns? How can you better "love your mother," the earth?

ADAM, EVE AND THE FALL

The second story of creation in Genesis (2:4–25) tells the story not of the creation of the universe but of the first humans, Adam (Hebrew, meaning "man") and the woman who is later named Eve. They live in a paradisal Eden. In the story the man is created first but none of the animals can provide him with true companionship, and thus the woman is created. There is in the passage a strong affirmation of human sexuality. Male and female fulfill each other.

Thus far, everything appears to be going according to plan. Now, however, the author of Genesis needs to explain how evil became part of the human condition. He tells the story of the serpent tempting Eve and the sin of both Adam and Eve and their expulsion from the garden of Eden.

What is the story trying to teach us? Eve is tempted by the serpent when he tells her, "You will be like gods," if she eats the fruit of the forbidden tree. Part of the sin of Adam and Eve is a rejection of their humanity. It is a rejection of the gift that God has given. It is a desire to be the center of the universe instead of a creature. The effects of the sins of Adam and Eve are immediate. They recognize their nakedness and they make clothing. The natural harmony and intimacy between the two has been shattered.

The biblical author wishes to make it clear that sin and evil are not part of God's plan. They stem from human choices and freedom misused. The effects of Adam and Eve's sin are contagious. Their son Cain kills his brother Abel. Sin is spreading like a sickness. We then read that after a while the whole world had become corrupt with the exception of Noah and his family.

What had begun as an individual offense has now spread and grown into the very fabric of human existence. Yet the story of Noah and the flood ends on a note of hope. God does not destroy the entire human family. God begins the creation anew by making a covenant with Noah.

For Personal Reflection and Discussion

In the Genesis stories, sin is almost contagious. This seems to be true. How does sin spread in our culture and society? What are some ways in which we "inherit" the sinful attitudes of the past or those existing within our society? How would you apply this to racism, violence, dishonesty or alcohol abuse?

JESUS, THE NEW ADAM

The stories in Genesis 1–11 are masterpieces because of their ability to get to the heart of the religious questions. They tell us that the world has been created by God's power and goodness. But **there now exists in the world a situation of sin, a tragic "fall" from grace.** The world and its people are scarred by sin, cut off from their God and in need of redemption. Yet there is hope that God will not abandon his creation. God will offer us a new beginning. The rest of the Bible is a story of the offer of that hope. God enters into a special relationship with Israel (a covenant) and promises them a way out of the darkness. He promises to offer them a new way of living which will restore the lost harmony between themselves and each other and God. **These promises are ultimately fulfilled in the person of Jesus, who was called the "new Adam." Jesus reveals the true meaning of our humanity and offers us hope in a world still scarred by sin.**

Jesus is acknowledged by Christians as the Savior of the world, the one who brings about the salvation of the human race. It is particularly in the death and resurrection of Jesus that God offers us salvation. Through Christ's life, death and resurrection, God has united himself in love with his people. **Jesus' death is the revelation of God's absolute and unconditional love for us.** He gives us his very life in and through his Son. **The resurrection of Christ is God's promise that his love is greater than all darkness,** redeeming sin and death. The resurrection reveals that ultimately sin and death are impostors: they do not have the power that people give them. Greater still is the power of God's love revealed in Christ.

Jesus not only reveals the saving love of God but shows us the way to that love. By walking with Christ we walk in a new way, a new path, with a new destination. The way of Jesus, which is love and compassion, truth and justice, trust and prayer, is the way to the Father.

For Personal Reflection and Discussion

God always offers us a new beginning. What have been some of the new beginnings that you have experienced? What relationship do you have that could use a new beginning? Why? What can you do about it?

SIN: ORIGINAL, PERSONAL, MORTAL, VENIAL, SOCIAL

If God is our Savior, what exactly are we being saved from? What are we being saved into? How will we be different? **According to the Bible, we are saved from "sin and death."** These are seen as the powers that separate us from God. Sin is our hard-hearted refusal to love and to trust in God. It is that which separates us from God. Death is more than the end of our earthly existence. Death is the end of hope. It is the despair that life has had no real meaning or purpose to it.

Let's take a closer look at the meaning of sin by examining some traditional descriptions of it:

Original Sin. One of the most misunderstood teachings of the church concerns the doctrine of original sin. Almost invariably, when students are asked to describe it, they respond, "It is the sin committed by Adam and Eve." But what does this mean? If we recognize that Adam and Eve are not historical figures, we realize that it cannot refer to eating the fruit offered them by the serpent. What, then, is original sin? To answer this, let's move away from the Bible and from theology and simply examine ourselves and the world that we live in. Read the newspaper today: something is terribly wrong with the world that we live in. It is filled with violence, racism, dishonesty, carelessness, cynicism, and anger. It reeks of war, hunger, homelessness, abuse, greed and drug addiction. But if we look again, we can also see love, forgiveness, service, courage, care, education, healing, hard work, and hope. This is a schizophrenic planet. It is both good and evil. If we look at ourselves we can probably find the same picture. We are capable of genuine love and forgiveness, but we also betray our best selves. We are drawn to the good; we are inclined to do the self-centered.

This state of social and personal brokenness is what is called original sin. Original sin is meant to describe something that is very real: the experience of evil and the lack of harmony that we find both in the world and in ourselves. Many people think of it as the sin that a baby is born with and that gets washed away at baptism, but it is much more real and complex than that. We are all affected by this situation, this web of sin. It is part of the air that we breathe. This sinful situation cries out for freedom and liberation and salvation. Jesus seemed to take this reality for granted. He said that he came to call sinners to repentance. He insisted on the need for a change of heart. He came to offer us a "way out" of the web of sin. Christians believe that salvation has already been offered to the world in Jesus. Original sin lives on, but it is not the only reality. The reality of Christ has changed the world forever. If we live in Christ and his Spirit, we are free from the bonds of evil in the world, and we are free to help bring about God's reign on earth.

For Personal Reflection and Discussion

Are you in need of salvation? Why or why not?

Personal Sin. Original sin describes a situation, not a decision. Personal sin is when we decide to sin, when we cooperate with the evil in the world and in ourselves. **Sin is always a failure to love in some way.** It is destructive of ourselves and of our relationships. Personal sins are the sins that we commit and that we are responsible for. Some, of course, are much more serious than others. The Catholic Church has traditionally distinguished between mortal and venial sins. **Mortal sins are those that are so serious that they truly cut us off from God at the core of our selves.** Some theologians describe mortal sin as a general direction in life: a basic choice to live selfishly. Others emphasize individual acts which are terribly harmful and which reflect a hardened, self-centered heart. **Venial sins** are considered "less serious." These are the sins that **disrupt and hurt our relationships with other people and with God,** but are not so devastating that they destroy the relationship. It should be pointed out, however, that all sins are serious in one way or another in that they hurt our relationship with God, others and ourselves.

For Personal Reflection and Discussion

What are the most serious sins that confront young people today? What sins are destructive not of others but of ourselves?

Sins of Omission. Sin is essentially a failure to love God, others or ourselves. Some of the worst sins that we might commit are called sins of omission. It is very possible to do nothing wrong and to still commit very serious sins. Apathy, not caring, is among the deadliest of sins. In the parable of the good Samaritan, the men who passed by the beaten man in the ditch did no wrong, but they did nothing right either!

For Personal Reflection and Discussion

Can you think of a time you did nothing when you should have done something?

Social Sin. Normally sin is applied to individual choices. Today, however, theologians and Pope John Paul II speak of something called "structures of sin." These are elements within society that are "sinful" in themselves in that they are destructive of human dignity. Thus, any situations that encourage violence, greed, poverty, racism, etc., could be called examples of social sin or structural sin. For example, in the United States at the current time, women are paid about seventy percent of what men are paid for doing the same work in the corporate world. Likewise women almost always suffer economically from divorce while men's lifestyles are rarely affected. Another example of structural sin is the relationship between countries of the developed world and the undeveloped and developing countries. It is not uncommon for the developed countries to benefit economically from the resources of poor countries by using their natural resources and hiring their people as a cheap form of labor.

For Personal Reflection and Discussion

What other examples can you think of concerning "social sin"?

WHAT ARE WE SAVED FOR?: GRACE AND LOVE

Thus far we have been focusing on the negative aspects of the theme of salvation. We have been looking at the brokenness, sinfulness and evil in the world and in ourselves. But an equally important aspect of salvation is the new life that we are called into. There are many different ways of describing this new life. **It is called grace,** which is the life and love of God at work in us. **Jesus calls it the reign of God,** a relationship between God and his people which reflects the harmony that we were created for. Because we will touch on these themes later in the book, here we will summarize some of the key ideas of the new life that Christians are called to live:

1. **God's saving love changes us.** It gives us a new perspective and vision of life. It calls us to grow as human beings. It brings us out of fear and hopelessness. Let's look at a more specific example. I have taught many students who come from families where a parent is an alcoholic. These children of alcoholics often suffer from terrible self-images. They live in shame and denial; they have a hard time forming lasting friendships. Some become behavior problems in school; others do extremely well in order to be the hero of the family. All of these children are in some way in need of help. Many of them in fact deal with the problem. They move beyond the denial and free themselves (somewhat) from the devastating effects of alcoholism in the family. These stu-

dents really have grown, taken risks and changed. They have been drawn out of their fear and live much more freely and happily. This was the same type of effect that Jesus had on many people. He called them to a new way of understanding themselves. He transformed fishermen into apostles; through encountering him, prostitutes recognized their dignity and people were often healed of those attitudes that had them imprisoned in their own minds. Christians are called a "new creation" by St. Paul. Our lives are to have a different focus. We are to live "in Christ." We are to be free to love.

2. **Salvation deals with the whole person.** Too often when we think of salvation, we think of something that happens to our souls. But the salvation that God offers us affects the whole person: mind, emotions, and body. When Jesus came upon the blind, the sick and the lame, he healed them. The saving power of God was not limited to a "spiritual" message alone. For a drug addict, the call to salvation has physiological consequences: it means freedom for his body from the devastation of drugs.

3. **Salvation begins in the here and now.** Most Catholics that I have met have an other-worldly understanding of salvation. They see it as something that happens after death. But that is only half-true. God's saving love is offered to us in this life. When Jesus was on earth he spoke mostly about how we should treat each other in the here and now. Our job as Christians is to be open to God's reign here on earth (as Jesus prayed, "Thy will be done on earth as it is in heaven"). We are to create friendships, families and societies in which the presence of God's love and justice can be found.

4. **Salvation is a process.** Some Christians talk about "being saved" as if this is a once-and-for-all event. Sometimes these are "born again" Christians who have gone through a powerful conversion in their lives and accepted Jesus as their Lord and Savior. Catholic Christianity agrees with the importance of accepting Jesus as one's Lord and Savior. However, since salvation is primarily a relationship, they view it more as a process than as a once and forever event. An alcoholic who has stopped drinking calls himself or herself a recovering (not recovered) alcoholic. Such persons are in the midst of a process. It is similar with salvation and faith. They are processes.

5. **Salvation is completed in eternity with God.** Our hopes are not limited to this world. The resurrection of Jesus reveals that the love and power of God is stronger than death. The love that God offers us does not end with our death. We are promised to share in the resurrection of Christ. Traditionally, Christians have called this "heaven." Whatever we call it, salvation means hope beyond death.

For Personal Reflection and Discussion

Have you ever met any "born again" Christians? How would you describe them? Has your faith changed you in any way?

HEAVEN, HELL AND PURGATORY

As we have seen, salvation reaches its final climax only after death. Let's take a closer look at what is meant by the categories of heaven, hell and purgatory.

Heaven. To me the most common images of heaven seem closer to hell: hanging out on a cloud playing a harp for eternity. If God wants people in heaven, there should be a better offer than that! In the Bible, heaven is described mostly through images. In the Hebrew scriptures, life after death was not an important theme or belief for the Jews until about five hundred years before the birth of Christ. In the time of Moses and David and Solomon, there does not seem to be any real notion of heaven as eternal life. When these ideas do begin to arise, they are descriptions not of what will happen to individuals after death, but rather of an end-time in which God's justice will be revealed and his promises fulfilled. One of the most common images used was that of the banquet:

> On this mountain the Lord of hosts will provide for all peoples a feast of rich food and choice wines, juicy rich food and pure, choice wines. On this mountain he will destroy the veil that veils all people, the web that is woven over all nations; he will destroy death forever (Isaiah 25:6–7).

The actual word "heaven" is not an important one in the New Testament concerning the final fulfillment of a person's life. In the New Testament, Jesus talks about the coming of the reign of God. He is concerned with this reign as both a present reality and a future fulfillment. God's reign is characterized by divine love and its effects on human beings. In his parables, Jesus also compares the reign of God to a great banquet or party. It is a banquet to which God invites all, but we can refuse that invitation. At the time of Christ, the Jews were divided in their belief concerning an afterlife. Jesus clearly sides with those who believe in such a final state of existence. He warns against the dangers of living only for the happiness offered in this world.

In his epistles, St. Paul makes it very clear that the resurrection of Christ is that which is promised to all those who believe. He compares Jesus to Adam: "Death came through a man; hence the resurrection of the dead comes through a man also. Just as in Adam all die, so in Christ all will come to life again" (Romans 15:21–22).

A final fulfillment of life after death is related more to the word "resurrection" than to "heaven." **This final fulfillment is not so much a place as it is a relationship.** Those who are "in Christ" are "in heaven." This relationship has already begun on earth, so we can begin to get a faint notion of what the future holds. It is reflected in those times, moments, and people where God's love is most powerfully present. It can be present in the birth of a child, in the love of a husband and wife, in peace between nations, in the care for the poor and the hungry, in the celebration of the eucharist, in a moment of forgiveness. As such, heaven is both an individual and a communal experience.

Finally, heaven is a gift from God. It is God's love offered to us in its full and final sense. On the one hand, we can't possibly earn it. Nothing we do can make God owe us his eternal love. It is his gift. On the other hand, we must accept it. We must not reject it. This brings us to the notion of hell.

For Personal Reflection and Discussion

Use your imagination: What is heaven going to be like? What will be the best thing about heaven? What would you especially want to see included in the experience?

Hell. Hell is the common term used to describe the place of everlasting torment for the damned and devils. If heaven is commonly thought to be "up," hell is down in the underworld. But hell, like heaven, is not so much a place as a relationship, or, better yet, a destroyed relationship. In the New Testament, Jesus uses a common image to describe hell: "If your right hand is your trouble, cut if off and throw it away! Better to lose part of your body than to have it all cast into Gehenna" (Matthew 5:30). Gehenna was a place outside Jerusalem which had been the site of human sacrifices by pagans and at the time of Jesus was likely a garbage pit with "unquenchable fires."

There are a number of ways of trying to understand the church's teaching about hell. The first has to do with justice. Just as a criminal is sentenced by a judge, so God sentences those who have lived sinfully without repentance. The injustices which took place on earth are reversed in the divine judgment. We see something of this idea in the parable of the rich man and Lazarus (see Luke 16). Because the rich man has ignored the beggar at his gate, he is sentenced to eternal damnation.

A second way of understanding hell would be a deterrent to immoral behavior on earth. It seems that Jesus used it in this sense in the passage above concerning Gehenna. Hell is God's way of bringing about the right behavior.

Today most theologians interpret hell as a statement about human freedom. We have the power to accept God's invitation to love others or to reject it. If we reject, we impose hell upon ourselves. It is not a judgment delivered by God as much as a judgment delivered by ourselves. This is an important factor. When the question is asked "How can an all-loving and merciful God possibly send people to hell?" the answer is that they choose it for themselves. God offers them salvation and grace. They reject it.

It is important to recall that the church does not teach that anyone in particular is in hell, only that hell is indeed a possibility. It is possible that God's grace does triumph over all. But Jesus warns against such a presumption when he says: "Enter through the narrow gate. The gate that leads to damnation is wide, the road is clear and many choose to follow it. But how narrow is the gate that leads to life, how rough the road, and how few there are who find it" (Matthew 7:13–14).

For Personal Reflection and Discussion

How would you describe hell? What would be hell for you? There is absolutely no way of knowing the answer to this question, but take a guess: On the average, how many people out of a hundred go to heaven? Compare your answer and your reasons with those of other people.

Purgatory. In addition to the church's teaching about heaven and hell, there is a third option after death. It is called purgatory. This is one of the teachings of the church that is not directly in the Bible. Purgatory is a place or a state of being in which people are "purged" of their sins in order that they may be able to encounter God in eternal life. The idea behind this is that before a person may encounter the fullness of God's love, he or she must be free from anything that would block out such love (sin). This is purgatory. This process may be aided with the prayers of the living. Those who are in purgatory are the just who shall be saved.

Earlier in this book, we said that faith will always have practical consequences. It is hard to see how they apply here. But there is an important practical consequence: to maintain our relationships beyond death. If you have lost a loved one to death, that relationship continues on the level of the spirit. People we love become a part of us and they live on in us. The doctrine of purgatory encourages us to continue to keep those relationships alive through memory and prayer.

For Personal Reflection and Discussion

Do you maintain relationships with those you love who have died? If so, how do you maintain the relationship?

Questions for Review

1. What are the main concerns of the first eleven chapters of Genesis? What questions do they address?
2. What is the difference between religious meaning and scientific meaning when it comes to the creation stories in Genesis?

3. What are the three main points of the first creation account in Genesis?
4. What is the author trying to teach in the story of the fall? What does the story tell us about sin and evil?
5. In what way is Jesus the "new Adam"?
6. What is original sin?
7. What is the difference between mortal and venial sin?
8. What is meant by social sin?
9. Describe fully what is meant by the Christian understanding of salvation. What are we saved from? What are we saved for?
10. Explain: "Heaven is more a relationship than a place."
11. Can we earn a reward in heaven?
12. What was one of the images used by Jesus for hell? How can an all-merciful God possibly send someone to hell?
13. Describe what is meant by purgatory.

4

The Word of God

GOD AND REVELATION

In the last chapter we looked at the reality of salvation, God's offer of forgiving love for a human race in need of reconciliation. In this chapter we will examine the Catholic Christian understanding of revelation. Revelation simply means God's self-communication and the communication of the divine will to his creatures. We have talked about the human need and search for God. But Christian faith is based on the belief that God communicates himself to us. **God is also searching for us. This means that God has taken the initiative and found a way to speak to the human race.** But how does God do this?

For Personal Reflection and Discussion

What are some ways in which God can communicate with us today?

COMMUNICATION: HUMAN AND DIVINE

Let's begin by looking at the way that human communication works. By communication, we mean not so much saying words but sharing oneself. I can talk to a rock if I want to, but I am not really communicating with it. **In order for me to share myself with someone else, the other person has to be open to receiving me and understanding me.** My best friend is someone who is really "in tune" with me. I can share myself with him or her, and he or she usually understands. A friend can connect in a way that a stranger cannot.

Now let's apply this to God communicating with us. **In order for God to do this, there must be something in us that is open to receiving this communication.** It seems that human beings have a special advantage here. We are open to God's communication in ways that the rest of the creation is not (at least as far as we know). What's the difference? Very simply, we are persons. We have a "self." As far as we know the rest of the creation lacks this. This self allows us to enter into relationships with others more deeply. It also gives us a relationship with ourselves. We ask: "Who am I? What do I want to do with my life? What is really important?" The earth, plants, trees, and my dog Rover can't do this. **Human beings are the only ones capable of being in love with each other, of sharing themselves with another. This is what allows God to share and communicate with us, because God is love.**

This probably sounds very abstract, but it is also very important. Human beings have been created with a capacity for love. It is this capacity that allows us to "hear" God's self-communication. **If this is true, then all human beings are at least potentially open to hearing God's word.**

But how does God speak? Does God have a voice? Perhaps the best way to say this is that **God speaks to us through us.** In other words, God does not speak directly to human beings. **He communicates through his creation and his creatures.** He communicates through the beauty of nature, the birth of a child, the love between people, our ability to think, our consciences, our ideas, through books and poetry, through our goodness and generosity. God is, in fact, always communicating through his creation.

For Personal Reflection and Discussion

Has there ever been a time when you thought that God was somehow "present" to you? Describe the experience fully. What happened? What were you feeling?

GOD REVEALED IN JESUS

Many people think that in the past (in the days when the Bible was being formed), God used to communicate directly with

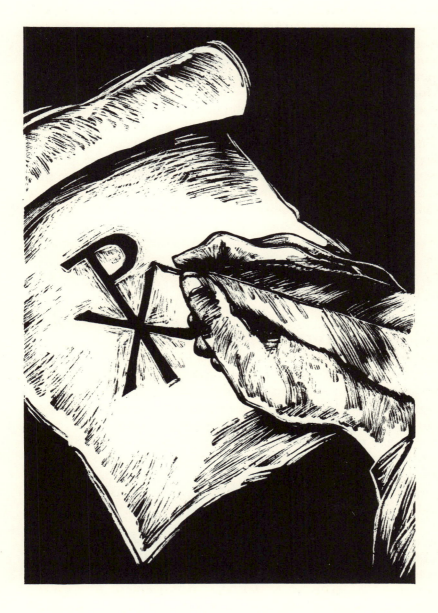

people. Since then he has stopped. For example, many people envision God dictating the commandments to Moses: "O.K., Moses. Number one: 'I am the Lord your God; you shall have no other gods besides me.' " This is a very simplistic notion of revelation. The commandments are certainly inspired by God. But the inspiration came through the insight, wisdom and prayer of Moses as well.

Christians believe that while God communicates to all human beings, **the fullness of this communication has been revealed in and through the person of Jesus Christ.** However, Jesus did not simply appear out of nowhere. He came as part of a people and promise. The story of Jesus makes sense only in light of the story of God's people, the Jews, for the God of Jesus is also the God of Abraham, Moses, David and the prophets.

For Personal Reflection and Discussion

If God could communicate a message to teenagers today, what do you think he would say? How can you help spread that message for him?

THE BIBLE AND TRADITION

The story of God's revelation to his people Israel and through his Son Jesus is found in the Bible. Any discussion of God's revelation must include an examination of the Bible as the word of God. **The Bible (or scripture as it is also known) has a unique and primary role in the Christian understanding of God's revelation. However, the Bible is not the only source of revelation for Christians.** For the word of God is a living word speaking anew to each generation. It is the task of Christians of each generation to move more deeply and fully into their understanding of God's revelation in Christ. This is the role of "tradition." **Tradition means not simply the ideas, rituals and formulas passed down from one age to the next but rather the ongoing interpretation and understanding of God's revelation.** Together, the Bible and tradition reveal **one source of revelation: God in and through Christ and the Spirit.**

For Personal Reflection and Discussion

What are some of the "traditions" in your family related to Christmas? How do these traditions help bring out the meaning of the day? What traditions would you like to create for your family in the future for Christmas?

UNDERSTANDING THE BIBLE

Some people decide that they are going to try to read and understand the Bible. They pick it up and begin on page 1 and try to make their way through the whole thing. They usually don't get very far. Their assumption is that the Bible is a book and that you should read it like any other book: from start to finish. This is usually a bad idea because in fact **the Bible is not a book. It is many books.** These books were written over a period of more than one thousand years. One book does not necessarily follow the next in a logical or chronological sequence. In short, it can be very confusing. Yet, in spite of all that, it remains the number one best-seller in the world year in and year out. People continue to turn to it in time of need and in search of inspiration. It remains at the heart of Christian faith as God's word.

There are two different (although related) ways of reading the scriptures: first, with the curiosity and intelligence of a scholar seeking to understand the meaning of the various books; second, with the openness and reverence of a believer seeking to hear God's word being spoken to me in my life. In this chapter, we hope to shed light on both.

For Personal Reflection and Discussion

Do you ever read the Bible on your own outside of a religion class? If so, why? If not, why not?

CONFLICTING INTERPRETATIONS

Not all Christians interpret the Bible in the same way. There are basically two different ways of interpreting the Bible. One interpretation is that of fundamentalism. **Fundamentalists believe that the Bible "says what it means and means what it says."** In other words, they interpret the Bible in a very literal fashion. If the Bible says that God created the world in six days, then that is what happened. If it says that the sun stopped in the sky, then the sun stopped. Fundamentalists believe that the Bible is God's word in the sense that God literally gave the precise words to the human authors that he wanted to be written. One might call this the "dictation theory of inspiration." God dictates the words to the human authors.

Most Christians (and most Jews as well) do not accept this form of interpretation. They **interpret the Bible contextually.** That is, they understand the words in the Bible in the broad context in which they were written. One must take into consideration the time and place in which the words were written, the author's concerns, the type of literature, the historical and intellectual circumstances, and the author's sources. In other words, **the Bible is the word of God, but God speaks through the faith, intelligence, abilities and limitations of the human author.** Thus, not every word in the Bible is of equal weight or value or of equal inspiration. Some parts of the Bible are clearly more important than others. For Christians, the New Testament is more important than the Old Testament, and within the New Testament the gospels are more important than the other twenty-three books.

The Catholic Church believes that the Bible is truly the word of God, written not solely by people but through God's guiding inspiration. However, it believes that **the inspired meaning can only be understood if we read the Bible in the context in which it was written.** It does not accept fundamentalism as a good approach to understanding the scriptures.

TOOLS OF INTERPRETATION

In order to interpret the Bible, scholars use a variety of techniques to help them uncover its meaning. Here we will briefly summarize a few of these:

1. **Literary analysis** (or criticism). The Bible consists of a variety of "literary forms." These include religious history, myth, poetry, gospels, epistles, etc. **In order to understand what we are**

reading it is essential to have a sense of its literary form. For example, the book of Job in the Old Testament tells of God inflicting incredible torture on Job in order to test his faith. This is a great work of fiction which seeks to teach a religious message about suffering and the will of God. It would be very misleading if we read the story as actual events, and we would most likely miss its point. Likewise, the first eleven chapters in Genesis are sometimes referred to as "myth." This is a very specific literary style. Myth does not mean "untrue" as it is sometimes used. Myth is a literary form which seeks to reflect on life's great mysteries through the use of story. Adam and Eve, Cain and Abel and Noah were not historical figures, and we might misinterpret the story if we think that they are.

2. **Historical analysis.** This is a broad term to describe the **study of the times, culture, surrounding nations, and influences on the biblical writers.** This is especially important because we believe that God acts in and through history, not in some timeless vacuum. This is particularly helpful in trying to interpret the historical and prophetic books of the Old Testament as well as many of the books in the New Testament (see below). Scholars today have access to more historical information than preceding generations because of extraordinary findings in archeology in the twentieth century.

3. **Redaction analysis.** A redactor is an editor, or, in this case, the biblical author. **This technique tries to focus on the intent of the author.** It takes for granted that the author will shape his writing according to his individual concerns. The four gospels in the New Testament, for example, reflect different (as well as similar) images of Jesus often shaped by the gospel writer's concerns.

4. **Study of biblical languages.** The Old Testament was written originally in **Hebrew.** The New Testament was written in **Greek.** Scholars have retranslated the Bible by going back to the original languages and better capturing the original meanings of the words.

THE OLD TESTAMENT

In a Catholic Bible, there are forty-six books in the Old Testament (also called the Hebrew scriptures). The Catholic Bible includes seven books not included in the Hebrew or Protestant Bibles (see chart at the end of the chapter). These books were part of the Septuagint (the Greek translation of the Hebrew scriptures) and were accepted by the Catholic Church as valid books but were later rejected by Jewish tradition and by Protestants. The Jewish tradition uses three divisions for these writings: the law, the prophets and the writings. Christian Bibles usually employ four categories:

1. The Pentateuch (Greek for "five books") or the Torah
2. Historical books
3. Prophetic books
4. Wisdom literature

The Old Testament is the story of a people who entered into a covenant with their God. The were a "chosen people" not because they were superior to other nations but because they had been chosen by God to be a light to other people, a sign of the greatness of their God.

The Pentateuch describes the early roots of these people. It begins with a **"pre-history" in Genesis 1–11** describing the creation of the world, the destruction of the harmony between God and his creatures, and **the patriarchs,** Abraham, Isaac, and Jacob. The book of Exodus describes the central event in Jewish history: the deliverance of the Hebrews from slavery in Egypt, the **covenant** established with Moses on Mount Sinai (ca. 1250 BCE), and the journey to the promised land. Also included are scores of **laws** which were to guide the people of Israel in the ways of the Lord.

The historical books describe much of the history of Israel. After the exodus from Egypt, they wandered in the desert for forty years before finally entering the promised land under the leadership of **Joshua.** The twelve tribes of Israel were still a loose confederation that gradually developed into the single nation of Israel. Under the kings **David and Solomon** (1020–930 BCE), Israel reached its peak of power and prestige. This peak was short-lived as a **civil war** divided the people into the northern kingdom of Israel and the southern kingdom of Judah. The northern kingdom lasted only about two hundred years before its destruction by the powerful Assyrians. Judah continued to survive but had to pay continual homage to Assyria. When the Babylonians defeated the Assyrians, the kings of Judah resisted their domination and were destroyed and taken into the exile known as the **Babylonian captivity** (ca. 586 BCE). The exile lasted nearly fifty years before the Persian king Cyrus conquered the Babylonians and allowed the Jews to return home. After their return, the Jews were still very much under the governance of the Persians. **Ezra and Nehemiah** spearheaded a religious reform that led to many of the practices of modern Judaism. In 332 BCE, Alexander the Great conquered the Near East and actively spread Greek culture among the Jews. In 175 BCE, **the Maccabees** fought for and gained a short-lived independence which ended in 63 BCE when the **Romans** occupied Palestine. They eventually allowed a Jewish ruler, **Herod the Great,** to govern the country for them. He was the king at the time of Christ's birth. (The history of Roman rule is not included in the historical books which go as far as the Maccabean revolt.)

The prophetic books are often divided among the greater and lesser prophets. These are determined by the length of the books as much as anything else. **The prophets were the great mouthpieces of the Lord who called the people back to fidelity to God and the covenant.**

Wisdom literature was unlike the other books in the Old Testament for many reasons. In the Wisdom books we find **little interest in the great themes of the covenant and salvation history.** They are rather more interested in religious issues that affect all people. They take a more contemplative and philosophical approach to these issues.

THE NEW TESTAMENT

With the life, death and resurrection of Jesus, Christians believe that God had offered a new covenant (or testament) to his people. The New Testament is a collection of writings in the early church which reflect the church's belief in Jesus. These writings were chosen by the church to be part of their sacred scriptures. (Those books which are officially part of the Bible are called the "**canon**.") In the New Testament there are twenty-seven books and four different types of literature:

1. Four gospels
2. Twenty-one epistles
3. One book of religious history
4. One book of "apocalyptic literature"

The Gospels. The four gospels (Matthew, Mark, Luke and John) have a special place of importance in the New Testament. In them we find the teaching and preaching of the early church about Jesus put in written form. **The word "gospel" means good news. This "good news" went through three phases of development:**

1. **First, there was the actual teaching and life of Jesus.** He called his message a gospel, the good news of God's love and mercy.
2. **Second, there was the teaching and preaching of the early church, called the oral tradition.** The stories told by Jesus and about Jesus were passed by word of mouth from community to community.
3. **Third, there were the actual written gospels.** It is generally accepted by scholars that the gospel of Mark was written first and that Matthew and Luke used his gospel in forming their own (these three have a similar structure and are called the "synoptic gospels"). John was last and used many different traditions. His gospel is quite different from the other three. In fact, all four give a unique perspective to the person and message of Jesus. (We will see more of this in the chapter on Jesus.)

Perhaps the biggest error is to mistake the gospels for biographies. They are not. They were meant to help the early Christians come to know the meaning of Jesus and his teaching. They were not greatly concerned with precise historical details. On the other hand, the gospels do give us a great deal of historical fact about the life, teaching and death of Jesus.

The Acts of the Apostles is the one book in the New Testament which might be labeled as "**religious history**." It was written by the evangelist Luke and is the second volume of his work. It tells the story of the early church, focusing at first on the community in Jerusalem and then on the journeys of Paul. It is not history in the same way that the gospels are not biography. They are written from the point of view of faith. **Luke wishes to show that a new age of history has begun: the age of the Holy Spirit.** Acts describes the power of the Spirit as the church develops from a small sect in Jerusalem and spreads throughout the entire Middle East. His book ends with Paul in Rome, showing that the message of Christ has spread to the center of the known world.

Epistles. The epistles are the most numerous "books" in the New Testament. However, they were not written as books. **They were letters** written to various communities in the early church. **These epistles can be divided into the Pauline and "catholic" epistles.** The Pauline epistles claim to have Paul as their author. Paul was the great missionary and theologian of the early church. He wrote letters to many of the communities that he had visited. In these letters we are able to get a good look at the faith and concerns of the early Christian communities. Many scholars question whether Paul did in fact write all the epistles attributed to him (see chart). The "catholic" epistles do not refer to the Catholic Church. They are catholic in that they are universal. They were intended for the Christian community at large without indicating any specific community. The letter to the Hebrews is not really a part of either group, but since it was once considered a letter of Paul's, we will list it among the Pauline group.

The book of Revelation is the favorite book of Hollywood directors. From it they gather the symbolism for such movies as "The Omen," "The Seventh Sign," and others. Reading this book in the twentieth century is a very difficult and confusing project. It is a form of "**apocalyptic literature**." This type of writing was **highly symbolic and was usually written in a time of crisis** (like the book of Daniel in the Old Testament). The book of Revelation, also known as the Apocalypse, was written when the church was being persecuted by the Roman empire. Its many symbolic references to the enemy are usually meant to attack the Romans. It has, unfortunately, been highly abused in the twentieth century. Some people claim that its symbols refer to events that are occurring today. This misses the entire point of why the book was written in the first place. The book of Revelation encourages Christians to hope in the face of the greatest odds and darkness, and as such it can be a book for all generations.

THE BIBLE IN THE CHRISTIAN COMMUNITY

For nearly two thousand years the Bible has continued to speak to those who seek to hear God's word. The Bible is a book that continues to nourish the spiritual life of Christians and Jews alike. It is a treasure of insight and wisdom into the relationship between ourselves and God. **If the Bible is to be a living word for us, we must learn to use it for prayer and meditation.** A scripture scholar who knows the details of the Bible but does not know its deepest meanings really knows little about the scriptures.

For Personal Reflection and Discussion

Do you have a favorite "saying" in the Bible? What is it? What does it mean to you?

THE LITURGY OF THE WORD

Part of the celebration of the mass each week includes selections from the Bible. Normally, the readings include:

1. an Old Testament passage
2. a psalm (read as a response)
3. an epistle from the New Testament
4. a passage from one of the gospels

During the year the same readings are read everywhere in Catholic churches throughout the world. The church uses a three year "cycle" of readings which are contained in a book called

THE BOOKS OF THE BIBLE

THE OLD TESTAMENT (those italicized are found in Catholic Bibles but not in Hebrew or Protestant scriptures)

Pentateuch (Torah): Genesis, Exodus, Leviticus, Deuteronomy, Numbers

Historical Books: Joshua, Judges, 1 and 2 Samuel, 1 and 2 Kings, 1 and 2 Chronicles, Ezra, Nehemiah, Ruth, Esther, Lamentations, *Judith, Tobit, Baruch, 1 and 2 Maccabees*

Wisdom Literature: Job, Psalms, Proverbs, Ecclesiastes, Song of Songs, *Ecclesiasticus, Wisdom of Solomon*

Prophets—Major: Isaiah, Jeremiah, Ezekiel, Daniel

Prophets—Minor: Hosea, Joel, Amos, Obadiah, Jonah, Micah, Nahum, Habakkuk, Zephaniah, Haggai, Zechariah, Malachi

THE NEW TESTAMENT

Gospels: Matthew, Mark, Luke, John

Religious History: Acts of the Apostles

Epistles—Pauline: Romans, 1 and 2 Corinthians, Galatians, Ephesians, Philippians, Colossians, 1 and 2 Thessalonians, 1 and 2 Timothy, Titus, Philemon, Hebrews

Epistles—Catholic: James, 1 and 2 Peter, 1, 2 and 3 John, Jude

Apocalypse: Revelation

a lectionary. In cycle A (years 1993, 1996, 1999, etc.), the gospel of Matthew is read on Sunday. In cycle B (1994, 1997, etc.), the gospel of Mark is read. In cycle C (1992, 1995, etc.), the gospel of Luke is read. In addition, each year the gospel of John is read during the Easter season (the seven weeks from Easter to Pentecost).

The Old Testament reading and the psalm response is chosen to fit in with the theme of the gospel passage (e.g., forgiveness, faith, God's love, etc.). The epistle may have nothing to do with this theme. We read through different epistles regardless of whether they fit the theme or not.

It is the role of the priest or deacon to preach about the meaning of the readings as they apply to our lives today. The readings used throughout the year are an excellent way of developing our relationship with God.

For Personal Reflection and Discussion

What cycle are we in as you read this? What are the readings for next Sunday (find a lectionary, or look in the back of your Bible, or consult the missalette in church)? What is the "theme" for the gospel? How is the Old Testament reading related to it?

THE BIBLE AND PRAYER

Surveys indicate that most adults and teenagers pray on some type of a regular basis. But what is prayer? Simply put, prayer is communication with God. Part of this communication is speaking: letting God know what is going on in our minds. But part of the communication is also listening: trying to "hear" what God is saying to us. One way in which we can listen is to reflect on God's word. Here are some practical suggestions for developing a life of prayer with the scriptures:

1. Plan your readings ahead of time. It is generally not a good idea to just open the Bible and read.
2. Find a quiet place where you know you will be free of distractions for a while.

3. Relax. Try to slow yourself down. Close your eyes and breathe slowly and deeply for about two or three minutes.
4. Read the passage you have chosen.
5. Ask yourself the following: What is this passage trying to say to me? How does it apply to my life now? Don't overload your circuits by trying to figure out how this reading will change your life. Take it a day at a time. Ask: How will I respond to this reading today? (You might want to keep a journal to briefly reflect on the reading.)
6. Finish with a closing prayer from your heart, asking God for his aid in living his word.
7. Don't always expect to feel inspired. Sometimes God may feel close or he may feel a million miles away. Remember that prayer is a commitment and a relationship.
8. Don't give up. If you stop praying for some reason, don't be afraid to get back on the track. Maybe you needed the break. Remember that God is more interested in your return than in your absence.

Questions for Review

1. Define revelation.
2. How does God communicate with his creatures?
3. What do Christians believe is the fullness of God's self-communication?
4. Define tradition.
5. What is the difference between fundamentalism and contextual interpretation?
6. What is meant by literary, historical and redaction analysis of the Bible?
7. What are the four divisions of the Old Testament?
8. What is the key event in forming Israel as a people of God?
9. What is a prophet?
10. How is wisdom literature different from the other books in the Old Testament?
11. What is the "canon" of the Bible?
12. What are the four literary forms that can be found in the New Testament?

13. Describe the three stages of development for the four gospels.
14. What is the main theme of the Acts of the Apostles?
15. What is an epistle? What is the difference between a Pauline and a catholic epistle?
16. What is apocalyptic literature? What is the main point of the book of Revelation?
17. Where do the four readings used at mass usually come from?

5

The Christian Understanding of God

As we saw in the last chapter, Christians believe that God has initiated a relationship with his creatures. God is revealed to us. But one thinks of the proverb, "Never feed a person more than he can digest." **God's self-revelation is limited by our human capacity to understand it.** This revelation was only gradually understood. It found its climax in the person of Jesus in whom God is fully revealed. Still, our understanding of this God is also something that grows and develops in time. Our own relationship with God must grow as we grow.

As we reflect on the Christian understanding of God, we will try to do this from two perspectives: scriptural images of God and theological ideas about God.

For Personal Reflection and Discussion

How did you understand or picture God when you were a little kid? Has your understanding of God changed at all? How?

BIBLICAL IMAGES OF GOD IN THE OLD TESTAMENT: YAHWEH, SAVIOR, LAWGIVER, CREATOR, JUDGE, MOTHER

We have seen that the Old Testament is a collection of forty-six books inspired by God. These books are very diverse in their themes and ideas. Scholars have tried to find a thread to connect all the books, a common theme. Scripture scholar John McKenzie says that there is **one thread running throughout the Old Testament:**

It can only be the discovery of Yahweh, the God of Israel. . . .
The discovery of Yahweh was something like the discovery of

America; it took several centuries before Israel really began to realize what it had discovered. Yet Yahweh is a single reality (*A Theology of the Old Testament,* Doubleday, N.Y. p. 29).

Israel's understanding of God was something that grew and developed in time. We will look briefly at some of the most important images of God revealed in the Old Testament. An image is a way of "picturing God" which includes both the mind and the heart. No image of God will ever be complete. The variety of images are meant to show the complexity of trying to describe a God who is beyond human words. That is why a number of images are needed to help balance the other images. They all should give us at least a glimmer of insight into the truth.

Yahweh. According to the book of Exodus:

"But," said Moses to God, "when I go to the Israelites and say to them, 'The God of your fathers has sent me to you,' if they ask me, 'What is his name?' what am I to tell them?" God replied, " 'I am who am.' This is what you shall tell the Israelites: 'I AM sent me to you' " (Exodus 3:13–14).

The name I AM is the English translation used for Yahweh. The meaning of the word is not clear, although it does appear to come from the Hebrew word meaning "to be." It likely means something similar to "the one who causes all to be." For the Jews, giving something a name meant having a type of authority over it (recall how Adam was instructed to name the animals). For this reason the name Yahweh was not allowed to be spoken by the Jews. It was the sacred and holy name. Thus, while God is given a name, the name is unspeakable. Both its meaning and its sanctity tell us something very important about the God behind the name: God is unlike any of his creatures and infinitely superior to them. Creatures come and go, but God **is** and God controls all. The God of Israel is the transcendent God: infinitely greater than his creatures. We see this notion of God's transcendence constantly emphasized throughout the Old Testament. **The name Yahweh teaches us that God is beyond any of the images or ideas that we apply to him.**

For Personal Reflection and Discussion

Draw a picture of God. Try to find a way to symbolically represent God in the drawing. What does the picture tell us about your understanding of God?

Savior. Just as the Declaration of Independence and the U.S. Constitution gave birth and identity to the United States as a nation, so **the exodus formed the people of Israel.** The Jews were a loosely knit group of people living under the enslavement of Pharaoh when God chose Moses to liberate his people from bondage. This liberation found its climax at the Sea of Reeds where the Jews escaped while Pharaoh's chariots were submerged under the sea. We find in the book of Exodus a folk song celebrating this great victory:

> I will sing to the Lord for he is gloriously triumphant;
>   horse and chariot he has cast into the sea.
> My strength and my courage is the Lord,
>   and he has been my savior.
> He is my God, I praise him;
>   the God of my father I extol him.
> The Lord is a warrior;
>   Lord is his name!
> Pharaoh's chariots and armies he hurled into the sea;
>   the elite of his officers were submerged in the Red Sea.
>   (Exodus 15:1–4)

For the Jews, their miraculous escape from bondage against all odds revealed **a God who freed them from slavery and who fought on their side against the Egyptians.**

Many people today would question this understanding of God as a warrior. Yet many Christians today who are living in hunger and oppression refer to the God of the exodus as their model because he frees them not only from spiritual oppression but from political oppression and slavery as well.

For Personal Reflection and Discussion

What do you think of the notion of God reflected in this ancient folk song? Do you think it is still a good image for us today?

Lawgiver. The Jews are a people called by God into a special covenant. God reveals that he has saved them from the Egyptians for a special reason:

> You have seen for yourself how I treated the Egyptians and how I bore you up on eagle wings and brought you here to myself. Therefore, if you hearken to my voice and keep my covenant, you shall be my special possession, dearer to me than all other people, though all the earth is mine. You shall be to me a kingdom of priests, a holy nation (Exodus 19:4–6).

But the covenant was a two-way pact. God promised himself to Israel, and they in turn were bound to follow his law. The ten commandments represent some of the highlights of the law of Yahweh. He was a God who placed demands on the people. They were to be a holy nation, and the way to holiness was through the law of God.

> Then God delivered all these commandments:
> "I, the Lord, am your God, who brought you out of the land of Egypt, that place of slavery. You shall have no other gods beside me. . . .
> You shall not take the name of the Lord your God in vain. . . .
> Remember to keep holy the sabbath. . . .
> Honor your father and your mother. . . .
> You shall not kill.
> You shall not commit adultery.
> You shall not steal.
> You shall not bear false witness against your neighbor.
> You shall not covet your neighbor's house.
> You shall not covet your neighbor's wife. . . ."
> (Exodus 20:1–17)

The law of God was more than rules for good conduct; it was the will of God for human beings which rooted them in the righteousness of God and gave them firm foundation for living. This is expressed in the first psalm:

> Happy the man who follows not
>   the counsel of the wicked
> Nor walks in the company of sinners,
>   nor sits in the company of the insolent,
> But delights in the law of the Lord
>   and meditates on his law day and night.
> He is like a tree
>   planted near running waters,
> That yields its fruit in due season,
>   and whose leaves never fade.
> [Whatever he does, prospers.]

The law provided the basis for the covenant on Sinai, but **the prophet Jeremiah looked forward to the day when a new law would come, a law written not on stone to be obeyed, but a law written within the hearts of the people:**

The days are coming, says the Lord, when I will make a new covenant with the house of Israel and the house of Judah. It will not be like the covenant I made with their fathers the day I took them by the hand to lead them forth from the land of Egypt; for they broke my covenant and I had to show myself their master, says the Lord. . . . I will place my law within them and write it on their hearts; I will be their God, and they shall be my people (Jeremiah 31:31–33).

For Personal Reflection and Discussion

What is the difference between obeying the law and having the law "written in your heart"? Give a specific example.

Creator. Israel was not the only ancient nation whose religion included stories of the creation. Its stories do, however, offer a different understanding of creation. In other "myths," creation springs from a battle between the gods. One of these myths is known as the Enuma Elish. In it the creation is caused by a battle between the god Marduk and his mother Tiamat. Marduk kills her and creates the earth from her slain body. People are created as the servants of the gods. The universe is the result not of God's creative power but of hostile forces at war. It is important to remember that the Genesis stories are not just "another myth." They are part of God's inspired word. In Genesis we have two creation accounts. The first emphasized creation springing from the power of God's word. The second reveals creation as the result of God's work. **The Israelite view of creation sees it in much more positive terms without the powers of good and evil at war with each other.** This is very evident in Psalm 104:

> Bless the Lord, O my soul!
>   O Lord, my God, you are great indeed!
> You are clothed with majesty and glory,
>   robed in light as with a cloak.
> You have spread out the heavens like a tent-cloth;
>   you have constructed your palace upon the waters.
> You make the clouds your chariot;
>   you travel on the wings of the wind.
> You make the wind your messengers,
>   and flaming fire your ministers. . . .
> May the glory of the Lord endure forever;
>   may the Lord be glad in his works!
> He who looks upon the earth, and it trembles;
>   who touches the mountains and they smoke!
> I will sing to the Lord all my life;
>   I will sing praise to God while I live.

We have already seen how the creation of human beings represents the culmination of the creation: they are created in God's image.

The notion of God as creator was very important to the Jews, but it could only be understood in the context of the God who acted in history and who saved his people. The God who was praised as creator is the one who liberated his people from slavery and formed a covenant with them.

For Personal Reflection and Discussion

Recently we have begun to realize how precious and fragile this earth is. The environmental movement has challenged us to evaluate the way we use or abuse the earth. Write a psalm of praise and thanksgiving for God's gift of creation.

Judge. The God of the Old Testament is a God who sides with the poor and oppressed against their oppressors. He is a God who calls his people beyond religious rituals to the true practice of their faith: care for the poor, the orphan and the widow. This challenge of God usually comes through the mouths of the prophets. The common notion of a prophet is someone who foretells the future, but in the Bible the prophet is primarily someone who speaks on behalf of God. **Prophets served as the "conscience of the people,"** and often the truth that they proclaimed was one that the people would rather not hear.

Amos was one of the great prophets of God's justice. The Israelites had developed many rituals to worship Yahweh. These often included the sacrifices of animals and the chanting of songs at the feast. At the time of Amos (ca. 750 BCE) there was a great gap between the few rich and the many poor. Amos spoke on behalf of Yahweh:

> I hate, I spurn your feasts,
>   I take no pleasure in your solemnities. . . .
> Away with your noisy songs!
>   I will not listen to the melodies of your harps.
> But if you would offer me holocausts,
>   then let justice surge like water
>   and goodness like an unfailing stream.
>   (Amos 5:21–24)

> Hear this, you who trample upon the needy
>   and destroy the poor of the land.
>   (Amos 8:4)

For Personal Reflection and Discussion

You are God's prophet speaking a hard truth to his people. What is your message?

Mother. One of the great misconceptions that many Christians have is the idea that the God of the Old Testament is a God of law while the God of the New Testament is a God of love. It is the same God, and Yahweh is a God of profound love for his people. The prophet Isaiah expresses this love beautifully. After the Babylonian captivity, the people felt abandoned by God. Isaiah reassured them that God's love is like that of a mother for her infant:

> But Zion said, "The Lord has forsaken me;
>   my Lord has forgotten me."
> Can a mother forget her infant,
>   be without tenderness for the child of her womb?
> Even if she should forget,
>   I will never forget you.
> See, upon the palms of my hands I have written your name. . . .
> (Isaiah 49:14–16)

Psalm 139 tells of God's intimate knowledge of all his children. He is not only the creator of the universe, but the creator of all of us:

> O, Lord, you have probed me and you know me,
>   you know when I sit and when I stand;
>   you understand my thoughts from afar. . . .
> Truly you have formed my inmost being;
>   you knit me in my mother's womb.
> (Psalm 139:1–2. 13)

For Personal Reflection and Discussion

Usually Christians speak of God as Father, but Isaiah compares God to a pregnant woman. What can we learn about God from the image of "mother"?

NEW TESTAMENT IMAGES: ABBA, FATHER, PARABOLIC IMAGES

Abba, Father. Jesus used the Aramaic word **Abba** to refer to God. The word is a term of affection much like "daddy" or "pop" in English. The word was used by children, both young and old, for their earthly fathers. It was a term that was both intimate and respectful. Although the actual Aramaic word is referred to only once in Mark 14:36, Jesus refers to God as "Father" and "my Father" constantly in all four gospels. He also invites his disciples to do the same. St. Paul uses the term as well in his epistles to describe the vocation of the Christian:

> All who are led by the Spirit of God are sons of God. You did not receive a spirit of slavery leading you back into fear, but a spirit of adoption through which we cry out "Abba!"

By calling God "Abba," "Father," Christians are reminded of the deep intimacy between God and his children. These texts are sometimes used to teach that God is male, but that is not the point. **Jesus is not trying to teach us about God's gender but about his unconditional love for us.** (We will say more about this later in the chapter). Jesus' best description of God as Father comes in his famous parable of the prodigal son (which would be better titled as the parable of the loving father). In the parable (Luke 15:11–31), a son insists on having his share of his inheritance before his father dies. His father sells half his estate, and the son goes away and spends the money on reckless and immoral living. Only after he has humiliated himself does the son make his way home to beg his father's help and be hired as a servant on his farm. But the father will not hear of it. He throws his arms around his wayward son and throws a party for him. He is truly delighted to have him home safe and sound.

For Personal Reflection and Discussion

How is the image of God as Father different from Isaiah's motherly image? What differences do these images teach us about God? How might a person's understanding of God as Father be distorted if he grows up in an unhealthy relationship with his own father?

Parabolic Images. Many of the images of God used by Jesus are more subtle because they are parts of his parables, and he does not explicitly make a connection between the image and God. In these parables God is being compared to a diverse group of images:

1. God is like the shepherd who searches out his lost sheep (Luke 15:1–7).
2. God is like the woman who searches for her lost coin (Luke 15:8–10).
3. God is like the farmer who sows his seed everywhere (Matthew 13:4–9).
4. God is like the farmer who sows good seed (Matthew 13:24–30).
5. God is like the power in the mustard seed which is transformed into the largest of shrubs (Matthew 13:31–32).
6. God is like the yeast which makes the dough rise (Matthew 13:33).
7. God is like the owner of a vineyard who gives his workers more than they have earned (Matthew 20:1–16).

Notice that some of the images refer to men, some to women, and some to nature. Each seeks to make its own point about God and his relationship to us.

For Personal Reflection and Discussion

Choose three of the parables listed above and read them in their entirety. What do you think each is trying to teach us about our relationship with God?

JESUS AS THE IMAGE OF GOD

We have briefly examined some of the images that Jesus himself used for God. However, after the death and resurrection of Jesus, **the early church recognized that Jesus himself was the true and full "image" of God.** More than any other image, Jesus himself reveals who God is for Christians. The author of the epistle to the Colossians writes:

> He is the image of the Invisible God,
>   the firstborn of all creation.
> In him everything in heaven and on earth was created,
>   things visible and invisible . . .
>   all were created through him and for him.
>   (Colossians 1:15–16)

On the same theme, the author of the letter to the Hebrews writes:

> In times past, God spoke in fragmentary and varied ways to our fathers through the prophets; in this, the final age, he has spoken to us through his Son, whom he has made heir of all things and through whom he first created the universe. This Son is the reflection of the Father's glory, the exact representation of the Father's being, and he sustains all things through his powerful word (Hebrews 1:1–3a).

And the gospel of John focuses very much on this theme, as Jesus says to his apostles, "Whoever has seen me has seen the Father" (John 14:9).

For Personal Reflection and Discussion

Which of the following best describes your understanding of Jesus as the image of God: Jesus the teacher? The crucified Jesus? The baby Jesus? Jesus the friend of sinners? Jesus the healer? Why?

THE HOLY SPIRIT

The early church discovered something extraordinary in Christ: that God had visited his people through him. Yet, after Christ's resurrection and ascension into heaven, the **church continued to experience the abiding presence of God in their midst.** Jesus had not abandoned them to their own devices. **God continued to be present to them in and through the Holy Spirit.** In the gospel of John, Jesus promised his followers that he would not abandon them:

> I will ask the Father, and he will give you another Paraclete to be with you always: the Spirit of truth. . . . The Paraclete, the Holy Spirit whom the Father will send in my name, will instruct you in everything, and remind you of all that I told you (John 14:16–17. 26).

In this passage the Holy Spirit is described as a "paraclete" or "advocate." This was a legal term that described someone's legal representative. The Spirit is the representative of the Father and the Son.

Luke describes the initial experience of the Spirit at the feast of Pentecost:

> When the day of Pentecost came, it found them gathered in one place. Suddenly from up in the sky there came a noise like a strong driving wind which was heard all through the house where they were seated. Tongues as of fire appeared, which parted and came to rest on each of them. All were filled with the Holy Spirit. They began to express themselves in foreign tongues and make bold proclamation as the Spirit prompted them (Acts 2:1-4).

In this passage, Luke uses the symbols of wind and fire to describe the Spirit. Both can be found in the Old Testament as symbols for the presence of God. The wind and fire are symbols from nature which describe the power of the Spirit to transform the disciples. They leave behind their fear and become bold witnesses of faith. They are able to communicate with men and women of different nations and languages.

For Personal Reflection and Discussion

How would you describe the Holy Spirit to someone who had never heard that there was such a thing?

CHRISTIAN THEOLOGY: THE TRINITY

Thus far, we have been examining the various images and understandings of God in the Bible. The Christian understanding of God does not finish there. The Church continued to try to understand who God is.

The early church faced a problem. They knew that there was only one God. They also believed that Jesus was God, but that he was not the Father. Likewise, the Spirit was also the presence of

God but was not completely identifiable with the Father and the Son. Would they have to change the basic belief of Judaism: that God is one? Were there three Gods?

In order to be able to solve this dilemma, the Christian community had to rethink their understanding of God. Eventually the church concluded that there is only one God but there are three persons in the one God: Father, Son and Spirit. If we try to understand this mathematically, we are doomed. There is no way that one plus one plus one can equal one. Nor is each person one-third of God. Each is truly God, yet each is distinct from the other.

It would be misleading to think that we can understand this in a pure logical form. It is important to remember that the Trinity is the ultimate Christian mystery: it transcends the human mind's capacity to know. Nor did some theologian sit down and reflect on God and conclude that God must be a Trinity. The dogma of the Trinity comes from the Christian experience of God's revelation. God has revealed himself to us as Father, Son and Spirit. Faith tells us that the three are totally united with each other yet distinct from each other. Let's see what we can learn from each of these persons:

1. The Father is the first person of the Trinity. He is the source of all, and from him the Son is begotten. The first person of the Trinity refers to God as the creator, the source of all being. By calling him "Father," we remind ourselves that the creator is one who enters into a loving relationship with his creation.

2. The Son is the second person of the Trinity. The Son is the expression of the Father. He is also referred to as God's word or logos. Just as an artist expresses himself by painting a picture, the Father expresses himself as the Son. It is the Son who took on flesh in the person of Jesus Christ. We have seen how the Son was understood in the New Testament as the full expression of the Father. God the Son reveals to us that God is not only the infinite source but the incarnate God as well. He is the God who became one of us.

3. The Spirit is the third person of the Trinity. The Spirit is the love that is generated by Father and Son. This love is made available to us as a power of God's love inside us. This is the love that allows us to share in the very life of God.

In less abstract terms, it is the Holy Spirit inside us that allows us to recognize God as our Father, to offer him praise and worship, to turn to him for mercy and forgiveness. It is the same Spirit in us that allows us to see the presence of Christ in all men and women and to accept Jesus as the Lord of our lives.

For Personal Reflection and Discussion

Which of the three persons of the Trinity do you relate to the most at this stage of your faith? Why?

SPECIAL QUESTIONS: GOD'S EXISTENCE, GENDER AND THE PROBLEM OF EVIL

1. How do we know that there is a God since he is not visible?
    We know that there is a God because he has revealed himself to us. However, this is the knowledge of faith. We believe in the God who has revealed himself to us.

2. Is it possible to prove that there is a God?
    It's not completely possible to prove it in the normal manner of "proving" something. Yet there is considerable evidence which could be called a "proof":
    a. St. Thomas Aquinas, the most influential Catholic thinker in history, believed that God is the "first cause" of creation. When we look at the world in which we live, we can ask ourselves: "Where did everything come from?" We can trace back the natural causes as far as we want, but eventually we must say that there must be a being who is not caused but who causes everything else to be. This being is God. It is important to realize that God is unlike any other type of being. **God is not a being, he is being itself.** The mere existence of creation implies a creator, that which is infinitely greater and unlike the creation.
    b. In addition, when we look at the creation, we can see that it has been created with extraordinary intelli-

gence. The working of the human body alone is a miracle greater than the parting of the Red Sea. **The intelligence within the creation points to an intelligence beyond it which is responsible for it. This is what we call God.**

c. The human experience of goodness also points to the presence of God. Humans are free to live as they choose. Humans experience within themselves a call to goodness, a conscience which tells them that it does matter how they live. If there really is a good life to be lived, there must be an ultimate source of this goodness. If there is not, then good and evil are something that each person can decide for himself or herself. If I want to be a hit man for organized crime, that's O.K. because it is my choice. I determine what is good or bad. But we know that it is much better to live like Mother Teresa than a drug dealer because we have a conscience. **This conscience points to the ultimate good, God.**

d. Humans experience within themselves a capacity to think, to reflect, to appreciate beauty and goodness. **This is the spiritual dimension of being human and it points to an ultimate spiritual reality which is God.**

3. Is God a man?

Most people believe that God is male, but in Christian theology **God is pure spirit. He is not a creature, so he does not have a sexuality.** God is neither male nor female. Yet since we talk about God as a person, we describe him most often as male because the Bible uses so many male images. But it is important to remember that there are other images as well, and they are only images. God is our loving Father, but God is also our loving Mother. It is important and helpful to be able to see both the masculine and the feminine within God.

4. If God is all-powerful, why does he permit evil things to happen?

A final answer to this question cannot be known, but we might shed some light on the issue.

a. God created humans to love him and other people. In order for this to happen they must be free. (Otherwise they are simply programmed robots.) **Humans have abused their freedom and brought about great suffering and evil in the world.**

b. Some suffering is not brought about by sin. People get incurable and painful diseases. Children are killed in earthquakes and accidents. Some die at birth. Why doesn't God do something for them? It would seem that while God is perfect, his creation must be imperfect (or it would be God), and this imperfection brings about suffering for people. From the point of view of faith, there is no suffering or evil great enough to overcome God's love. We, however, do not get to see the "big picture," God's ultimate design in which he will redeem all suffering through love.

Questions for Review

1. What single theme connects all the books of the Old Testament?
2. What was the name revealed by God to Moses? What does it tell us about God?
3. What image of God is contained in the Israelite folk song in Exodus 15?
4. What was the role of the law in the covenant?
5. How did Jeremiah envision a new law?
6. How are the Genesis stories of creation different from those in the Enuma Elish?
7. What was the mission of the prophet Amos? What did that mission tell us about God?
8. What feminine image does Isaiah use to describe God?
9. What does the name "Abba" mean? What does it tell us about Jesus' understanding of God? What parable most fully describes this Abba?
10. What nature images of God does Jesus use in the parables?
11. For Christians, where is the image of God most complete?
12. What word does John use to describe the Holy Spirit? What does this tell us about the Spirit?

13. What words does Luke use to symbolize the Spirit? Why?
14. What does the doctrine of the Trinity tell us about God?
15. According to Catholic Christian theology is God a man?
16. If God is all-powerful, why does he not end all wars to-
    morrow?

6

The Life of Jesus

What makes Christian faith Christian? In a word—Christ. **The heart, soul, and center of Christian faith is a person, Jesus Christ.** It is impossible to know anything about Christianity or Catholicism without the focus being on Christ. Since almost all of our knowledge of Jesus comes from the four gospels, it is to the gospels that we look in order that we may come to know more deeply and fully the center of our faith: Jesus Christ.

JESUS OF HISTORY, CHRIST OF FAITH

Scholars sometimes distinguish two levels of knowledge of Christ: the Jesus of history and the Christ of faith. **"Jesus of history" is the historical person Jesus of Nazareth**—the facts of his life: what he did and said and how he affected the lives of those who knew him. The **"Christ of faith" refers to what we believe about Jesus of Nazareth** (for example, he is the Son of God). In the four gospels we find the Christ of faith, but we are also given information about the Jesus of history as well. This chapter will focus on what we know about Jesus. Another chapter will focus on what we believe about him.

For Personal Reflection and Discussion

You are speaking with someone who has never heard of Jesus of Nazareth. Make a list of facts that we know about him (not what we believe).

THE WORLD OF JESUS: THE MESSIAH, JESUS THE JEW, JEWISH GROUPS

It is almost impossible to understand someone without knowing something about the world in which he or she lives. People are very much shaped by their society and culture. Likewise, if we want to get to know Jesus, we must know the world in which he lived.

At the time of Jesus' birth, **Palestine was part of the Roman empire.** The Romans allowed **Herod the Great** to rule as king beginning in 37 BCE and ending shortly after the birth of Jesus. Matthew's gospel tells the story of Herod killing the innocent infant boys in Bethlehem in an attempt to kill the newborn king of the Jews. Whether or not this event actually happened, it certainly would have been in keeping with Herod's personality. He was a paranoid who killed members of his own family to protect his own power.

After Herod's death, his kingdom was originally divided among his three sons, Herod Antipas, Archelaus and Philip. Herod Antipas ruled Galilee, Philip ruled the regions to the east, and Archelaus was the tetrarch of Idumea, Samaria and Judea. Archelaus was hated by the Jews, and the Romans eventually replaced him with a Roman governor. The most famous of these governors was **Pontius Pilate.**

For Personal Reflection and Discussion

Imagine what it would be like to live in a country occupied by a foreign nation. How do you think this would affect the mentality of the people?

The Messiah. The Jewish people continued to hope that God would one day fulfill his promises. They awaited the coming of the messiah who would free them from their bondage to Rome and restore Israel to its former prominence. **The word "messiah" means "the anointed one" and originally referred to David and the Jewish kings.** The kings were anointed to show that they were

God's representatives and that their power was dependent on their fidelity to God who was the only true king of Israel. In time, as the monarchy became corrupt and eventually vanished, there developed the hope that God would send a true messiah. Yet there was no single clear belief on who the messiah would be or what he would accomplish. For some the messiah meant the coming of the "day of Yahweh." It would be a decisive event in which God's reign would be established. For others the coming of the messiah was seen in terms of national liberation, while others believed that when the messiah came the Torah would finally be observed with fidelity. When John began his baptism, it flamed the hopes of the Jews. Perhaps God would finally act on behalf of his people.

For Personal Reflection and Discussion

People today are still looking for a messiah: someone or something that will make their lives fulfilling. There is a tendency in our culture to make messiahs out of military power or financial success.

Who are the heroes of American society? Do you think they show us a great way to be human beings?

Jesus the Jew. It was in this context of hope that Jesus was raised in Galilee and began his public ministry. **The first thing that we must recognize about Jesus is his Jewishness.** When we look at portraits of Jesus today, they are often reflections of the culture from which they are produced. The white-skinned, blue-eyed Jesus who looks at us from our portraits is not meant to be an accurate physical portrayal of Jesus of Nazareth. In the east Jesus looks Oriental; in Africa he is black. These artistic renderings point to the truth that Christ is the savior of all and the body of Christ embraces all cultures. However, the Jesus of history was Jewish. He was circumcised, prayed in the synagogues, worshiped in the temple, studied the Hebrew scriptures and identified strongly with the message of the prophets. He was born into the faith of Israel, and his teaching and message must be understood in that context.

For Personal Reflection and Discussion

All prejudice is un-Christian but the most absurd is antisemitism. Our Lord was Jewish. Mary was Jewish. St. Peter and all the apostles were Jewish.

What are some ways to fight against prejudice within ourselves and our society?

Jewish Groups. When we read the gospels, we see that within Judaism there were many different beliefs and ways of life. In a sense it was not unlike Christianity today in which we can find monks and activists, priests and laypersons, Catholics and Protestants, nuns and mothers. Likewise, the people of Israel were not a monolithic group.

One of the groups often mentioned in the gospels were **the Pharisees. These were laymen who believed in a strict interpretation of both the oral and the written law.** The written law was the precepts of the Torah. The oral law was the rabbinic interpretations of those laws. The name "Pharisee" means "the separate ones," for they refused to associate with those less pious than themselves. The gospels portray Jesus and the Pharisees as often in conflict with each other. The Pharisees took exception to his interpretation of the law and his association with public sinners.

The **scribes** are often mentioned with the Pharisees. They **were the educated class who were experts in the Jewish law.** Many of them belonged to the Pharisee party. Like the Pharisees, they are most often mentioned in the gospels to be in opposition to the teaching and actions of Jesus. They would have resented Jesus teaching on his own authority since they believed that the law was the only true source of righteousness.

The priests of Israel were called Sadducees. They were members of an aristocratic class who wielded both political and religious power. The Sadducees were in charge of the temple and its worship. Unlike the Pharisees, they accepted only the written Torah and no further additions. They resented the Pharisees and their intrusion on the religious life of the people. One famous Sadducee was the high priest Caiaphas who presided over the trial of Jesus which led to his eventual death.

During Jesus' life there were a group of Jews who believed that the Romans must be expelled from their land. They were called **zealots.** They **used terrorist tactics and were hated by both the Romans and most of the Jews.** The zealot movement was fairly calm during the life of Jesus, but they instigated a revolt against Rome in the late 60s that led to the eventual destruction of the temple.

One of the groups mentioned in the gospels is the **Samaritans.** Today when we hear the word "Samaritan" we usually think of the good Samaritan and a person who helps another in need. This is ironic because the Jews certainly did not think of the Samaritans as "good." In fact, they hated them. **There was a long-standing feud between the Jews and the Samaritans.** Originally part of the faith of Israel, the Samaritans had intermarried with pagans and built their own temple on Mount Gerizim. When Jesus made the Samaritan the hero of his parable, it was done for shock purposes. It would be like making Martin Luther King, Jr. the hero of a story told to the Ku Klux Klan.

For the common people, their faith revolved around the local synagogue and the sabbath. The sabbath was the seventh day of the week, set aside for God. It was a day of rest and prayer. The synagogue was the local place of prayer. The sabbath and the synagogue allowed the faith of Israel to be celebrated by all and to be made part of the daily life of the people.

The synagogues are not to be confused with the temple. **There was only one temple, which was considered the dwelling place of God.** It was located in Jerusalem on Mount Zion. Jews would make a pilgrimage to the holy city and the temple for the great festivals of Passover, Pentecost and Tabernacles. Jesus was on pilgrimage for the Passover when he was arrested and put to death.

For Personal Reflection and Discussion

Can you think of a parallel in Christianity for the following: the Pharisees, the Sadducees, the Samaritans, the sabbath and the temple?

Now that we have looked at the world in which Jesus lived, let us turn our attention to Jesus himself. We have already seen that the gospels are not really the same as biographies, but that does not mean that they are misleading or untrue. We can discover a great deal about Jesus from the gospels even if not every word or detail happened exactly as described.

The birth of Jesus (see Matthew 1–2 and Luke 1–2). Every little child knows the story of Jesus' birth. **The basis for the Christmas stories comes from two of the gospels: Matthew and Luke. Other than these two gospels, there is no information concerning Jesus' birth anywhere in the New Testament.** In studying these accounts of Jesus' birth, sometimes called the infancy narratives, scholars today are convinced that the stories have been shaped by their authors into "mini-gospels" which are concerned more with the meaning of the birth than the birth itself. The two versions are startlingly different from each other. Luke mentions the appearance of the angel to Mary, the trip to Bethlehem, the birth in the stable, and the visit by the shepherds. Matthew mentions none of these. Instead, he relates an angelic appearance to Joseph, a visit from the three wise men, and an attempt on the life of Jesus by King Herod, none of which can be found in Luke. What is going on here? **Why are the accounts so different?** Because Matthew and Luke were working from different "oral traditions" and they wanted to emphasize different messages. (We will see more about this in a later chapter.) If we look at what they have in common, it may help us to get to the facts of the matter:

1. Jesus is conceived when Joseph and Mary are engaged but before they are living together.
2. The conception is a miraculous one. Mary is a virgin when it occurs.
3. An angel appears and declares that the child has been conceived through the power of the Holy Spirit and they are to name him Jesus.
4. Jesus is born of Mary in Bethlehem.

The Catholic Church has always insisted on the historical accuracy of the virginal conception of Jesus. They have taught that this is not a symbolic story but a miraculous event.

For Personal Reflection and Discussion

It is impossible to recover the actual events of Jesus' birth beyond the shadow of a doubt, but the details are not really the important thing at all. The stories in Matthew and Luke give us the true meaning of Christmas: in the birth of this infant, God has visited his people and brought them salvation.

How are you doing with Christmas? Has any of its real meaning been preserved in your celebration of it? What can you do this Christmas to remember the real reason for the season?

The gospels give us no historical information about Jesus as he was growing up. The one story of Jesus teaching in the temple (Luke 2:41–52) is most likely a legend rather than fact.

The Baptism of Jesus (read Mark 1:1–11; Matthew 3:13–17). **Jesus' baptism by John in the Jordan is the beginning of his public ministry.** Until this time, we know almost nothing about his life. The only information that the gospels give us is that he was from Nazareth, that he was a carpenter, and that he was about thirty years old. After the baptism, however, Jesus put his carpentry behind him and began to travel through the countryside teaching and preaching.

John's baptism was not the baptism that Christians receive. People were not becoming Christians. It was a baptism of repentance. John proclaimed the coming of the new age when God would finally act. The baptism was to prepare a person for the coming of the Lord.

It is difficult to know with certainty why Jesus went to John to be baptized. Whatever the reason, it gives us a clue about the type of messiah that Jesus will be: one who wades into the waters of sinful human beings. He is not a powerful, aloof king. Nor is he a monk. In his baptism, Jesus identifies with sinners and the common people of Palestine.

For Personal Reflection and Discussion

John was a prophet who called the people away from their practical concerns to face the demands of God in their life. Can you think of any contemporary "John the Baptists"?

JESUS' TEACHING AND MESSAGE:
THE COMING OF THE REIGN OF GOD

Here are some typical responses to the question: What was the message of Jesus Christ?

Woman:	Jesus told us to love one another.
Man:	I think that Jesus came to tell us to obey the commandments.
Teenager:	Jesus said that everyone is loved by God, no matter what one's race or religion.
Senior citizen:	The message of Jesus Christ is very simple: "Do unto others as you would have them do unto you."
Young Man:	In a word: forgiveness. God is all-forgiving, and we should be willing to forgive others as well.
Young Woman:	Jesus came to teach us about God. He taught us the way God expects us to live, which is to love each other.
Senior Citizen:	If I had to summarize the teaching of Jesus in one word, I would say "compassion." Jesus taught us to live lives of compassion for the poor and the sick and the outcasts of society.

For Personal Reflection and Discussion

If you had to explain the message of Jesus Christ to someone who had never heard of him, what would you say?

The Coming of the Reign of God. The main themes of Jesus' message are well known by most Christians. Jesus taught about love, compassion, forgiveness, and reconciliation. Yet **they can all be placed under one heading: the reign of God. Scripture scholars agree that the central theme of Jesus' message was the coming of the reign of God.** The very first words from the mouth of Jesus in the gospel of Mark place this theme at the core of Christ's proclamation: "Now is the time of fulfillment. **The reign of God is at**

hand. Repent and believe in the gospel." If we wish to understand the message of the master, we must first understand what he means by the reign of God.

For the people of Israel, the reign of God represented the time in which God would fulfill his promises, when God's people would worship him from their hearts. It is the time foreseen by Isaiah when the lion and the calf lie down together. It is the great banquet to which all nations will be called. The reign of God is the end of the reign of sin and death. For the Jews, God's reign signified the end time when God would act with justice for his people.

God's Reign Is Near at Hand. Jesus appears on the scene and says, "The time you have waited for is here. It is coming. God's reign is at hand." **For Jesus, God's reign is already breaking through to his people.** We see Jesus describing God's reign by using very ordinary and commonplace circumstances in the lives of his listeners. What is this reign of God? It is like yeast, or a seed, or a woman who loses a coin or a man who finds a pearl, or a farmer who sows seed. For Jesus, the reign of God is near.

For Personal Reflection and Discussion

God's reign is present in this world—but incomplete, and awaiting fulfillment in the future. A popular word for God's reign is "heaven." How is this reign present now in your life and in the world that you live in?

The Parables. The best place to look for Jesus' understanding of the reign of God is in his parables. The parables were stories and images used by Jesus in his teaching. Not only do they center around the reign of God, but scholars agree that the parables found in the gospels find their source in the actual words of Jesus. What is the reign of God like? Let us look at one of the images Jesus uses to describe it:

> The reign of God is like yeast which a woman took and kneaded into three measures of flour. Eventually, the whole mass of dough began to rise (Matthew 13:33).

Likewise, God's reign is the result of the extraordinary power of God at work in the world. God's reign is not a human achievement alone. Such power comes from God.

There is something of a contradiction in the message of Jesus. **On the one hand, God's reign is brought about by the power of God. On the other hand, humans are needed to "knead the dough."** It seems to be a collaborative effort between God and his people. The temptation is either to think that we can build the kingdom of God alone or to put it all in God's hands.

For Personal Reflection and Discussion

When it comes to building God's reign, traditional Christian wisdom has said, "Pray as if everything depends on God; work as if everything depends on you." Both elements are essential to the task. How are you helping to bring God's reign to the people in your life?

Open Your Eyes and Your Heart. In the story *The Little Prince,* the fox advises the Prince that "it is only with the heart that one can see rightly. That which is essential is invisible to the eye." Jesus also encouraged his listeners to look at life differently, for they might be surprised at what they find. For Jesus, the reign of God had already begun in his preaching, his miracles and his offer of reconciliation to sinners. Part of the message of Jesus was a wake-up call to the people: NOW IS THE TIME OF FUL-FILLMENT! DON'T MISS IT! **Jesus called his listeners to be attentive and responsive to the presence of God in their midst:**

> He said to the crowds: "When you see a cloud rising in the west, you say immediately that it will rain and so it does; and when you notice that the wind is blowing from the south, you say that it is going to be hot—and so it is. You hypocrites! You know how to interpret the appearance of the earth and the sky; why do you not know how to interpret the present time?" (Luke 13:54–56).

For Personal Reflection and Discussion

Sometimes the best things in life are right under our nose. We just need to look at them differently. We need to see them through the eyes of the heart.

Who have you been taking for granted recently? Look again—this time from the heart.

God's Reign Is a Party! In the Hebrew scriptures, the image that is used for heaven more than any other is that of a banquet. The prophet Isaiah writes, "On this mountain, the Lord of hosts will provide for all peoples a feast of rich food and choice wines, juicy rich food and pure choice wines" (25:6), and Jesus often adopts this image himself. The reign of God is a party. It is a time of rejoicing, of celebration. It is a time of fellowship and community. It is a time when the burdens of the world seem lost to us, when we are drawn up into a different and better reality.

In the parable of the great feast (Luke 14:15–24), Jesus tells the story of a man who gives a great dinner to which many are invited. One by one, they excuse themselves. But the man will not cancel his party. Instead he instructs his servants to go into the streets and alleys of the town and invite the poor, the crippled, the blind and the lame. "Make people come in, that my home may be filled!"

God calls us to happiness, to friendship, to joy, to rejoicing!

For Personal Reflection and Discussion

Sometimes high school parties are not real celebrations. They are an excuse for a bunch of lonely people to get together and get wasted. The same can be said for many adult gatherings as well. Do the parties that you attend really celebrate your friendships? Or are they an excuse to hide from loneliness and confusion? Do we really know how to celebrate and enjoy ourselves? It's one of the requirements for following Christ.

Let's Change Our Hearts and Let Go of the Anger. If God's reign is a joyous celebration hosted by a loving Father, how is it that Jesus is put to death? Who could be threatened by such a message?

There is a flip side to this coin. If we are God's children, then we must live like God's children. Recall Jesus' words in Mark's gospel: "The reign of God is at hand. **Repent** and believe the good news." Repenting is part of the package. What is this repenting all about? It's really very simple. It means that we don't love as well as we can, and each day is a new challenge to let go of the anger, hurt, and selfishness that prevents us from loving more deeply. It means we must let go of our self-centered ways.

For Personal Reflection and Discussion

Take a look at a relationship in need of repair. What can you do in your own heart to help repair it?

Jesus Asks for a Commitment. In the gospel of Matthew Jesus says:

The reign of God is like a treasure buried in a field which a person finds and hides again, and out of joy goes and sells all that he has and buys that field (Matthew 13:44–46).

In this parable, we hear that the reign is a gift that is not deserved but joyously stumbled upon. However, that is only part of the message. More importantly, the man goes and sells everything and buys the field. He is willing to make the necessary sacrifices, for he has found a real treasure. God's gift calls for a response from us, a new way of living. **We can't call ourselves Christians unless somehow it really affects our lives.**

For Personal Reflection and Discussion

On a scale of 1 to 10, how high a priority is your relationship with God at this stage of your life?

The Inseparable: Love of God and Love of People. When asked to choose the most important commandment of the law, Jesus chose two. The first: "You shall love the Lord your God with all your heart, with all your soul, with all your strength and with all your mind." The second is like it: "You shall love your neighbor as yourself." **For Jesus, there are two absolutes: love of**

God and love of other people. And they cannot be separated from each other. Jesus makes this point in the parable of the rich man and Lazarus:

> There was a rich man who dressed in purple garments and fine linen and dined sumptuously each day. And lying at his door was a poor man named Lazarus, covered with sores, who gladly would have eaten his fill of the scraps that fell from the rich man's table. Dogs even used to come and lick his sores. When the poor man died, he was carried away by angels to the bosom of Abraham. The rich man likewise died and was buried, and from the nether world, where he was in torment, he raised his eyes and saw Abraham far off and Lazarus at his side (Luke 16:19–23).

In this parable the rich man goes to hell not because he was cruel to the beggar at his gate but because he ignored him. He did no harm, but he offered no love either. For Jesus, love means more than being nice or not hurting people. Love means opening your heart to those who are in need. The rich man is separated from God because he failed to love another human being.

For Personal Reflection and Discussion

Jesus combines two commandments: one for love of God and the other for love of people. Both of these elements are essential to Christian faith: we must develop our relationship with God and with other people. The temptation is to do one but not the other. For some, religion is just going to church. For others, it means just trying to be a good person. For Christians, it is both and more.

It also helps, of course, to love yourself. What do you think is meant by a healthy love of oneself?

THE MINISTRY OF JESUS: MEALS, MIRACLES, MERCY

Jesus: The Reign of God in Person. We have seen what Jesus had to say, but what did he do? How did Jesus live and relate to other people? As you might suspect, there was a close relationship between the words and the deeds (ministry) of Jesus. The ministry of Jesus was based on relationships. He was not an organizer or a writer or a social worker. Jesus had a unique ministry because he had a unique role in all of history. **Through his actions and relationships Jesus gave witness to the meaning of his message. The reign of God was present in and through this person,** and it was evident in the startling way in which he was able to touch and change the lives of those around him.

We find a good summary of Jesus' ministry in the gospel of Luke. Jesus had just returned to his hometown of Nazareth after his baptism. He went into the synagogue on the sabbath, and when he was given the scroll of the prophet Isaiah to read, he turned to this passage:

> The spirit of the Lord is upon me; therefore he has anointed me. He has sent me to bring glad tidings to the poor, to proclaim liberty to captives, recovery of sight to the blind, and release to prisoners, to announce a year of favor from the Lord (Luke 4:18–19).

Jesus fulfills the prophecy of Isaiah. He has come in a special way for the poor, the captives, the blind, and the prisoners. Jesus identifies himself as bringing "glad tidings" to those who live on the margins of society.

For Personal Reflection and Discussion

If Jesus were walking the earth today, what do you think he would be doing? How should the church be extending the ministry of Jesus to the outcasts of society?

Jesus: "The Friend of Sinners." One of the nicknames that was given to Jesus by his enemies was "the friend of sinners." This in itself tells us a great deal about Jesus. Consistently throughout the gospels, Jesus reaches out to sinners and offers them God's mercy.

> When the scribes who belonged to the Pharisee party saw that he was eating with tax collectors and offenders against the law, they complained to his disciples, "Why does he eat

with such as these?" Overhearing the remark, Jesus said to them, "People who are healthy do not need a doctor; sick people do. I have come to call sinners, not the self-righteous" (Mark 2:16–17).

The fact that Jesus forgave sins is extremely important in helping us understand who Jesus was and how to understand his mission. In the Catholic Church we can go to the sacrament of penance, but the Jews of Jesus' time believed it was a scandal for any man to offer forgiveness for sins committed.

Jesus said to the paralyzed man, "My son, your sins are forgiven." Now some of the scribes were sitting there asking themselves, "Why does the man talk in that way? Who can forgive sins but God alone?" (Mark 2:5–7).

Only God can forgive sins. **By forgiving sins, Jesus was taking on an authority that belonged to God. Once again, we see that he personally embodies the reign of God.**

For Personal Reflection and Discussion

A bumper sticker reads: "Christians are not perfect, just forgiven." It seems that being a sinner is a prerequisite for following Jesus. This does not mean that Jesus encourages sin, but if we are honest, all of us should admit our need for God's mercy.

Jesus describes himself as a doctor in the passage above. In what way are you in need of healing?

Jesus and Food. Jesus and food? What does food have to do with the ministry of Jesus? Believe it or not, a great deal.

In the passage above, Jesus is criticized not only for associating with sinners but for eating with them. ("Why does he eat with such as these?") Meals were not just a way of filling one's belly. They were a sign of friendship and solidarity. **By sharing a meal with someone, Jesus was extending his friendship to them.** So Jesus did more than just tell people that their sins were forgiven. He ate with them and offered them his friendship.

Jesus also ate with his friends, with the wealthy, with the

common people, and with the Pharisees, and finally he shared a "last supper" with his apostles. On all these occasions, **Jesus was offering a sign of the great and final banquet which is God's reign.**

For Personal Reflection and Discussion

In the age of fast food, we are quickly losing the meaning of meals. Meals are meant to do more than give us food. They also create community. What are some of the meal "traditions" in your own home?

The Miracles of Jesus. Today many people are skeptical about the possibility of miracles. We define a miracle as a suspension of the law of nature, but in Jesus' day, the "laws of nature" were unknown. A miracle was a "sign" of God's power.

The miracles of Jesus were an extremely important part of his ministry. **If his words proclaimed the coming of God's reign, his miracles revealed that reign coming with power.** Biblical scholars believe that some of the miracle stories have grown out of legend for teaching purposes, but there is little doubt that Jesus was in fact a miracle worker. Most of the miracles of Jesus were healing miracles and exorcisms. They were signs of God's reign overcoming the powers of sickness and evil in the world. They were part of the good news of God's care for his children. In the following passage, Jesus performs a miracle which is also a "sign" of the priority of love over rigid legalism:

> He returned to the synagogue where there was a man whose hand was shriveled up. They kept an eye on Jesus to see whether he would heal him on the sabbath, hoping to be able to bring an accusation against him. He addressed the man with the shriveled hand: "Stand up here in front!" Then he said to them: "Is it permitted to do a good deed on the sabbath—or an evil one? To preserve life—or to destroy it?" At this they remained silent. He looked around at them with anger, for he was deeply grieved that they had closed their minds against him. Then he said to the man, "Stretch out your hand." The man did so and the hand was perfectly restored (Mark 3:1–5).

For Personal Reflection and Discussion

Sometimes we lose sight of the fact that the laws of nature are miraculous! Make a list of life's daily miracles.

Questions for Review

1. Explain the difference between Jesus of history and Christ of faith.
2. What was the political situation in Palestine at the time of Christ?
3. What was the original meaning of the messiah? How did the meaning change?
4. Define: Pharisee, scribe, Sadducee, Samaritan, synagogue, sabbath and temple.
5. Why do Matthew and Luke have different accounts of the birth of Christ?
6. What do their accounts have in common?
7. Why was John baptizing in the Jordan?
8. What was the main theme of Jesus' preaching?
9. What do the parables of the yeast and the treasure tell us about the reign of God?
10. According to Jesus what are the two great commandments?
11. Why was it startling to the Jewish religious leaders that Jesus would forgive sins?
12. What do meals have to do with the ministry of Jesus?
13. What is the relationship between the words and miracles of Jesus?

7

The Death and Resurrection of Jesus

Imagine what it would have been like to have been one of Jesus' disciples: to travel with him, to listen to his words, to watch in awe as he healed the sick and the blind. Something extraordinary was happening in this carpenter from Nazareth. This is a man like no other. Your heart soars with hope and excitement. And then, all of a sudden, it's over. Your master has been arrested in the middle of the night, tried by the Romans and brutally executed. One night you were celebrating a meal together. Less than twenty-four hours later, Jesus is dead. Now all that you know is fear and grief and despair.

This was how Christianity began. Jesus himself began in a womb, and in a family's love. But Christianity began with despair and death. However, what seemed to be doom in fact turned out to be salvation. What seemed to be evil turned out to be God's love in its most powerful form. What seemed to be the death of hope was hope's birth. Conceived on the cross and delivered from the tomb, the world had been born again.

In this chapter, we turn our attention to the center of Christian faith: the death and resurrection of Jesus. We will focus on the following questions:

1. Why was Jesus put to death?
2. How did the early church understand his death?
3. What is the meaning of that death for Christians and the rest of the world?
4. What happened at the resurrection of Jesus?
5. What is the meaning of the resurrection for Jesus and for us?

For Personal Reflection and Discussion

The cross is the symbol of Christian faith. Take a good look at a cross or crucifix. What does that symbol mean to you?

BACKGROUND INFORMATION

Most Christians today seem to assume a natural connection between faith and the immortality of the soul. It would be hard to imagine otherwise because Christian faith is based on the resurrection of Jesus and the hope of a future resurrection for all who believe. We speak confidently of our hope that the death of a beloved one is not the end. We live in the hope that he or she is united with God in heaven. When a child asks us what happens to people when they die, we try our best to explain what heaven is all about.

Because Christian faith is so connected to eternal life there is often the presumption that all religious people believe in the immortality of the individual. This is simply not so. In fact, many of the Jews who lived at the time of Christ did not believe in life after death. In all likelihood, the greatest religious leaders in the Old Testament did not believe in life after death. Ancient Israel believed in a God of history, a God who was very much part of this world although infinitely greater than it. **The salvation promised by God was seen primarily as God fulfilling his promises to Israel. This was very different than the notion of survival of the individual soul.** At first this salvation from God was seen within the context of human life and history. In time, however, Israel lost its prominence and was defeated by foreign powers. Confidence in human institutions and human power waned and the Jews began to look for a new day when God would restore his people. Israel developed a general "eschatological" (meaning the end-time) hope that, in the end, God would triumph and restore his people. This notion was captured in the image of the "day of Yahweh" or the reign of God. As the prophet Isaiah extolled, "On this mountain the Lord will destroy the veil that veils all people, the web that is woven over all nations; he will destroy death forever. . . . On that day it will be said: 'Behold our God to whom we looked to save us!' " (Isaiah 25:6–9). Still, the salvation envisioned by Isaiah is not the same as individual resurrection. There are only vague allusions to individual immortality. There is the belief that Yahweh will save the righteous man, but this salvation is not the same as our notion of resurrection. For some of the Jews, immortality took the general form of living on in one's ancestors, a notion that remains popular today. **Most scholars today believe that the Jewish belief in individual resurrection did not begin until the second century BCE.** This resurrection was not limited only to the just. The wicked shall also live beyond the tomb but in divine punishment.

For Personal Reflection and Discussion

Conduct a survey of your friends, relatives, neighbors etc. Ask the question: What happens to us when we die?

During the lifetime of Jesus there seems to have been a variety of opinions within Judaism. The Pharisees believed in a final resurrection at the end-time in which the just and the unjust would be judged. The Sadducees rejected any such notion. In fact, Mark's gospel tells us of a discussion that took place between Jesus and the Sadducees:

One Sadducee said: "Teacher, Moses wrote for us that if someone's brother dies leaving a wife but no children, his brother must take the wife and raise up descendants for his brother. Now, there were seven brothers. The first married a woman and died, leaving no descendants. So the second married her and died, leaving no descendants, and the third likewise. And the seven left no descendants. Last of all the woman also died. At the resurrection, when they arise, whose wife will she be? For all seven had been married to her." Jesus replied: "You are misled because you do not know the scriptures or the power of God. When they rise from the dead they will not marry, but they are like angels in heaven. As for the dead being raised, have you not read in the book of Moses how God told him, 'I am the God of Abraham, the God of Isaac, and the God of Jacob.' He is the God of the living, not of the dead" (Mark 12:19–27).

Since the Sadducees accepted only the written law and did not believe in the resurrection, they sought to trip Jesus up. Jesus explained to them that their understanding of the resurrection was too materialistic. They saw it simply as a continuation of human life as we know it. **Jesus pointed to a whole new reality that would be brought about by the power of God.**

For Personal Reflection and Discussion

Jesus says that the dead are like angels in heaven. Unfortunately we don't really know what angels are like. What might Jesus mean by this statement?

DID JESUS PREDICT THE RESURRECTION?

In light of Jesus' belief in resurrection, the disciples seem rather dull and thick-headed in their inability to grasp the significance of Jesus' death. In fact, it appears that Jesus predicts his death and resurrection:

> He began to teach them that the Son of Man had to suffer much, be rejected by the elders, the chief priests and the scribes, be put to death and rise three days later (Mark 8: 31–33).

Didn't Jesus tell his disciples almost exactly what would happen? Scripture scholars believe that this passage, written after the resurrection, may have been influenced by the fact of the resurrection. **However, Jesus did identify himself as a suffering servant. He may have understood his death as the final act of fulfilling his mission, confident that God would not abandon him to the tomb.** He may not have predicted the events of his death and resurrection quite so clearly as Mark states it, but he certainly may have foreseen what would occur in Jerusalem and believed that his death would not be the failure of his mission. However, his followers seemed oblivious to the message of suffering and death. **Messiahs are not supposed to suffer! The idea that the messiah would suffer and die for the people was completely foreign to the**

Jews of Jesus' era. When Jesus predicts his future suffering and death, Peter immediately begins to argue with him.

> Peter then took him aside and began to remonstrate with him. At this, he turned around and, eyeing the disciples, reprimanded Peter: "Get out of my sight, you satan! You are not judging by God's standards but by man's" (Mark 8:32–33).

Death and resurrection are simply not part of the plan. The messiah is to be triumphant. This is one reason why the resurrection is such a shocking revelation.

For Personal Reflection and Discussion

Can you think of any examples of people today looking for messiahs who are powerful and mighty rather than loving and merciful?

PRACTICING WHAT HE PREACHED

In the previous chapter we discussed the connection between the words and the deeds of Jesus. Jesus' death was the ultimate expression of his words and his life. He taught his disciples that life's meaning was found not in selfishness but in self-surrender:

> Whoever would preserve his life will lose it, but whoever loses his life for my sake and the gospel's will preserve it. What profit does a man show who gains the whole world and destroys himself in the process? (Mark 8:35–36).

> I solemnly assure you, unless the grain of wheat falls to the ground and dies, it remains just a grain of wheat. But if it dies, it produces much fruit (John 12:24).

For Personal Reflection and Discussion

Jesus' deeds and words are connected. He preaches what he practices. In what area of your life do you need to make a closer connection between your words and deeds?

THE FINAL DAYS OF JESUS:
ENTRY INTO JERUSALEM, THE TEMPLE SCENE,
THE LAST SUPPER, ARREST AND TRIALS

The Entry into Jerusalem. The synoptic gospels mention only one trip by Jesus to Jerusalem. The gospel of John describes three visits to the city by Jesus and his disciples. (Scholars tend to favor John's version as more plausible in light of the amount of hostility that Jesus faced.) In any event, all four gospels agree that Jesus' final visit is occasioned by the Jewish feast of the Passover. It was common for the Jewish people to make a pilgrimage to the holy city for this great feast. The city would have been teeming with such pilgrims. It was in this context that Jesus is welcomed into the city:

> They brought the colt to Jesus and threw their cloaks across its back, and he sat on it. Many people spread their cloaks on the road, while others spread reeds which they had cut in the fields. Those preceding him as well as those following him cried out: "Hosanna! Blessed is he who comes in the name of the Lord! Blessed is the reign of our father David to come! Hosanna in the highest!" (Mark 11:7–10).

The image of Jesus riding on the donkey reflects the one in the book of the prophet Zechariah in the Old Testament:

> Rejoice heartily, O daughter Zion; shout for joy, O daughter Jerusalem! See, your king shall come to you: a just savior he is, meek, and riding on an ass, on a colt the foal of an ass (Zechariah 9:9).

Jesus' entry on the colt reveals the type of messiah that he is. A warrior messiah would ride a horse ready for battle. Jesus comes in peace.

The Cleansing of the Temple. One of the events that led to Jesus' death was his action in the temple in Jerusalem. When Jesus reached the temple area, he found the outer precincts filled with money-changers and those selling animals for sacrifice in the temple. There was nothing very new about any of this. When the pilgrims visited the temple, they needed the Jewish coin (the shekel) to pay the temple tax. Since many pilgrims came from areas outside of Palestine, they exchanged their foreign coins for shekels. Likewise, the doves sold were used for sacrifice in the temple. This busy activity was being done in the outer courtyard of the temple area which was called the court of the Gentiles, because non-Jews were allowed in this section of the temple. Jesus, however, was not pleased:

> He entered the temple precincts and began to drive out those who were engaged in buying and selling. He overturned the money-changers' tables and the stalls of the men selling doves. . . . Then he began to teach them: "Does not scripture have it, 'My house shall be called a house of prayer for all peoples'? But you have turned in into a den of thieves" (Mark 11:15–17).

Jesus' attack on the traders in the temple was an attack on the carnival atmosphere in which some profited from the celebration of the Passover. Jesus sees this as a violation of the true spirit of the Passover and the temple which is one of prayer and worship. Such an attack by Jesus, however, was seen as an attack on the temple itself and those who controlled it. At his trial before the Jewish elders and priests, this threat against the temple will be used against Jesus.

For Personal Reflection and Discussion

This scene in the temple seems uncharacteristic of Jesus. He loses his temper. Is this anger wrong? There is a difference between the anger of hatred and "righteous anger." When we see injustice and evil we should be angry! If we aren't there is something wrong. What situations in the world today call out for the righteous anger of justice?

The Last Supper. On the night before his death, Jesus gathered to celebrate a final meal with his disciples. According to the synoptics, this was the passover meal (the seder). John writes that the meal was eaten on the night before the Passover, on the evening of preparation. Even if John is more accurate on this detail (which most scholars believe), the meal was given a Passover character by Jesus. In the course of the meal, Jesus took the bread and declared, "This is my body." With a cup of wine, he said, "This is my blood, the blood of the covenant, to be poured out on behalf of many" (Mark 14:22–24). **In the meal, Jesus symbolized his imminent death. His body, like the bread, would be broken for others. His blood, like the wine, would be poured out.**

We have seen that Jesus shared many meals with people as part of his ministry. But this was truly his last supper, and in it he would proclaim the meaning of all that went before. This meal revealed all that he had been and all that he would be: a life poured out on behalf of others. (We will say more about this meal in our treatment of the eucharist.)

The Arrest and Trials of Jesus. After the meal, Jesus goes off to the Mount of Olives to pray. The account of this prayer in the gospels gives us insight into **the contrast between Jesus and his apostles, between his faith and non-violent courage and their weakness and violence.**

Jesus' trust in God does not strip him of human emotion and his desire to live. Jesus prays that he will be able to avoid the death that awaits him. He is filled with fear and distress. "He kept saying, 'Abba (O Father), you have the power to do all things. Take this cup away from me. But let it be as you would have it, not as I'" (Mark 14:36). The apostles, by contrast, have fallen asleep. It is more than they can bear.

When the crowd comes to arrest Jesus, he is given one last opportunity to become a military messiah. A man draws his sword, but Jesus will not hear of it: "Put your sword back where it belongs. Those who use the sword are sooner or later destroyed by it" (Matthew 26:52).

Jesus is taken to the sanhedrin, which was the Jewish council of elders and led by the high priest Caiaphas. There he was questioned without any conclusion until the high priest addressed the question to him: "Are you the Messiah, the Son of the Blessed One?" (Mark 14:61b). Jesus' response is unclear. In Mark he says, "I am." In Matthew and Luke he replies, "It is you who say it." (In other words, he does not claim it, although he doesn't completely deny it.) He then says, "And you will see the Son of Man seated at the right hand of the Power and coming with the clouds of heaven." (All three synoptic gospels agree in general with these words.) At this, the high priest tears his robes to indicate that he has heard blasphemy, a charge that could merit the death penalty.

It is very difficult to know what exactly took place at this hearing or trial since none of the apostles were there. However, whatever took place, it was enough for the Jewish temple authorities to bring Jesus to the Roman governor Pontius Pilate for a trial. The gospel versions of the Roman trial vary quite a bit. They all agree that in the end Pilate sentenced Jesus to death. The charge against Jesus had to be a political one (Pilate was uninterested in Jewish internal religious affairs). **Jesus was executed as a false king, as is indicated by the charge hung on the cross,** "Jesus of Nazareth, King of the Jews."

Scholars believe that the portrait of Pilate in the gospels has been softened a great deal. In Matthew he washes his hands of the responsibility, and in Luke he declares Jesus to be innocent three times. **In fact, Pilate was a callous and bloodthirsty antisemite who hardly would have had qualms of conscience over Jesus' execution.** The gospels place the lion's share of blame on the Jewish authorities, but the death of Jesus was more likely a collaborative effort between the Roman and Jewish authorities.

For Personal Reflection and Discussion

Throughout the world today, thousands continue to be unjustly imprisoned and unfairly tried. The passion of Jesus continues in these who are persecuted. To learn more about them, contact Amnesty International USA, PO Box 96756, Washington, D.C. 20077-7131.

THE CRUCIFIXION

Of all the things that we know about Jesus, nothing is more historically certain than the fact that he was crucified. **This Roman form of execution was reserved for foreigners because of its brutality.** (Roman citizens were beheaded.) All four gospels agree that Jesus was beaten and abused by the soldiers before the crucifixion itself (although in Luke the soldiers are part of Herod's guard). The crown of thorns placed on Jesus' head and the royal cloak placed around him mocked him according to the charge against him: King of the Jews.

The crucifixion took place outside the city at a site called Golgotha (the skull place). The prisoner would be forced to carry the crossbeam, although Jesus seems to have been aided by Simon the Cyrene because of his weakened condition. There were a variety of forms of Roman crucifixion, one of which included nails through the wrists and the ankles. (Only the gospel of John refers to the use of nails.) Victims died of suffocation, collapsing under the weight of their own bodies. This procedure was sometimes hastened by breaking the legs of the prisoner (not necessary for Jesus) or thrusting a lance through his side (mentioned in the gospel of John, to be certain that Jesus was dead).

The gospels differ in conveying the words of Jesus on the cross. It is difficult to know exactly what happened or what was said by Jesus on the cross. There is a strong relationship between the events at Golgotha and Psalm 22 in the Old Testament.

Matthew 27:39–40.
41–42. 45–47

People going by kept insulting him, tossing their heads and saying, "So you are the one who was going to destroy the temple and rebuild it in three days! Save yourself, why don't you? . . . He saved others but he cannot save himself! So he is the King of Israel! Let him come down from that cross and then we will believe in him. He relied on God; let God rescue him now if he wants to. . . ." Then toward midafternoon, Jesus cried out in a loud tone, "Eli, Eli, lema sabacthani?"—that is, "My God, My God, why have you forsaken me?"

Psalm 22:1–5. 7–9

My God, my God, why have you forsaken me, far from my prayer, from the words of my cry? O my God, I cry out by day and you answer not; by night, and there is no relief for me. Yet you are enthroned in the holy place, O glory of Israel! In you our fathers trusted; they trusted and you delivered them. . . . But I am a worm, not a man, the scorn of men, despised by the people. All who see me mock at me; they mock me with parted lips, they wag their heads: "He relied on the Lord; let him deliver him, let him rescue him, if he loves him."

For Personal Reflection and Discussion

The cross is a symbol of both divine love and human evil. How is the cross of Christ present in our world as both divine love and human evil?

THE RESURRECTION

With the crucifixion, Jesus' entire message and mission seemed to come to a crashing halt. The book of Deuteronomy claimed, "Cursed be everyone who hangs on a tree." Public execution was a sign of being cursed by God, certainly not blessed. **It appeared that the crucifixion of Jesus validated the claim of his enemies.** This was a false prophet—a pretender messiah.

And then: the unthinkable, the unimaginable. God raises Jesus from the dead. The women visit the tomb of Jesus to anoint his body and discover it to be empty. This empty tomb at first is only a sign of confusion and wonder. Where is the body of Jesus? Has it been stolen?

> On the first day of the week, at dawn, the women came to the tomb bringing the spices they had prepared. They found the stone rolled back from the tomb; but when they entered the tomb, they did not find the body of the Lord Jesus. While they were still at a loss over what to think of this, two men in dazzling garments stood beside them. Terrified, the women bowed to the ground. The man said to them: "Why do you search for the Living One among the dead? He is not here; he has been raised up" (Luke 24:1–6a).

There are no witnesses to the resurrection itself. The women discover a tomb that is empty. But the meaning of the empty tomb eludes both them and the apostles until the risen Lord makes himself known to them. Descriptions of the risen Lord in the gospels take the form of stories in which the gospel writers are trying to describe the undescribable. When we examine these accounts we can conclude the following about the resurrection:

1. **Jesus' resurrection is a transformation, not a resuscitation.** Jesus does not return to the same human form that he had before

death. He does not merely "sit up" in the tomb and walk outside, returning to life as he knew it. This would be resuscitation, like the raising of Lazarus (John 11). Lazarus will have to die again. But Jesus has entered into a whole new way of being, freed from former limitations. For example, he simply appears in a locked room:

> On the evening of the first day of the week, even though the disciples had locked the doors of the place where they were for fear of the Jews, Jesus came and stood before them. "Peace be with you," he said (John 20:19).

For Personal Reflection and Discussion

St. Paul tries to describe this transformation using the image of a seed and a plant. What other images from nature are "signs" of resurrection?

2. **The risen Lord is really Jesus.** Some people claim that Jesus did not really rise from the dead. He simply lived on in the memory of his disciples. The resurrection is not something that simply happened in the hearts of the disciples. Jesus did more than live on in their memory. He conquered the tomb. The risen Lord is really the same Jesus who lived among them and was crucified on a cross. The gospel of John makes this point by referring to the wounds of Jesus.

> It happened that one of the twelve, Thomas (the name means twin), was absent when Jesus came. The other disciples kept telling him: "We have seen the Lord!" His answer was, "I will never believe it without probing the nail-prints in his hands, without putting my finger in the nail marks and my hand into his side."
> A week later, the disciples were once more in the room, and this time Thomas was with them. Despite the locked doors, Jesus came and stood before them. "Peace be with you," he said, and then to Thomas: "Take your finger and examine my hands. Put your hands into my side. Do not persist in your unbelief, but believe!" (John 20:24–27).

This passage and others like it (see Luke 24:36–39) make it clear that the risen Lord is more than a ghost or a memory. **The**

resurrection of Jesus is somehow a "bodily" one even if the body of Jesus has been profoundly transformed.

3. **The appearances of the risen Lord are experiences of revelation and faith.** Those who meet the risen Lord see more than a person. They understand him to be Lord and Savior. Meeting the risen Lord is not like seeing another person: it is to encounter Christ in one's heart and soul. It is a personal experience of conversion and belief. This is communicated in the gospel stories in a variety of ways. The disciples on the road to Emmaus (Luke 24:13–29) walk with the risen Jesus but do not recognize him until "the breaking of the bread." They have done more than see Jesus: "Were not our hearts burning inside us as he talked to us on the road and explained the scriptures to us?" Likewise, Mary Magdalene sees the risen Lord and thinks him to be the gardener until he calls her by name: "Mary!" It is when the Lord speaks to her heart that she recognizes him.

4. **The resurrection reveals Jesus to be the Lord and Savior.** The resurrection of Jesus is not a philosophical idea about the immortality of the soul. It is a divine statement about Jesus of Nazareth. In the resurrection, Jesus is now known as Lord and Savior. In the death and resurrection of Jesus, God has spoken his word to the world, and it is a word of hope and a word of life. Because of the resurrection, the words, the deeds and the person of Jesus Christ take on a unique significance in human history. Thomas' response to Jesus is the proclamation of faith: "My Lord and my God" (John 20:28). It is only after the resurrection that such a proclamation can be made.

There may in the future be men and women of great eloquence, of holy compassion and mercy, of brilliance and insight and love for God. There may be great teachers and prophets and saints. But in the death and resurrection of this man, Jesus of Nazareth, Christians believe that God has been revealed to us and has offered us salvation. Jesus is unique in all history. This is why Easter is for Christians the greatest of all feasts. It is literally the basis of our faith. As Paul tells the Corinthians, "If Christ is not raised, your faith is worthless . . . we are the most pitiable of men" (1 Corinthians 15:17–19).

For Personal Reflection and Discussion

We hear a great deal about putting Christ back in Christmas. What about putting him back into Easter? What can you do this year to help bring out the true meaning of the holy days?

The resurrection of Christ is not only a statement about Jesus; it is also the revelation of what God has planned for all who believe in him. For the early church, Jesus is not only raised from the dead but he is the source of hope for all who believe in him. His death and resurrection becomes the pattern for living as his follower. Thus Paul writes to the Romans: "Are you not aware that we who are baptized into Christ were baptized into his death? We were indeed buried with him through baptism into death, so that just as Christ was raised from the dead by the glory of the Father, we too might live a new life" (Romans 6:3–4).

For Jesus, the way to eternal life is through the self-surrender that is love. **His resurrection affirms not so much that death will unite us with God but that love will unite us with God.** This is what Paul means when he writes to the Philippians:

> I wish to know Christ and the power flowing from his resurrection; likewise to know how to share in his sufferings by being formed into the pattern of his death. Thus do I hope that I may arrive at resurrection from the dead (Philippians 3:10–11).

For Personal Reflection and Discussion

Can you find any patterns of death and resurrection in your own life? Make a time-line of your life, listing key experiences. Where among these can you find the cross and resurrection?

Finally, the cross and resurrection must be understood together, for they are inseparable. If the cross is the symbol of self-surrender and love, the resurrection is the fruit and joy of that love. If the cross is the symbol of the human ability to destroy the good, the resurrection is the hope in fighting against all evil. If the cross is the death that brings grief and pain, the resurrection reveals the meaning of that death which is union with God.

Questions for Review

1. How did the Pharisees and Sadducees differ in their interpretation of life after death? Whom did Jesus side with?
2. Why was Jesus' notion of the messiah so shocking to Peter?
3. What is the connection between the words and the deeds of Jesus concerning dying to oneself?
4. What did Jesus' entry into Jerusalem reveal about the type of messiah that he would be?
5. Why were merchants selling in the temple area? Why did this upset Jesus?
6. How was the last supper a foreshadowing of the death of Jesus?
7. What were the charges leveled against Jesus by the Jews and the Romans?
8. What do we know about Pilate's relationship with the Jews from history?
9. Who discovered the empty tomb? What was their initial reaction?
10. What is the difference between resurrection and resuscitation?
11. How are the cross and resurrection "patterns of life" for the Christian?

8

Christology:
The Church's Belief in Jesus

Then Jesus and his disciples set out for the villages around Caesarea Philippi. On the way, he asked his disciples this question, "Who do people say that I am?" They replied, "Some, John the Baptist, others, Elijah, still others, one of the prophets." "And you," he went on to ask, "who do you say that I am?" (Mark 8:27–29).

"WHO DO YOU SAY THAT I AM?"

The question that Jesus asked his disciples is the critical question. We can read about Jesus, study about his life, consult the scholars, and interpret his message, but the bottom line is: Who is he? Is he a great teacher? a prophet? the Messiah? the Son of God? Christology is the attempt of the church to answer this question, to describe who Jesus is. Now that we have looked at the life, death and resurrection of Jesus, we will turn our attention to christology: the church's understanding of the person and meaning of Jesus.

All Christians have a personal christology. Our own christology is the way that we answer the question: "Who do you say that I am?" Some people emphasize the humanity of Jesus, others his divinity; some emphasize his relationship to the poor, others his role as teacher, while others recite the official teaching of the church. All of these descriptions of Jesus are, in their own way, true. Yet none of them captures the whole truth.

For Personal Reflection and Discussion

Which of the following best describes your understanding of Jesus: teacher, friend of sinners and the poor, Lord, Messiah, Son of God, Savior? Why?

NEW TESTAMENT CHRISTOLOGIES: SYNOPTICS, JOHN

The Synoptic Gospels. Who are you? The answer to that question may depend on whom we ask. A friend might describe you very differently than a parent. One teacher's description might be very different from that of a different teacher. Human beings are complex and not easily described. We have many different facets to our personality. The same is true with the person, Jesus Christ.

There has always been in the church a pluralism of christologies—different ways of describing the mystery of Jesus Christ. There is no single "christology" in the New Testament. There are many diverse christologies. These christologies, however, do not contradict each other. They complement and enhance each other. Perhaps the most obvious example of this pluralism is the fact that we include in the scriptures not one gospel but four. While they share much in common, they have their own unique emphases.

In Mark, the focus is on Jesus as the suffering Messiah. Scholars believe that Mark was writing for an audience (probably in Rome) which was undergoing a great deal of persecution. It is not surprising, then, that Mark makes this such an important issue in his gospel. He wants to assure his readers that Jesus himself had to endure what they endure. Mark shows that Jesus' mission was ultimately fulfilled not through his great teaching or powerful miracles, but in his death. Mark seems to interpret the suffering and death of Jesus in light of the writing of the prophet Isaiah who described a servant of God who would heal his people through his sufferings.

Matthew has a different focus. **For Matthew, Jesus is the fulfillment of the Old Testament and the great teacher who fulfills the Torah.** He begins his gospel with a genealogy which traces the

family tree of Jesus back to Abraham. He is intent on showing Jesus' connection to the hopes of Israel. Matthew tells his infancy narrative by structuring it around five quotations from the Old Testament. In each instance, Jesus is seen to fulfill the Old Testament. Likewise, Matthew adds a great deal of Jesus' teaching to his gospel. But he makes it clear that in his teaching Jesus has come not to abolish the law and the prophets but to fulfill them (see Matthew 5:17).

Luke wishes to show that Jesus is the Savior of all people, Gentiles as well as Jews. He is the Lord not only of Israel, but of the world and all history. Luke also includes a genealogy, but, unlike Matthew, he traces Jesus' ancestry all the way back to Adam (obviously symbolically) because Adam is the father of the entire human race. In his second volume, the Acts of the Apostles, he traces the spread of Christianity to the Gentiles and the center of the known world, Rome.

In addition, Luke also shows special interest in portraying Jesus as the friend of the poor, the oppressed and the sinner. **For Luke, the love of God has no boundaries.**

For Personal Reflection and Discussion

Which of the themes in the synoptics is closest to your own understanding of Jesus?

Jesus in John: The Word Made Flesh. John emphasizes that Jesus is the eternal Word of God in the flesh. He emphasizes the union between Jesus and God much more than the synoptics. John has the most highly developed christology of any of the gospels. In the Prologue, he develops his christology of the Word:

> In the beginning was the Word;
> the Word was in God's presence,
> and the Word was God.
> He was present to God in the beginning.
> Through him all things came into being,
> and apart from him nothing came to be. . . .
> The Word became flesh
> and made his dwelling among us,
> and we have seen his glory:

the glory of an only Son coming from the Father,
filled with enduring love. . . .

For while the law was given through Moses, this
enduring love came through Jesus Christ. No
one has ever seen God. It is God the only Son,
ever at the Father's side, who has revealed him
(John 1:1-3. 14. 17-18).

Jesus is described as the Word of God made flesh. **He begins the prologue with the same words that begin the book of Genesis, because John is interested in portraying Jesus as the pre-existent Word of God who was present at the dawn of creation.** In Genesis, God creates through his word: "God said: 'Let there be light and there was light.' " It is God's creative Word that has taken flesh in the person of Jesus. In the final two verses, Jesus is compared to God's word given to Moses. That word is inferior to Jesus because it revealed God's law, but Jesus reveals God's love, and, in fact, God himself.

In addition to this prologue, John offers a christology throughout his gospel which he places on the lips of Jesus. Throughout the gospel there are a series of sayings of Jesus that begin with the expression, "I AM." This conjures up the Old Testament name for God as Yahweh and implies a unity between Jesus and God. This "christology" is less philosophical and based more on images than ideas:

"I myself am the bread of life, no one who comes to me shall
ever be hungry" (6:35).

"I am the light of the world. No follower of mine shall ever
walk in darkness" (8:12).

"I am the gate. Whoever enters through me will be safe"
(10:9).

"I am the good shepherd. The good shepherd lays down his
life for his sheep" (10:11).

"I am the resurrection and the life; whoever believes in me,
though he should die, will come to life" (11:25-26).

"I am the way, and the truth, and the life; no one comes to the Father but through me" (14:6).

"I am the vine and you are the branches. He who lives in me and I in him will produce abundantly" (15:5).

In each of these passages, we see Jesus' relationship to his followers and the effects of that relationship.

For Personal Reflection and Discussion

Which of the "I AM" sayings in John makes the most sense to you? Which is the best image for your relationship with Jesus?

TITLES OF JESUS IN THE NEW TESTAMENT

One way that the early church dealt with the question of Jesus' identity was by giving him titles. These titles had their roots in the Old Testament, and they always had to be reinterpreted when they were applied to Jesus.

The Messiah. Jesus' very name is more than a name. It is a christology: it is a description of who Jesus is. History calls him Jesus Christ. Christ, of course, is not the last name of Jesus. **It is a statement of faith.** Jesus is the Christ. **The word "Christos" is the Greek equivalent of the Hebrew "messiah."** As we have seen, the notion of messiah originated with the Jewish kings and gradually meant a figure who would save Israel and restore its former prominence.

The name Jesus Christ means that Jesus is the Messiah. Yet even that designation which is so central to Jesus does not really fit him. When Peter was asked by Jesus "Who do you say that I am?" he responded, "The Messiah." And he was right. But he was also wrong, because for Peter the Messiah was the triumphant messiah: the Davidic king who would restore Israel to glory, who would bring all people to true worship of Yahweh. When Jesus describes himself as a Messiah who must suffer and die, Peter will not hear of it, and he and Jesus begin to argue. Jesus is the Messiah but he is not the messiah expected by the people of

Israel. He is the Messiah, but it is he who defines what it means to be a messiah. When the early church used the title "Messiah" to describe Jesus they did so knowing that the meaning of that title had been transformed. Yes, Jesus was the Son of David, the fulfillment of God's promises to Israel. But he was a messiah who freed them not from the Romans but from sin. He was a messiah who offered a new way of relating to God and a new way of living.

Lord. Another problem faced by the early church was the attempt to describe the relationship between Jesus and God the Father. For the Jews there was only one God, and the Father was God and Jesus was not the Father, so how does one speak of the divine authority and role of Jesus? There were two titles that helped the church accomplish this.

The first of these titles was "Lord." Jesus was more than just a righteous man or a holy man or prophet or great teacher. He was Lord. He had been exalted by God and raised up by God. The word "Lord" has two meanings. It can mean "master" and refer to an earthly authority, or it can refer to God. **It is applied to Jesus after the resurrection to indicate his authority over all creation.** It is this word "Lord-Kyrios" that is used to designate God himself in the Greek Old Testament. We see this is in the hymn used by Paul in his letter to the Philippians:

> Though he was in the form of God,
> he did not regard equality with God as something to be
>   grasped.
> Rather, he emptied himself
> and took the form of a slave,
> being born in the likeness of men.
> He was known to be of human estate,
> and it was thus that he humbled himself,
> obediently accepting even death,
> death on a cross!
> Because of this, God highly exalted him
> and bestowed on him the name
> that is above every other name,
> so that at Jesus' name
> every knee must bend

of those in the heavens, on the earth, and under the earth
and every tongue proclaim
to the glory of God the Father:
Jesus Christ is Lord (Philippians 2:6–11).

The hymn emphasizes that Jesus is made Lord because his absolute fidelity to God is obedient unto death. He has been raised up and given the name above all others. Jesus' exalted role is bestowed on him at the resurrection. We see this theme in the earliest Christian preaching found in the Acts of the Apostles. Peter addresses the crowds on Pentecost and says: "Therefore, let the whole house of Israel know for certain that God has made him both Lord and Messiah, this Jesus whom you crucified" (Acts 2:36). Jesus' lordship begins at the resurrection.

For Personal Reflection and Discussion

According to the hymn in Philippians, Jesus is exalted and glorified, because he does not seek glory or exaltation but instead humbles himself. Can you think of any examples in your own life when you found true happiness by putting the needs of others before your own?

Son of God. Another way in which the church describes Jesus' special relationship to the Father is through the use of the title "Son of God." We are so used to hearing this title in the context of the Trinity that it is hard to imagine its original sense. For us, Son of God means God. But the theology of the early church was not so developed. **In the Old Testament, a son of God could refer to anyone blessed by God or it could refer to the people of Israel as a whole.** Once again, the church uses the title and transforms its meaning. After the resurrection, Jesus is known as the Son of God in a unique way. Once again, it is Christ who gives the term its meaning. **It points to Jesus' special relationship with the Father, one that all Christians are called to by grace.** This title helps the church explain Jesus' relationship to God and provides the language that will eventually be used to articulate the doctrine of the Trinity.

The letter to the Hebrews shows the close connection between the Sonship of Jesus and our own relationship to God:

Since, then, we have a great high priest who has passed through the heavens, Jesus, the Son of God, let us hold fast to our profession of faith. For we do not have a high priest who is unable to sympathize with our weakness, but one who was tempted in every way that we are, yet never sinned.

Son though he was, he learned obedience from what he suffered; and when perfected, he became the source of eternal salvation for all who obey him (Hebrews 4:14–15; 5:8–9).

Jesus' Sonship is here depicted as something that is perfected by his fidelity to God in and through his humanity. **This is a very important point because Jesus as God's Son is presented here as the model for all human beings.**

For Personal Reflection and Discussion

The author of the letter to the Hebrews says that Jesus was tempted in every way that we are, and that he learned obedience to the will of God through suffering and struggle. Do these ideas fit into your understanding of Jesus? If not, perhaps you have stripped Jesus of his true human nature.

Servant of God. As we have seen, the church had to find a way to interpret the meaning of Christ's passion and death because it was so unexpected. One way in which this could be done was by appealing to the suffering servant of Isaiah. **In chapters 40–55, Isaiah writes of a cryptic figure called the servant of Yahweh.** It is unclear precisely to whom he was referring, but the passages spoke eloquently to the early church as a description of Jesus. **In particular, these servant poems could help the church understand the passion and death of Jesus.** No wonder that we read from these passages at the Good Friday liturgy:

He was spurned and avoided by men, a man of suffering, accustomed to infirmity, one of those from whom men hide their faces, spurned and we held him not in esteem. Yet, it was our infirmities that he bore, our sufferings that he endured, while we thought of him as stricken, as one smitten by God and afflicted. But he was pierced for our offenses, crushed for our sins; upon him was the chastisement that makes us whole, by his stripes we were healed. We had all gone astray like sheep, each following his own way; but the Lord laid upon him the guilt of us all (Isaiah 53:3–6).

Son of Man. The most peculiar of the New Testament titles is one that is found in the gospels, "Son of Man." It is unusual because it has very little background in the Old Testament (see Daniel 7), yet it is the title that Jesus uses most often to describe himself. He uses the title often in reference to his suffering. There is little we can say about the meaning of the title because its background is so vague. **It is possible that Jesus used the title because it did not have any strong, clear expectations and he could give it his own meaning.**

PAUL'S CHRISTOLOGY

The greatest thinker of the New Testament was Paul (or Saul) of Tarsus. He was not one of the original apostles; in fact he persecuted the early church. However, he underwent a profound conversion in which the risen Lord appeared to him. He went on to become the greatest theologian and missionary of the early church. Paul, more than even the gospel writers, was able to interpret the meaning of Christ's life, death and resurrection. His focus, however, was not so much on who Christ was, but on what Christ had done for us, his role in salvation history.

Paul's christology focused almost entirely on the death and resurrection of Jesus. Paul mentions virtually nothing about Jesus' preaching or miracles or deeds. For Paul it was the death and resurrection of Christ that was the great event of salvation which dramatically altered the human race's relationship with God. Paul's teaching is complex and difficult to understand. We will simply try to summarize his key points:

1. The law of Moses is not sufficient to bring about our salvation, for on their own humans are incapable of living up to the demands of the law.
2. We are saved, not by the law, but by God's grace, the free gift of his love to us.

3. The grace of God has been revealed in and through the death and resurrection of Jesus.
4. Christ is the new Adam who offers us a new way of being human in fidelity to God's love. Those who are "in Christ" are a new creation.
5. Those who believe in Christ live in his Spirit. Through the Spirit we receive the grace of God which offers us salvation.
6. The resurrection of Christ is the first-fruits of all creation. In it we are called to live in hope.

For Personal Reflection and Discussion

Paul emphasizes God's grace, the pure gift of his love for us. We don't earn it. But when we know we are loved, our lives should never be the same. It should overflow with the love of God for others. We should be somehow "different" and more free. Does your faith make a real difference in your life? How?

THE COUNCILS OF NICEA AND CHALCEDON: TRULY GOD AND TRULY HUMAN

As we have seen, the New Testament authors used images, titles, hymns and stories to express their understanding of Jesus Christ. They did so using the Old Testament as their background for explaining who Jesus is. However, as the church developed, it moved away from Judaism as its cultural roots. **Christianity grew and developed not among the Jews but among the Greek-speaking people.** These people also tried to explain who Jesus was. However, **they were more interested in philosophical descriptions than in biblical ones.** They also asked different questions. The main concern of the New Testament was to show who Jesus was in relation to us and to God—in other words, what his **function** was. The later Christians tried to explain more about **who Jesus was in his essence and being.**

The most important question that had to be answered was: "Is Jesus Christ God?" While the New Testament clearly indicates the unity of the Father and the Son, it was not directly interested in this question. One of the bishops of the early church, a man named Arius, taught that Jesus Christ was not fully God. Since there was only one God, Jesus must belong to the order of creation. He is God's created Son, and superior to the rest of the creation, but he is a mediator between God and humans. This teaching was rejected by the leaders of the church at **the Council of Nicea in 325. They stated that Jesus is one in being with the Father.** He is not created by the Father but "begotten" of the Father. In this, the Son of God is clearly distinct from any creature. He does not belong to creation but to the very being of God. The official teaching of the Council of Nicea has made its way to us as the Nicene Creed which we recite at mass.

After the Council of Nicea, there was no question about the church's teaching concerning the divinity of Jesus as the Son of God. However, all the problems were not yet over. **While it was clearly taught that Jesus was truly God, the matter of his humanity still needed to be clarified.** After a series of extended arguments, councils and synods, the Council of Chalcedon declared in 451 that Jesus Christ was:

> the same perfect in divinity and perfect in humanity, the same truly God and truly man composed of rational soul and body, **the same one in being with the Father as to divinity and one in being with us as to humanity,** like unto us in all things but sin. . . . We confess that the one and the same Lord Jesus Christ, the only begotten Son, **must be acknowledged in two natures,** without confusion or change, without division or separation. . . . The character proper to each of the two natures was preserved as they came together in one person and one hypostasis.

These arguments may seem as though they are hair-splitting attempts to take the life out of Jesus and his message. The average Christian today is not concerned with these early debates within the church. But the conclusions that they reached are indeed important. What are these conclusions?

1. Jesus Christ is one person with two natures, both human and divine. The one person is the second person of the Trinity, the Word or Logos.

2. All that can be said about God can be said about Christ.
3. All that can be said about humanity can be said about Christ except that he was without sin.

This is the official teaching of the church. What does it mean?

Jesus Is Truly God in the Flesh. What if Jesus were not God? What if he were "only" God's greatest prophet and messenger, one who shows us the path of true life to God? What difference would it make?

If Jesus were not God, then God would remain outside the human situation. He may care about his creatures and love them dearly, but he has not united himself with them. He has not become one with us.

Because Jesus is God, we believe that the human and the divine are joined forever. The sacred has entered into the human condition, and therefore the human condition can never be the same. We can find God most powerfully on this earth not in the beauty of nature or in the drama of ritual but in other flesh-and-blood human beings. In the incarnation, God has united himself with us in and through his only Son.

If Jesus was God, there are some difficult questions to be raised. Did he have the mind of God? Did he only appear human? Did he know future events (like the fact that one day you would be reading this book)? Could the baby Jesus do calculus? These questions are difficult to know because the union of the human and divine in Jesus is a mystery beyond our comprehension. Most theologians today emphasize that if Jesus truly had a human nature, then he had to learn and grow as humans do, through experience and knowledge. He would have learned the way we all learn, as part of a culture and history. This is certainly the portrait of Jesus that we are given in the gospels and the New Testament.

The Humanity of Jesus. The teaching of the church is very clear that Jesus was fully human. He had a human mind and human body. He did not simply appear to be human.

What difference does it make? The answer is the same as the one above. **If Jesus was not truly human, then God has not united himself to us.** He has visited us, but he has not become one of us. As we have seen, Christ is called the "new Adam," "the first-born of all creation," because through his humanity he has revealed to us the true meaning of all humanity.

Although Jesus is truly unique (no other person is the Son of God made flesh), he is also the model of all humanity. **For we are all called to be sons and daughters of God by God's grace.** We are all called to share in the resurrection and to live a life of union with God.

For Personal Reflection and Discussion

In your own relationship to Jesus, do you tend to emphasize the human or the divine?

CONTEMPORARY UNDERSTANDINGS OF JESUS

The official teaching of the church remains the same more than fifteen hundred years after Chalcedon. **However, it is the task of each culture and generation to come to understand Christ anew.** This does not mean that we change the teaching of the church. For Christ is not a doctrine, but the power and presence of God in our midst. He is not a formulation to be memorized but a person to be encountered by his followers. **If the Councils of Nicea and Chalcedon are to have meaning, they must enable us to understand Christ present in our midst.**

For centuries the understanding of Christ in the church focused on his divinity (not surprisingly, since it was what made him unique). **Today, however, the focus is often on his human nature.** There is greater emphasis on his teaching, his attitudes, his values, and his challenges to us as his followers. This rediscovery of the Jesus of history is an important one if we are to be faithful to both natures. It is important to remember that the two are united and must be kept "in balance."

Today, there are still a wide number of christologies responding to the needs of the people:

- The sacred heart of Jesus is still an important image of Christ in many homes and families. It helps us to realize the closeness of Christ to all that we experience in our lives and loves.
- Among oppressed people of South America and throughout the world, Jesus is often described as a liberator, one who calls us to freedom from all oppression, especially political and economic oppression.
- Highly developed nations often portray Jesus as the model of humanity. Such nations have the leisure to ask questions about life's meaning for the "haves" of the world.
- Many intellectuals have begun to develop a "political" christology which helps to show the relationship between Christ and the world of politics.
- Peace groups focus on the non-violence of Christ.
- Millions of Christians develop a christology based on the eucharist.
- Many women point to Jesus' appearance to Mary Magdalene and his attitudes toward women in general. They have developed a christology which pays special attention to the needs of women in light of the oppression that they have suffered.

All of these "Christs" usually speak to a truth about Jesus and a need in his followers. In that way they are much like the gospels.

Questions for Review

1. What is meant by a "pluralism of christologies" in the New Testament?
2. What are the main focuses of Matthew, Mark, Luke and John in their understanding of Jesus?
3. Explain the meaning of the titles: Messiah, Lord, Son of God, Servant of God, and Son of Man.
4. How did Paul explain the lordship of Jesus in the hymn from Philippians?
5. What did the author of the letter to the Hebrews help the early Christians to understand about Jesus?

6. What were some of the key ideas in Paul's christology?
7. What was the chief teaching of the Councils of Nicea and Chalcedon concerning Jesus?
8. Why is it important to maintain both the humanity and the divinity of Christ?

9

Models of the Church

We now turn our attention to the church. For many people, young and old, faith in the church is more difficult than faith in God or faith in Jesus. It is one thing to believe in a God who is love and in a Savior who died for us. It is quite another to believe in a group of people as limited and as ordinary as you or I. The problem with the church is that it is so messy and human. If the church were only a divine reality, made up exclusively of saintly people, faith would be easy. But it is not. A divine Spirit lives in and guides the church, but its members are all too human.

For Personal Reflection and Discussion

Rate the strength of your faith in the following (on a scale of one to ten):

1. faith in God's love
2. faith in Christ
3. faith in the church

Which comes out lowest on the list? Why do you think this is so?

THE CHURCH AS MYSTERY

In this chapter we will examine the mystery of the church. In order to help us do so, we will borrow an idea from Avery Dulles, S.J. Dulles wrote a book entitled *Models of the Church* (Doubleday, NY, 1972) which has become one of the most influential works in religious education. Dulles' stroke of brilliance was to recognize that attempts to come up with a single definition or

description of the church was doomed to failure. **The church is a "mystery"** which defies any simple description. The word "mystery" does not mean a puzzle. It refers to a reality in which God acts and is present. **It possesses a richness and depth of meaning that cannot be fully captured.** In this sense, human beings are also a mystery. We too defy any one single description or definition. Dulles described five different "models" of the church. These models are different ways of understanding the church that are not exclusive of each other. Rather, they are essential elements of the church and enhance each other. Taken together, these models can help us better understand the nature of the church.

For Personal Reflection and Discussion

To help get a better sense of "models," we could use models to describe you. You are someone's child, a student, a friend. You can be described psychologically, biologically, sociologically and spiritually. If we asked your best friend, a teacher and a parent to describe you, how would they focus on different parts of you?

THE CHURCH AS COMMUNITY: FAITH, FRIENDSHIP AND SERVICE

The first model for our consideration is that of community. Today it is not uncommon for people to think first of a building when they hear the word "church." Or perhaps they think of "going to church." The earliest meaning of the word, however, described **a people of God.** The church was the faithful. The New Testament uses many different images to describe the church, but the one that has had the most lasting effect on the church's self-understanding is Paul's description of the church as the **body of Christ.** Paul was writing to the people living in the city of Corinth. This was a seaport city famous for its sexual immorality. Paul had a great deal of success in the community, but after he left, divisions developed within the church. There were arguments over who was the most important in the community.

Paul seeks to show them that in the church, all the various gifts and talents within the community are for the good of the whole group:

> There are many gifts but the same Spirit; there are different ministries but the same Lord; there are different works but the same God who accomplishes all of them in everyone. To each person, the manifestation of the Spirit is given for the common good. . . . But it is one and the same Spirit who produces all these gifts, distributing them to each as he wills.
>
> The body is one and has many members, but all the members, many though they are, are one body; and so it is with Christ. It was in one Spirit that all of us, whether Jew or Greek, slave or free, were baptized into the one body. All of us have been given to drink of the one Spirit. Now the body is not one member, it is many. If the foot should say, "Because I am not a hand I do not belong to the body," would it then no longer belong to the body? If the ear should say, "Because I am not an eye I do not belong to the body," would it then no longer belong to the body? If the body were all eye, what would happen to our hearing? If it were all ear, what would happen to our smelling? As it is, God has set each member of the body in the place he wanted it to be. There are, indeed, many different members, but one body. . . .
>
> You then are the body of Christ. Every one of you is a member of it (1 Corinthians 12:4–7. 12–18. 27).

There are many important ideas in Paul's image:

1. The church is composed of a wide diversity of people and gifts. **This diversity is an essential element in the church.** We are not to be clones of one another. Our unique gifts are for the good of the entire community.

2. Although the church is diverse in its members, **it is united by its Spirit.** The church is **one,** not because its members are alike but because their differences are united by the Spirit at work in each of them.

3. **The church is the presence (the body) of Christ on earth.** The risen Lord needs our bodies, hearts, courage, intelligence, goodness, generosity, care, to make himself present through us.

4. **Christ's body is made up of people who are not all saints.** Thus the church will be a combination of human and divine.

MODELS OF THE CHURCH

The church as a "mystery" of God's love cannot easily be described. By using models, we point to various aspects of the church. No model is complete unto itself, and each needs the others for balance and completion.

Model	Characteristics	Strengths	Limitations
Institution	hierarchy, organizations, rules, doctrines	order identity clarity	impersonal clericalism
Community	focuses on people	fellowship inclusive	lacks structure, direction
Sacrament	church as a "sign"; highly intellectual	sacramental spirituality	cut off from practical life
Herald	proclaims the word; focus on preaching of scripture	biblical basis	focus on words; can ignore deeds
Servant	works to transform the world for justice and peace	service, care for others	can lose faith dimension

The Spirit that unifies and inspires us is the divine element, but the fragile, sinful people who get unified and inspired is the human part.

Paul's vision of the church is one in which the entire community through its unique and varied gifts continues to make Christ present on earth. Perhaps the best way to be part of this body of Christ is to come to recognize the unique gifts that you have to offer, to develop them and give them away. To waste your gifts is to cheat not only yourself, but all who would be served by them.

Paul makes it clear that the greatest gift we can offer is that of ourselves, **for the greatest of all gifts is love:**

> Now I will show you the way which surpasses all the others. If I speak with human tongues and angelic as well, but do not have love, I am a noisy gong, a clanging cymbal. If I have the gift of prophecy and with full knowledge comprehend all mysteries, if I have faith great enough to move mountains, but have not love, I am nothing. If I give everything I have to feed the poor and hand over my body to be burned, but have not love, I gain nothing.
>
> Love is patient; love is kind. Love is not jealous, it does not put on airs, it is not snobbish. Love is never rude, it is not self-seeking, it is not prone to anger; neither does it brood over injuries. Love does not rejoice in what is wrong, but rejoices with the truth. There is no limit to love's forbearance, to its trust, its hope, its power to endure.
>
> There are in the end three things that last: faith, hope, and love, and the greatest of these is love (1 Corinthians 13: 1–7. 13).

The church as the Christian community is to be known and distinguished as a community of love.

This notion of the church as community places special importance on the local church. The church is not only the pope and bishops; the church exists wherever the people of God come together in faith. For most people this local experience of faith occurs within the parish. It is within the parish that all the gifts of the community must be used for the good of the whole and all the needs of the community must be ministered to.

Many people today are discovering that sometimes the parish structure is too large for the experience of Christian community. A growing movement in the church is the formation of small faith communities within the parish. These often meet for prayer, education, scripture study, or social functions. Sometimes these groups will reflect the specific interests of the people involved: the peace and justice group, teen groups, the elderly, the divorced or separated, the widowed, etc.

Within the New Testament there are two elements that especially characterize the Christian community. They are to be a **community of friendship (koinonia) and a community of service (deaconia).** Both of these elements are critical. The first recognizes the basic human need for friendship and social relationships. Thus parishes will sponsor athletic events, picnics, dances, teen clubs, etc. But the second element reminds us to make sure that we serve those in need, especially the poor and the sick.

Finally, there is one last element to the church as community. The universal church is also a "community" of faith. The bonds of the community are not social or personal but spiritual. Christians are united with one another in a faith which transcends all boundaries of race, language, culture or nationality. This spiritual connection is sometimes referred to as the **mystical body of Christ.**

For Personal Reflection and Discussion

Try to make a list of all the ways in which your local church functions as a community of service and one of fellowship.

THE CHURCH AS INSTITUTION: HIERARCHY, MAGISTERIUM

The next model is that of institution. This model is the most dominant one in the minds of many Catholics. When they think of the church, they think of the pope, the bishops, their pastor and priests, nuns, church teaching, etc. These are all key ingredients in the church as an institution. In saying that the church is an institution, we mean simply that it is an organization which has certain structures, standards, teachings and authority. In one sense it can be compared with IBM or General Motors. In order for computers and cars to be built, it is necessary for there to be an organization or institution capable of getting the job done. Of course the goal of the church is vastly different than those corporations, but the concept is similar. **A huge body of people with a goal must have some organization.**

The Catholic Church has a hierarchical structure of authority. This hierarchy (literally, "sacred order") is **built on the bishops and the pope. The bishops are considered to be successors to the apostles. The bishop of Rome, the pope, is the "first among equals" and the successor of Peter.** In this sense, the pope is the head of the universal church. This does not mean that he is the bishop of all Catholics; rather, he is to ensure the unity of the church in matters of faith. Individual bishops have as their task teaching, celebrating the sacraments and governing the church in the local **dioceses.** Bishops also teach as national bodies of bishops (e.g., the American bishops issued two important documents in the 1980s: one on the economy and the other on peace in a nuclear age). The bishops, together with the pope as their head, govern the universal church as well. Bishops throughout the world meet in **synods** in Rome on a regular basis to discuss issues related to the universal church.

The official teaching of the church may be communicated in a number of ways. Whenever a bishop preaches, he teaches on behalf of the church. Local bishops may also issue **pastoral letters** to guide the members of the church in matters of faith and morals. The pope may issue an **apostolic letter or an encyclical** in order to communicate with the universal church on a matter of faith or morals. The most authoritative teaching of the church comes from an **ecumenical council** which brings together all bishops throughout the world (with their advisors). The most recent ecumenical council was Vatican II, held in the years 1962–1965.

In essential matters of faith and morals, the teaching of the church is infallible (incapable of error). This **infallibility** belongs to the entire church whenever the bishops concur as a whole on a matter to be believed. It belongs also to the bishops in union with the pope whenever they teach definitively on matters of faith and morals and intend for such teaching to be infallibly declared. The pope also possesses infallible teaching authority when he "proclaims with a definitive act that a doctrine of faith and morals is to be held as such."

The teaching on infallibility is one of the most confusing and difficult in the church. For many people it is simply nonsense: How can any person or persons be infallible? Perhaps it should first be noted that the pope and bishops are fallible, that is, they are human beings capable of error. Their infallibility comes not from a divinely infused wisdom, but rather from the faith of the church. It is the faith of the church that is guaranteed to be true. Put simply, this means that the church's most essential teachings are not just opinions but reflect God's revelation. For example, is Jesus really Lord and Savior? Or is it something about which we can change our minds? The church says that this teaching (as well as others) is infallibly true. It is not something that we think is a good idea: it is part of God's revelation. The infallibility of the pope and bishops is limited to "matters of faith and morals" and reflects only those teachings which are essential to the faith. The church also notes that a teaching of the pope is to be considered infallible only when declared as such. (The exercise of papal infallibility has been extremely rare.)

The various teachings of the church can be divided as follows:

a. **Doctrines:** These are the official teachings of the church.

b. **Dogmas:** These are the doctrines which are essential to the faith. As such, they cannot be changed.

c. **Canon Law:** These are the official laws governing the church. (There are 1,752 canons regulating almost every aspect of the church.)

The pope administers his position as head of the church through the offices generally called the **Vatican.** He is assisted by a staff known as the **curia.** These are various Vatican positions and offices.

Cardinals are chosen from among the bishops of the world for two purposes: they are involved in the administration of the curia and they elect the pope. Only cardinals vote for the next pope.

The local bishop is represented in parishes throughout the diocese by the **pastor** and associate pastors (priests). The chief functions of these men is to celebrate the sacraments, preach and administrate the parish.

Religious sisters and brothers are called by special vocation to lives of **poverty, chastity, and obedience** in community. (Diocesan priests do not take vows of poverty, although like all Christians they are bound to the virtues of humility and generosity.) Nuns and brothers are referred to as "religious." Through their vows their lives are meant to give witness to the fact that there is more to life than wealth, sex, and independence. Nuns and brothers belong to various "orders" which usually have a certain charism or special task.

The **laity** are the baptized faithful who are not priests or "religious." The laity are to share their gifts with the church, but their main vocation is to bring their faith and the values of the gospel to the world.

What are the values of having such a highly organized, structured institution? The institutional church provides **order and identity.** It has given the church a clear sense of tradition and roots with the past. Catholics at least should know who they are and what their church stands for. The pope and bishops help to provide a sense of unity on both the local and the universal levels.

The institutional model is not without its problems. Like any organization, it can too easily get lost in its own bureaucracy. It can confuse the code of canon law for the sermon on the mount, and because of its hierarchical nature, it can lose sight of its heart and soul, the laity, and equate the church with the pope, bishops, priests, nuns, and brothers.

In the end it is impossible to imagine a church without institutional elements. In addition, the Catholic Church identifies the pope and bishops as essential elements within that institution. Church dogma and moral teaching give the faithful a sense of continuity, stability and direction. This is not to say that the institution cannot change and grow. Indeed, it does and it always must. But institutions like the Catholic Church will always have a tendency to move slowly, for they carry with them a tradition nearly two thousand years old.

For Personal Reflection and Discussion

People who have the institution for their main model usually think of the church as "they." The community model sees it more as "we." Which one of these two describe you better? When you think of the church, is it "they" or "we"?

THE CHURCH AS SACRAMENT

When we go to mass or celebrate the sacrament of penance or receive confirmation, these are all signs of a deeper reality. They are sacraments. **Sacraments are signs which not only point to an invisible reality (God's love and grace), but also make that reality present.** Thus, at the eucharist, we believe that Christ is truly present to us. In penance God's mercy is really given to us. In confirmation the Spirit is truly given to us. The sacraments are signs, but they are not **just** signs. God is really present in and through them. (We will say much more on this in later chapters.)

The church is also a sacrament. It is not one of the seven official sacraments of the church, but a more basic sacrament. The church is a sign of Christ present in the world, but it is more than just a sign. To some extent it truly is Christ present in the world. (This idea is part of Paul's teaching on the body of Christ which we saw earlier.)

In the sacramental model, the church is most fully and deeply itself in the celebration of the sacraments. Although the church is not limited to the sacraments, it is through them that the church expresses its meaning. It is a eucharistic community in which one enters into a new life of faith (baptism) and lives in the Spirit of Christ (confirmation). It is community of those in need of healing (anointing the sick) and forgiveness (penance). It is a community served by those chosen for a special ministry (holy orders) and symbolized by the love of a man and woman in marriage (matrimony).

The sacramental model of the church is a distinctively Catholic one. Although the Protestant churches have sacraments (but not all seven), this model is not one that fits their self-understanding very well.

The strength of this model is that it helps Christians to develop a sense of spirituality and identity through the sacraments. These sacraments continually get us in touch with the most basic elements of faith. On its own, however, this model can be cut off from the real world and the life of the church in the everyday experience of people. The chapters on the sacraments will help explain the meaning of this model more fully.

THE CHURCH AS HERALD

"Hark! The herald angels sing: glory to the newborn king."

Remember those herald angels in the Christmas carol? The word "herald" refers to a messenger. The herald angels brought the message of Christ's birth to the shepherds. This notion of proclaiming the message of faith and the word of God is behind the idea of the church as a herald. According to this model, the church is primarily a proclaimer of the good news of faith in Jesus Christ.

This idea of the church has **strong roots in the Protestant traditions. The focus is placed not on the church itself, but on the word of God.** This idea of church points away from itself to God's word. What is important is not doctrines, laws, sacraments, or even the people themselves. The heart of the matter is the word of God proclaimed for all the world to hear. This is the **"evangelical"** element of the church. This model of the church has a strong biblical basis. St. Paul writes that "faith begins with hearing." The early church saw much of its mission as proclaiming the good news. Today, we see this mission being carried out by preachers and television and radio evangelists. Some of these men, like Billy Graham, have achieved international fame.

The Catholic Church has recently rediscovered the importance of this model. More and more emphasis is being placed on the Bible. Lay people are being encouraged to read and study it. (In the not too distant past, it was almost unheard of for Catholic laity to be encouraged to read the Bible.) The Catholic Church has developed its own television evangelists and placed greater emphasis on the teaching and message of Jesus. This model places great emphasis on "evangelism": proclaiming the good news of Jesus Christ. It is extremely important for the church to find new and creative ways to evangelize: to proclaim the message in a way that really affects the lives of its listeners.

This model, like the others, however, cannot stand on its own, especially for Catholics. Its emphasis on the word of God is extremely important, but it runs the risk of substituting words for actions. It can proclaim God's reign without working to build that reign.

For Personal Reflection and Discussion

The gospel and homily are examples of this model at work in the Catholic Church. In many Protestant churches the preaching on Sunday lasts much longer than in the Catholic Church. They focus more on the herald model.

Can you think of a sermon that really affected you? If so, what was it about?

THE CHURCH AS SERVANT

The final model of the church, the servant model, places its focus not so much on proclaiming God's word but on serving God's people. In this context **the goal of the church is to work for love, justice and peace in the world.** Those who prefer this model believe that the church must "die to itself" and serve others. It takes seriously the mandate of Jesus in Matthew 25: "I was hungry and you gave me to eat, thirsty and you gave me to drink, naked and you clothed me, a stranger and you welcomed me, imprisoned and you visited me." The church's mission is to place itself at the service of those in need, especially the poor and the oppressed.

According to this model of the church, proclaiming faith in Christ is more than a matter of words or even of God's word. It is following the example of Jesus in reaching out to those in need.

This understanding of the church has grown and developed immensely in the past few decades. The Catholic Church gave it official recognition when a Synod of Bishops in 1971 wrote:

> Action on behalf of justice and participation in the transformation of the world fully appear to us a constitutive dimension of preaching of the gospel, or, in other words, of the church's mission for the redemption of the human race and its **liberation from every oppressive situation.**

What the bishops were saying is that redemption is more than a "spiritual" reality. An essential element in the church is to strive for the liberation of the whole person. This cannot exclude the spiritual, but **includes the liberation from hunger, disease, homelessness, psychological oppression, etc.**

In many parts of the world the servant church has become, by necessity, the dominant expression of the Catholic Church. This is most true in Central and South America where countless millions of Catholics live in dire poverty and often political repression. From these areas the church has developed what is called **a theology of liberation. The focus of this theology is the application of the gospel to the needs of the poor.** The church has developed a **"preferential option for the poor"** by which it evaluates political and social choices in terms of their impact on the poor. There has developed not only a church on behalf of the poor but a church of the poor. (This is in striking contrast with the past when the church was often aligned with the concerns of the wealthy in these countries.)

The servant model has grown tremendously in the past thirty years. However, it is not without its problems. The weakness of the servant model is the tendency to lose a sense of identity of faith. Christians must serve the world, but all people are called to do this as well. The servant model cannot lose sight of Jesus Christ as the true liberator of human beings. Likewise, the reign of God will always be much more than human achievement or political and economic development.

For Personal Reflection and Discussion

The bishops have said that this element of the church in service to others is essential to its meaning. Service must be part of the life of every Christian. How are you living this element of faith right now? If you are not doing much, what can you do?

Have we now discovered which of the models of the church is the true model? They all are and none are. That is the point of using models. The church must include all five of these elements in order for it to truly be the church. It must be a community of faith which uses the unique gifts and abilities of all its members. As a community, the church nourishes the life of faith and gives a basis for that faith. This community celebrates and renews its faith in and through the sacraments. This community will need structure and leadership if it is to grow and develop and pass its wisdom down to future generations. This is why the church is also an institution. However, the temptation for all institutions is to become self-preoccupied. This cannot be the case for the church. It does not exist simply for its own benefit but must be in service to God's word and proclaim that word so that all may hear the good news of Jesus Christ. This proclamation must be more than a matter of words. The church must work in the world for justice and peace, in service of those who are in need.

For Personal Reflection and Discussion

Which of the models of the church do you relate to the most? Why? Which is most foreign to you?

Questions for Review

1. Why is faith in the church more difficult for many people than faith in God and Christ?
2. What does it mean to say that the church is a "mystery"?
3. Why are models helpful in explaining the church?
4. Explain Paul's notion of the church as the body of Christ.
5. According to Paul, which is the greatest of the spiritual gifts?
6. Explain what is meant by *deaconia* and *koinonia*.
7. What is meant by the mystical body of Christ?
8. Why is it necessary for the church to be an institution?
9. What is the main role of the bishop?
10. What is the main role of the pope?
11. Define the following: diocese, synods, encyclicals, ecumenical council, dogma, doctrine, canon law, curia, cardinals, laity.
12. Explain what is meant by infallibility as it applies to the pope, the bishops and the entire church.
13. What are the strengths and weaknesses of the institutional model?
14. Explain what is meant by the church as a sacrament. What are some of the strengths and weaknesses of this model?

15. What does the herald model understand to be the mission of the church? What are the strengths and weaknesses of this model?
16. According to the servant model, what is the mission of the church? What is the theology of liberation? What are the strengths and weaknesses of the servant model?

10

The Church in History

In this chapter we will be dealing with the church in history, offering a brief sketch of some of the highlights of the history of the church. Our purpose is not so much to study history (because we don't have the space for that here) but to get a sense of how the church has grown and developed in time. Since our concerns are with events, there will be less attention given to personal reflection and discussion than in previous and future chapters.

JESUS AND THE CHURCH

It has sometimes been believed that the church was set up and organized by Jesus as if he gave his followers a blueprint of what he wanted them to do after he was dead:

> O.K., Peter, you be the Pope. The rest of you apostles I want to be bishops. Build churches that have altars and confessionals. Celebrate the mass every day. Everyone is to come on Sunday. There will be seven sacraments and a code of canon law. We will need Catholic schools and catechisms. Get busy, guys!

Scholars today recognize that Jesus gave his followers no such blueprint. What he did give them was much more important: he gave them his Spirit and he gave them his life and example. **The church as we know it today is a people of faith that have grown and developed through history.** There are elements to the church that are essential to it, but the church is primarily people. Therefore, it is a growing, living organism. When it does not grow, it becomes stifled and loses sight of its purpose on earth.

THE NEW TESTAMENT CHURCH: THE PAROUSIA, THE COUNCIL OF JERUSALEM, AUTHORITY IN THE CHURCH

It seems that after the death of Jesus, the apostles were much more interested in trying to survive than they were in organizing a church. They feared for their lives. Their hopes had crumpled all around them. But, miraculously, they found new hope. The grave had not been able to hold Jesus. His mission and work was not over. It was to carry on in them.

As we have seen, **the birth of the church came on the feast of Pentecost.** Even though the risen Lord had appeared to his disciples, it was not until Pentecost that they were freed from their fear and became bold witnesses of faith. On Pentecost the Spirit came to them with power:

> When the day of Pentecost came it found them gathered in one place. Suddenly from up in the sky there came a noise like a strong driving wind which was heard all through the house where they were seated. Tongues as of fire appeared, which parted and came to rest on each of them. All were filled with the Holy Spirit. They began to express themselves in foreign tongues and make bold proclamation as the Spirit prompted them (Acts 2:1–4).

As he promised, Christ had not left them alone. He had come to them through the power of the Spirit. In the story of Pentecost, the apostles had the power to speak in foreign tongues, and they were heard by people of different nations in their native languages. This is the reversal of the story of the tower of Babel in Genesis (chapter 11). Sin had divided the people into different languages; now the Spirit was reuniting them.

From the start there was a profound connection between the church and the Holy Spirit. We who live after the ascension have

not seen Jesus in the flesh. Our access to him is through his Spirit. **The church consists of those who are called to live in the Spirit of Christ and the Father.**

For Personal Reflection and Discussion

What do you think it means to "live in the Spirit of Christ"?

The Parousia. The early church believed that the final day of salvation was near. They believed that Jesus would return in glory to establish his kingdom. This return was known as the **parousia.** It would be the end of the world as they knew it. We see this concern reflected in 1 Thessalonians, the first letter written by Paul. The people in the city of Thessalonica were concerned about the fate of those who died before the parousia:

> We say to you, as if the Lord himself had said it, that we who live, who survive until his coming, will in no way have an advantage over those who have fallen asleep (1 Thessalonians 4:15).

Since the early church believed that the end was near, the mission of the church was to proclaim the good news as far and as wide as possible within the short time remaining. Little thought was given to the structure of the church. Later, as the church realized that the parousia might be delayed indefinitely, it became more urgent to structure the church for its future mission on earth.

Who Can Be a Christian? It is easy for us to forget that the earliest church was made up exclusively of men and women who were Jewish. For them, Jesus did not come to begin a new religion. He fulfilled their old one. Peter, Mary, and the apostles still considered themselves Jews after the death and resurrection of Jesus. They continued to pray the prayers of Judaism, to visit the synagogue and temple, to eat "kosher" food. **It was taken for granted that Jesus had come for the Jewish people since he himself was a Jew.**

In time, however, non-Jews (Gentiles) started to become interested in following Jesus. The early church had its first crisis:

Should the Gentiles be accepted into the church? If so, must they also become Jewish and follow the law of Moses? The first question was easily answered when Peter baptized a Roman centurion. But the second question was more difficult: Should the Gentiles also be forced to obey the law of Moses? It was an important question because if the Gentiles were forced to obey the law of Moses, it would forever wed Christianity with Judaism. In addition, the number of those welcomed into the church would be dramatically reduced.

The debate focused on a few specifics within the law: circumcision, eating of foods forbidden by the Torah, and sexual morality. The biggest obstacle would have been circumcision. This Jewish ritual would have likely been an obstacle that kept Gentiles away from the church. In the end a council was called in Jerusalem (see Acts 15) where the opposing forces met, and **it was decided that circumcision was not necessary,** although a compromise was reached concerning foods and sexual morality. **In effect, this Council of Jerusalem (as it is called) set the stage for opening Christianity's doors to those of any nationality or culture. It helped make the Christian church a "catholic" (universal) church.**

Authority in the Early Church. In the gospels Jesus makes it clear that Christian authority is to be unlike the authority that the world generally understands. For Christians, authority must mean service:

> Jesus called them together and said to them, "You know how among the Gentiles those who seem to exercise authority lord it over them; their great ones make their importance felt. It cannot be like that with you. Anyone among you who aspires to greatness must serve the rest; whoever wants to rank first among you must serve the needs of all" (Mark 10:42–44).

In the early church this authority of service had a certain structure to it. There were, at first, no officially ordained priests or ministers. It was clear, however, that **the church was built on the foundation of the apostles.** The gospels describe twelve especially chosen by Jesus as his closest disciples and as those sent out in his name. It appears that the apostles of the early church were not limited to these twelve, but among them Peter was given unique authority as the "head" of the apostles. The name Peter means "rock" in Greek, and in Matthew's gospel Jesus plays off the name to describe the role of Peter as he says:

> I for my part declare to you, you are "Rock," and on this rock
> I will build my church and the jaws of death shall not prevail
> against it (Matthew 16:18).

The Roman Catholic Church has always given this passage heightened meaning, interpreting it to mean that Christ wills his church to be led by Peter and by the successors of Peter (the popes). Thus, in the Catholic Church **the authority of the pope as head of the church is part of the official teaching of the Catholic Church.** (This is one of its critical distinctions from Protestantism.)

In addition to the apostles there were others who had roles of authority in the church. These roles were often based not on a special training program but on the unique individual gifts (or charisms) within the community. Paul outlines some of them:

> God has set up in the church first apostles, second prophets,
> third teachers, then miracle workers, healers, assistants, ad-
> ministrators, and those who speak in tongues (1 Corinthians
> 12:28).

In time, however, all the apostles died, and there developed a need for a more organized structure to meet the needs of communities and carry the church into the future. Three new types of leaders developed in the latter part of the first century AD. They were called episkopos, presbyters, and deacons. There was no clear distinction between the presbyter and episkopos at first. They were given leadership over a certain community and presided at the celebration of the eucharist. In addition, they were to guard the church against "false teachers." Deacons were chosen as "helpers" or servants within the community. Their ministries often had to do with care for the poor and the needy. **Gradually these three positions developed into what we now know as bishop (episkopos), priest (presbyter) and deacon.**

FAMOUS DATES IN CHRISTIAN HISTORY

Listing famous dates in history is not meant to be training ground for trivial pursuits. Each event has an important meaning and reminder for the present.

c. 30	Jesus is crucified by the Romans; the Holy Spirit descends upon the apostles
c. 36	The conversion of Saul (Paul) of Tarsus, Christianity's first great thinker and missionary
c. 50	The Council of Jersusalem; apostles meet in Jerusalem and free the Gentile Christians from the demand of circumcision
67	Persecution of church by Nero
70	Destruction of Jerusalem by Titus
70–100	Writing of the gospels
95–312	Various persecutions of the church by different Roman emperors
312/3	The conversion of the emperor Constantine: Christianity is granted legitimate status by the Edict of Milan
325	Nicea: the first great "ecumenical" council affirms the divinity of Jesus against the heresy of Arianism
400	Jerome translates the Bible into Latin (called the Vulgate)
431	Death of Augustine of Hippo, one of the most influential thinkers in the history of the church
451	The Council of Chalcedon declares that Jesus is the Second Person of the Trinity with both a human and divine nature
529	Benedict establishes a monastery at Monte Cassino and begins the influence of monasticism in the west
590–604	Pope Gregory the Great establishes the power of the pope as a model for the next seven hundred years
800	Pope Leo III crowns Charlemagne emperor of the Holy Roman Empire
1054	Schism between Constantinople (Orthodox) and Rome reaches final climax
1231	Pope Gregory IX authorizes the papal inquisition as a means of dealing with heresy
1309–77	The popes live in Avignon, France
1517	Martin Luther nails his 95 theses to the door of the Wittenberg church, beginning the Protestant reformation
1545–63	The Council of Trent begins a new era in the history of the Catholic Church, called the counter-reformation
1789	The French revolution marks the beginning of the end of the privileged church in Europe and the new era of enlightenment
1869–70	The First Vatican Council declares the infallibility of the pope
1891	Pope Leo XIII issues the encyclical Rerum Novarum, defending the rights of workers in the midst of the industrial revolution
1962–1965	The Second Vatican Council seeks renewal in the church

THE YEARS 67–312: GOLD TESTED IN FIRE

Being a Christian in North American society is hardly a risk. The overwhelming majority of the people who walk the streets of this country were baptized into Christ. This was not the case when Christianity began. At first the Roman authorities paid it little attention, but before long Christians began to become the target of extraordinary persecution. These began with the emperor **Nero** in the year 67. It is believed that the two great apostles, **Peter and Paul, were both killed in Rome during the persecutions of Nero.** From this time forward, Rome would always occupy a central place in Catholic faith as the seat of St. Peter. His successors, the bishops of Rome, would be given a place of special leadership and authority in the church.

For more than two hundred years, Christians were from time to time subjected to persecution. One of the worst of these was that of Diocletian. When he abandoned the throne, it would have been impossible for Christians to predict that they were soon to become the dominant religion of the empire and the most dominant force in shaping western civilization.

For Personal Reflection and Discussion

Can you think of any situations where the church continues to be persecuted today?

CONSTANTINE AND THE GROWTH OF CHRISTIANITY

When Constantine succeeded Diocletian, he brought with him a new element: a mother who was a Christian. While Constantine was still a pagan, he had a vision in battle which led him to believe he would be victorious under the sign of Christ. He was victorious, and later, with his co-emperor Licinius, he passed the **Edict of Milan** which granted freedom of religion to Christians. Roman emperors were accustomed to taking an active part in religious matters, and Constantine applied this to Christianity. It was he who called the bishops together for the great Council of Nicea.

The next centuries brought forth some extraordinary Christians. The so-called fathers of the church began to embark on extraordinary scholarship on behalf of the church. **Jerome** (ca. 345–420) was a monk who translated the Bible from its original languages into Latin. This translation is called the **Vulgate** and was later officially recognized as the official translation of the Catholic Church.

The most influential of the fathers of the church was **St. Augustine.** Originally from northern Africa, Augustine had a pagan father and a Christian mother, **Monica.** He was an extraordinarily brilliant young man who was prone to life's pleasures: gambling, prostitutes and drinking. He later calmed down, took a mistress who bore him a son, and taught in Milan. It was there that he met another great Christian, the bishop **Ambrose.** After much procrastination and another mistress, Augustine at the age of thirty-three finally converted to Christianity under the influence of his mother and Ambrose. He wrote a book describing his conversion, called *The Confessions,* which is one of the greatest descriptions of a spiritual journey ever recorded. Augustine quickly became a priest and shortly after was appointed bishop of Hippo. Augustine's most lasting influence was in the area of theology. Arguing against the heretics of his time, Augustine wrote about virtually every aspect of Christian faith, and his writings have remained influential to this very day.

The fifth century also produced **Leo the Great,** the pope who not only was a spiritual leader but also became the most powerful man of his time in the west. Not only did he preside over the Council of Chalcedon, but he also met face to face with Attila the Hun. **He set the tone for a powerful papacy which would be intimately involved in not only the affairs of the church but those of the state as well.** By the time of his death, the connection between church and state was inseparable.

For Personal Reflection and Discussion

What were some of the advantages and disadvantages of the church's being accepted by Rome?

MONASTICISM

In time, "conversions" to Christianity had little to do with Jesus Christ and much to do with one's local leader or king. **As Christianity became the preferred religion, masses of people were baptized. Christianity lost much of its original force** as the power of God's love and Spirit in the world. Many historians credit monasticism with preserving both the spirit of Christianity and the ancient wisdom of civilization. As people continued to long for a purer form of faith, they entered monasteries for a life of prayer and community. **St. Anthony** of Egypt is often credited as the founder of monasticism in the church. In the year 285 he withdrew into the desert as a hermit. Pachomius was at the same time beginning a communal experiment with monasticism. These movements to withdraw from the life of society became extremely important as the church became more closely wedded to the state. The most important figure in this movement was **St. Benedict** who built a monastery at Monte Cassino. The community was composed of ordinary people who lived by the motto "ora and labora" (work and prayer). Benedict's **Rule** became the standard for monastic life for centuries. The monastery was a self-contained community in which all the material as well as the spiritual needs of the monks were provided. **By copying the works of the fathers of the church and the classics of western civilization, the monks kept alive this tradition in an age in which the Roman empire was crumbling.** By the ninth century the monasteries had become the centers of learning and their abbots were powerful men.

THE SCHISM BETWEEN EAST AND WEST

The two great centers of Christianity were Rome and Constantinople. Although geographically they were not so distant, they became more and more separated by theology and politics. Those in the east (Constantinople) often resented the Roman claims to primacy. After the fall of the Roman empire, there was only one emperor (in the east). His failure to protect the west from invading peoples led the pope to crown **Charlemagne** as

Holy Roman Emperor in the year 800. This also brought about great resentment from the east. In 858, the emperor in the east removed the patriarch of Constantinople and replaced him with his own man named Photius, who refused to accept the authority of the pope. This argument was patched up but relations remained strained.

When Michael Cerularius became patriarch of Constantinople in 1043, he had little respect for the papacy. When the pope insisted that easterners living in the west conform to western rituals, Michael did the same to those westerners living in the east. One bad decision was followed by another. Diplomatic relations broke down, and the patriarch, the emperor, and their followers were all excommunicated in 1054. Despite repeated attempts at reconciliation, all hope was lost after the fourth crusade in which the city of Constantinople was sacked by armies representing western Christianity. The result was the break that divides the Roman and Orthodox churches to this day.

THE POPE GROWS IN POWER

The connection between church and state became so powerful that the church became increasingly corrupted by secular forces. Church offices were bought and sold by men interested more in wealth and power than faith. Church property was passed on to the children of priests or bishops (celibacy was not yet mandatory in the church), and bishops were appointed by secular rulers. **The power of the pope had virtually disappeared.** Into this mess came **Pope Gregory VII** (d. 1085) with a determination to reform the church. He did so by strengthening the structure of the institutional church and the power of the pope. Under his leadership, the church developed a wide array of offices under the pope (known as the curia). **Under Gregory, the papacy was granted extraordinary powers within the church** which were further developed by Innocent III. These reforms also gave rise to the dominance of the code of canon law. Under canon law the rules of the church were strictly codified. This had the advantage of clarity of purpose, but the disadvantage of redefining spiritual matters in legal terms. **The church was defined more and more in**

institutional terms with the pope as the supreme head and the laity and priests in totally subservient roles.

These were some of the best and worst days in the history of the church. Under Innocent III **the inquisition** began its terrible chapter in church history. However, at the same time **St. Francis** (d. 1226) and **St. Dominic** (d. 1221) were offering powerful signs of what Christian life was truly meant to be. They began religious orders of men interested in living the gospel in its pristine simplicity: lives of poverty, prayer, preaching and service. In addition, these orders gave rise to a renewal in theology in the church, led by the Dominicans Albertus Magnus and Thomas Aquinas and the Franciscans Bonaventure and Duns Scotus.

THE EXILE TO AVIGNON

The power of the papacy came to a crashing halt in September 1303. Pope Boniface VIII had issued a statement (called a bull, Unam Sanctam) declaring his authority over the French government. This initiated one of the most bizarre series of events in church history. He was soon arrested by the French king, Philip IV. After the death of Boniface, a French bishop, who was a friend of the king, was elected pope. He took the name **Clement V and moved his residence from Rome to the south of France in a town named Avignon.** He appointed many French cardinals, and they in turn elected another Frenchman as pope, John XXII, who moved all the papal offices to Avignon. Seven French popes lived in Avignon from 1309 to 1377. This was not a good time for the papacy, as it became increasingly concerned with finances and greatly increased taxation while some of the Avignon popes lived in open extravagance. Finally, Gregory XI decided to return the papacy to Rome under the influence of an extraordinary woman of her time, a thirty year old religious sister, **St. Catherine of Siena.**

Just when there appeared to be hope for restoring the papacy to its rightful position, things went from bad to worse. When Gregory VI died, the crowds in Rome insisted on the election of an Italian pope. The cardinals obliged, choosing Urban VI. They were not happy with this choice, however, and since they had elected him under duress, they left Rome and voted again. This time they chose a Frenchman who went to live at Avignon. **Now there were two popes.** A council was held at Pisa, seeking to choose a compromise candidate and unify the church. Instead, the two popes already chosen refused to let go of their authority, and then there were three popes. In 1414 the emperor Sigismund called a council to meet at Constance. The Roman pope re-signed, but before he did he recognized the validity of the council. The Pisa pope departed, the Avignon pope was deposed, and Martin V was elected.

THE REFORMATION

As the church entered the sixteenth century, one thing was perfectly clear: it was **badly in need of reform.** Unfortunately, those in the church with the power to lead this reform seemed to have little interest or ability in this regard. With the hindsight provided by history we can see some of the reforms that were necessary in the church:

1. There was a need to return to the message of the gospel and the person of Jesus. A great deal of the theology of the church had lost touch with its biblical roots.
2. There was need for reform in spirituality. At the time there was a great focus on life after death and especially on the souls in purgatory. There developed the practice of the church selling indulgences which could release a soul from purgatory.
3. There was great need for reform in the papacy. The era of the renaissance popes was a scandalous one in which many of the popes were more interested in pleasure and wealth than in the spiritual interests of the church.
4. There was need for reform within the church concerning the selling of offices and the lack of education and devotion among many priests.
5. The relationship between the church and secular governments was also in need of reform.

Although some good bishops and priests were seriously interested in reform, their powers were not great enough. The church was in a crisis. Into the midst of this crisis stepped one of the most important figures of western culture and Christianity: **Martin Luther.** Luther was a Roman Catholic priest and monk who was devoutly religious and somewhat scrupulous. On October 31, 1517 he posted his now famous **Ninety-Five Theses** on the door of the castle church at Wittenberg. Luther saw himself as a reformer, not as someone seeking to begin a new form of Christianity. The attempt at dialogue between Luther and church officials became a tragedy of errors. More and more, Luther hardened his position. He believed the following:

1. Salvation comes from faith alone. In no way did a person merit his or her eternal life with God through good works. It was grace alone that brought salvation.
2. The Bible is the sole authority in the life of the Christian. While church traditions may be helpful, they are completely secondary to the Bible.
3. Luther recognized only two sacraments as having a biblical basis: the eucharist and baptism. He believed that the mass should be said in the language of the people. He did not believe in celibacy for priests since it was not in the Bible.
4. He discredited all intermediaries between God and the believer. Thus there was no need for the rosary, prayers to saints, statues of saints, indulgences, etc.
5. He emphasized the role of the laity in the church and believed that all should have access to reading God's word.
6. Because of his belief in the Bible, he stressed the importance of preaching (which was often not done at all).

Luther was excommunicated from the Catholic Church on January 3, 1520. He was protected by German royalty, and his popularity and ideas spread rapidly.

Luther was not the only one taking the church by storm. In Switzerland **Ulrich Zwingli** was beginning a highly democratized approach to the faith that sought to get the church back to its biblical roots and away from any beliefs not rooted in the Bible. In France **John Calvin** was winning the hearts and minds of many with his teaching concerning predestination. Meanwhile, in England the king was not so much a reformer as a man seeking to divorce his wife. When the pope would not allow this, **Henry VIII** declared himself head of the church in England and along with most of the bishops of the country set himself against Rome. This marked the establishment of the Anglican Church.

THE COUNTER-REFORMATION

The results of the reformation were astounding on every level: political, religious, social and economic. Both the church and Europe were in a state of nearly unparalleled change. The Catholic Church had to respond to the challenges of the reformers. It was unable to do so until it had an able pope in Paul III. He called together the Council of Trent which was to become the most influential council in the church's history. The council met twenty-five times in three different sessions (1545–1547, 1551–1552, 1562–1563), was suspended for long periods of times, and was sometimes very poorly attended. Nevertheless it articulated the teaching of the church on many important issues and helped to begin a new reform within the church. As opposed to the reformers, it taught:

1. Salvation comes from God's grace but requires human cooperation as well.
2. The Bible is not the sole source of authority. The tradition of the church (the ongoing interpretation of the faith of the scriptures) is a source of authority along with the Bible.
3. The pope is the supreme head of the church.
4. There are seven sacraments divinely chosen by Christ and the church. Christ is truly present in the bread and wine of the eucharist.
5. The saints can act as intermediaries for us.
6. Mary has a unique role as the mother of God and the church.

The Council of Trent inspired a period of reform within the Catholic Church that was badly needed. Unfortunately, these reforms came only after the church had been torn asunder by the reformation. At Trent the church was on the defensive, and in many ways it would stay in this defensive posture until the Second Vatican Council in 1962. **Trent defined the life of the church for the next three hundred years.**

THE MISSIONS

At the same time as the church in Europe was undergoing reform and counter-reform, the Catholic Church was embarking on great missionary projects throughout the world.

In China the Jesuit Matteo Ricci had made his way into the upper echelons of society through his knowledge of the sciences. He studied the culture of the Chinese and soon began to converse with them about his religion. He had some success, but the Chinese were reluctant to adopt western culture since they already had a highly sophisticated civilization of their own. The missionaries tried to adapt Christian practices to Asian culture, but ultimately this was forbidden by Rome and the missions there could achieve little.

Meanwhile the Spanish and the Portuguese were in the midst of colonizing the new world. While Luther criticized the church, Cortez led his band of soldiers into Mexico and slaughtered the Aztec people and looted their invaluable gold. At nearly the same time, Francisco Pizarro was doing the same to the Incas of Peru. The Indian peoples were slaughtered for their wealth, and were considered sub-human. The missionaries who came to South America worked with the native people and converted many to Christianity. Unlike the situation in Asia, however, there was no attempt to assimilate the native customs into Christian faith. In order to accept Christianity, one was forced to accept the western culture that came with it. Often the missionaries were the chief defenders of the Indian people against such abuses as slavery. Eventually the king of Spain forbade slavery, under the influence of Bishop de Las Casas of Chiapa in the New World. Portugal, however, continued to permit slavery in its regions.

By the seventeenth century the Jesuits had established great missions in which the Indians could share in the wealth and authority of the plantations. These cut into the profits of the colonizers, and eventually these too were destroyed by those intent on material gain.

By the nineteenth century the missionary movements began to focus on Asia and Africa. There was tremendous success in the Philippines, while inroads were made in China, Hong Kong, Thailand, Malaysia and India. Likewise, many parts of Africa were responding to the message of the gospel.

For Personal Reflection and Discussion

The Catholic Church was becoming more and more catholic as it spread throughout the world. However, in many ways it remained a European church as it resisted the cultures of other people and imposed its own culture on them. Today this is one of the most important issues facing the church. It is often called "inculturation." How can the church remain one while taking on different cultural expressions? How can different cultures enhance the church?

Can you think of any ways in which cultures celebrate the Catholic faith differently?

THE ENLIGHTENMENT

The intellectual and religious upheavals that had occurred in Europe during the fifteenth and sixteenth centuries (the renaissance, the reformation and the counter-reformation) helped give birth to a period known as the enlightenment. **The philosophers of the enlightenment placed great value on human thought as a science.** That which can be known is that which can be observed and studied. The human mind cannot know anything about a "spiritual" realm of existence. The French philosopher Voltaire summed up the mentality: "What our eyes and mathematics demonstrate, we must take as true. In all the rest, we can only say: We are ignorant." Many of the philosophers of the enlightenment saw no problem remaining Christians, but, for others, Christianity had to be rejected as a religion of revelation and authority. The only revelations they would accept were those made by the human mind. Likewise, the mind was the only true authority. These thinkers also were greatly optimistic about the human capacity to think and thus make the world a better place. Such thinking threatened not only the church but society as well. Threats to the church were obvious. It undermined much of the authority of the church and its basis for authority—divine revelation. It was also a threat to kings who saw themselves as chosen to rule by God.

The French revolution followed on the heels of the enlightenment. The church was seen as an element of the old order of power and underwent extraordinary persecution during this revolution which further hardened Rome against the movement. This revolution brought an end to the hierarchical and feudal patterns of relationships upon which much of Catholicism had been built, but did so at a terrible cost. France went through a terrible period of terror, followed by the dictator Napoleon. Meanwhile other nationalistic movements would occur in Italy, Spain and Germany, in each case limiting the authority of the church.

Oddly enough, the Catholic Church regained some strength in Anglican England during the nineteenth century. Led by John Newman and Henry Manning, the "Oxford Movement" brought about the conversion of many Anglicans to Catholicism.

THE FIRST VATICAN COUNCIL

Pope Pius IX was pope from 1846 through 1878, the longest rule of any pontiff. During this time he actively condemned the onslaught of modern philosophical, social and economic ideas. This was done most exhaustively in his **Syllabus of Errors** (1864), in which he declared the church's traditional belief that there should be only one religion protected and endorsed by the government: Catholicism. (This position would be officially reversed at Vatican II in 1965.)

He also called the first ecumenical council in three hundred years: Vatican I. Although the council was never officially concluded, its main goal was to ensure the authority of the pope. It did this by declaring the pope to be infallible when speaking on matters of faith and morals.

THE INDUSTRIAL REVOLUTION

The nineteenth century is best known as the age of industrialization. With great breakthroughs in technology, the world began to work in new and different ways. The big loser, however, was the worker. The sources of wealth were in the hands of the few, and the masses of workers often had terrible wages and working conditions. Into this crisis came Karl Marx, the father of communism. He blamed capitalism itself for its abuses and excesses and called for a socialist order in which the worker would contribute according to his ability and receive according to his need. Religion for Marx functioned as escape from the demands of the real world. It was, in his words, "the opium of the people." It distracted them from their real mission in this world while pointing to life in the next.

Leo XIII, however, was a pope very much concerned with the realities of this world. He wrote an encyclical called **Rerum Novarum** in which he encouraged the development of trade unions, as well as just wages and working conditions. He criticized both extreme capitalism and extreme socialism. Leo also set the stage for a church which would begin to become more and more involved in the quest for social justice.

THE TWENTIETH CENTURY

During the twentieth century the church has involved itself in a wide spectrum of affairs. It began the century condemning "modernism," which was an intellectual movement that sought to bring some of the principles of the enlightenment to Christian faith. In time, however, the church became more open to modern ideas. There was growing concern for growth in the areas of liturgy, biblical studies, ecumenism and social justice. Perhaps no event of the first half of the century was more important than the encyclical **Divino Afflante Spiritu,** written by Pius XII, which opened the doors of modern scripture study for Catholic scholars. The effects of this document are still being felt in the church.

Another major thrust of the church of the twentieth century was its battle against communism. Because of its atheistic and materialistic doctrines, communism has been repeatedly condemned by the church throughout the world.

The unquestionable highlight of the century was the Second Vatican Council held in Rome from 1962 to 1965. Although its effects are still being weighed, it is considered by many historians to be the most important event in church history since the reformation. Because of its significance and its historical proximity, we will deal with this council in a separate chapter.

Questions for Review

1. What event is known as the birth of the church? Why?
2. What was the parousia and how did it influence the early church's self-understanding?
3. What issues were debated at the Council of Jerusalem? What was decided? How did these decisions influence the future of the church?
4. How did Jesus describe the nature of authority among his followers?
5. What passage from the gospels has the Catholic Church pointed to as a sign of the authority of the pope?
6. What were episkopos, presbyters and deacons?
7. Why did the city of Rome take a special importance for the church?
8. How did Constantine influence the relationship between the church and the Roman empire?
9. What were the contributions made by Jerome, Augustine and Leo the Great?
10. What were the great benefits of monasticism to the church and society?
11. What brought about the split between east and west in the church?
12. How was the thirteenth century both the best and the worst of times for the church?
13. Describe the disaster of the Avignon popes.

14. What were some of the causes of the reformation?
15. What were some of Martin Luther's key ideas and beliefs?
16. How did Zwingli, Calvin and Henry VIII contribute to the division in the church?
17. What were the main conclusions of the Council of Trent?
18. What were some of the benefits of the missionaries in South America? What were some of the tragic elements of European expansion into South America?
19. How did the enlightenment challenge the church?
20. What was the chief idea supported by the First Vatican Council?
21. What was the purpose of the encyclical *Rerum Novarum*?
22. What was the main achievement of the encyclical *Divino Afflante Spiritu*?

11

The Second Vatican Council

It is impossible to understand the church today without understanding the events and results of the Second Vatican Council. Although it concluded more than a quarter-century ago, its effects are still being felt throughout the church. It brought about a period of renewal in the Catholic Church more dramatic than at any other time in history.

BACKGROUND TO THE COUNCIL:
THE ELECTION OF JOHN XXIII

As we have seen in the previous chapter, the church had been in a defensive position for many of the four hundred years following the reformation. In the twentieth century it gradually started to come out of its cocoon again. There was much talk of reform in the church and some small signs that it was on its way. However, **when Pope Pius XII died in 1958, little did the church know that it was about to embark on a new era of its history.** The election of **Angelo Roncalli** as the new pope was seen as a choice of moderation. He was elderly with a reputation for holiness, but few imagined that he would bring about an extraordinary process of change in the church. In fact, he may have been elected because it was thought that he would not rock the boat. Instead he sent the Spirit blowing through the church's sails. He chose the name **John XXIII,** and from the beginning he gave a new direction to the papacy. He described himself as a shepherd and a priest. He visited the sick, the elderly and those in prison. Perhaps most importantly, **John XXIII believed in the goodness of the world and in the possibilities of progress.** He said:

> The prophets of doom always talk as though the present, in comparison to the past, is becoming worse and worse. But I see mankind as entering upon a new order, and I perceive in this a divine plan.

John XXIII was an optimist. He saw in human progress the hand of God, and he believed that the church must open itself up to the modern world. If the church could not speak to real problems of men and women in the world, it would become increasingly irrelevant to their lives. **He also believed that the divisions of the church brought about in history by the schism of east and west and the reformation were a scandal.** He believed that the church is one and must work for reunification. With these ideas in mind, the pope called for an ecumenical council, a meeting of all the bishops throughout the world to reflect on the meaning of the church in the modern world. This purpose was, in itself, revolutionary. In the past, ecumenical councils were called in response to heresies. **Vatican II was to be different. Its purposes were not to condemn, but to build up and renew and help the church face the challenges of the twentieth century.** The council would not (could not) change the basic teaching of the church, but as the pope said in his opening address to the council:

> The substance of the ancient doctrine of the deposit of faith is one thing, but the way in which it is presented is another. It is the latter that must be given much consideration.

In other words, John XXIII was saying that the essential teaching of the church must not change, but it must be communicated in such a way that it is helpful for real people living in the real world. It must adapt its style to the time and place.

For Personal Reflection and Discussion

Why is it important for the church to keep a balance between the past and the future? What is it trying to maintain from the past? Why is it necessary to change for the present and future?

THE COUNCIL MEETINGS

The Second Vatican Council met in four sessions from 1962 through 1965. The sessions generally went from October to the beginning of December. Those who came to the council included all bishops throughout the world and their advisors. In addition, observers were welcomed from the laity and from the Protestant and Eastern Orthodox churches. At the opening session which attracted worldwide public attention, there were more than 2,500 participants. Pope John XXIII died in June 1963 between the first and second sessions. He was succeeded by **Paul VI** who continued the council, and under his leadership not only its work but also its spirit was maintained.

One would like to think that the bishops would get together and the Holy Spirit would gently and swiftly guide them in the right direction. The Spirit, however, works through human beings, and human beings are not so easy to manage. At the council there were many different points of view, ranging from very conservative bishops who wanted little change, to the very liberal bishops who wanted drastic and sweeping changes. The largest group was in the middle. It was clear, however, that the council would be a defeat for the minority who wanted to maintain the status quo.

Various "commissions" would meet and write statements concerning different issues. These would be debated (sometimes fiercely), rewritten and revised, until eventually a document would receive a two-thirds majority vote from the bishops. When this occurred, the document was officially accepted and became part of the highest teaching authority of the church. In the course of the council, sixteen documents were produced on a variety of topics. The single most important topic was clearly the church itself. This was not a council debating the person of Jesus or the meaning of salvation or the number of sacraments; rather the focus was on the meaning and role of the church itself.

For Personal Reflection and Discussion

The process of the council is an example of how the divine works through the human. God doesn't send the Spirit down

with a note indicating what direction to move in. Rather, the
Spirit worked through the faith and intelligence of the men who
governed the council. How does God communicate to you?
In the same way, by making use of your faith, intelligence,
goodness, etc. Can you think of an example in your own life of
a time when you believed that the Spirit was leading you in some
direction?

What were the conclusions reached by the Second Vatican
Council? They are too broad and sweeping to be treated fully
here. Instead, we will try to focus on the key areas and ones that
have had the most dramatic effects on the church.

THE CHURCH: LUMEN GENTIUM

The *Dogmatic Constitution on the Church* (also known as
Lumen Gentium) is one of the most important documents of the
Council. This document describes the very nature and meaning
of the church. Its main significance is found in its spirit as well as
its words. Unlike previous teaching on the church, this document
does not define the church primarily in terms of the hierarchy. Such
a document was presented at the council and rejected. Instead,
the church is at first described as a **"mystery"** (see chapter on
models of church). It is a mystery because God's grace is at work
in it, and it is more than human words can adequately describe.
Secondly, the church is called the **people of God,** a biblical image
which emphasizes the call of God and the responsibility of an
entire people to respond to that call and be a light to the world.
The church, as the people of God, is a pilgrim people, a people
on a journey who have not yet fully realized their goal and purpose. By saying this, the council wished to move away from the
previous notion that the church was a "perfect society" (as it was
sometimes defined). It is only after these descriptions that the
church is described as a hierarchy. In other words, the hierarchy
gains it meaning from the entire people of God and the mystery
of God's love.
    In addition, one of the chapters of this document is entitled
"The Call of the Whole Church to Holiness." The council clearly

wished to break down the walls separating laity from clergy which often relegated the laity to second-class citizenship in the church. It made it clear that holiness was not intended only for an elite group in the church. Rather, **holiness is the vocation of all Christians.**

Finally, the council recognized that the church is broader than the Roman Catholic Church. It includes all the baptized. (We will discuss this at greater length later in the chapter.)

For Personal Reflection and Discussion

According to the council, all Christians are called to live a life of holiness. What does this mean for you? Have you ever met someone whom you would describe as being holy?

AUTHORITY IN THE CHURCH

The Second Vatican Council **affirmed the role of the pope as the supreme head of the church, but it did so in a new context.** The authority of the pope is discussed in the context of the authority of the bishops:

> This council has decided to declare and proclaim before all men its teaching concerning bishops, the successors of the apostles who, together with the successor of Peter, the vicar of Christ and the visible head of the whole Church, govern the house of the living God (*Lumen Gentium,* no. 18).

Although the unique authority of the pope is affirmed, he is seen as the head of the body of bishops. This mentality is called **collegiality,** in which the pope is joined with all bishops as those called to authority in the church. This does not in any way take away from the authority of the pope. It does, however, return that authority to its original setting. Peter was one of the apostles, even though the head one. The pope is one of the bishops, although "first among equals."

We saw in the previous chapter that this authority of the pope and bishops is primarily to teach on behalf of the church and to govern the church in practical affairs. The council also

reaffirmed the infallibility of the pope, the bishops in union with the pope, and the whole church in essential matters of faith.

For Personal Reflection and Discussion

The notion of "collegiality" is one of mutual cooperation and respect among bishops. In this sense, all the bishops are "empowered" to lead the church. Rather than simply be representatives of the pope throughout the world, they teach from their own authority. Can you give any examples from school, home or work of how authority can empower people rather than simply rule them?

ECUMENISM

In the gospel of John, Jesus prays for his followers in the following words:

> I do not pray for them alone. I pray also for those who will believe in me through their word, **that all may be one, as you, Father, are in me, and I in you:** I pray that they may be one in us, that the world may believe that you sent me (John 17: 20–21).

Jesus' prayer for unity among his followers reached the hearts of many at the council. The divisions that existed among Christians were a scandal to the faith. Throughout the twentieth century, many of the Protestant churches had begun a process of dialogue aimed at uniting the churches (known as the ecumenical movement). The Anglican and Orthodox churches became part of this dialogue, but the Catholic Church remained an outsider, praying for unity, but uninvolved in the dialogue. The Catholic Church was waiting for the other churches to "come back." They were seen as fallen away and in error. Unity would be achieved only when they returned to the true church, the Catholic Church.

This attitude died at the Second Vatican Council. **Pope John XXIII made it one of the council's chief objectives to enter into the process of attaining Christian unity.** Observers were invited

CHRISTIAN DENOMINATIONS

The unity of the church has been splintered for nearly one thousand years. Below is a sample of some of the major Christian denominations, with their origins and key beliefs.

	Origin	*Beliefs and Practices*
Eastern Orthodox	Conflicts between Constantinople and the west concerning the authority of the pope; worship and theology of Holy Spirit led to a final split in 1054.	Accept the authority of both scripture and tradition. View the church as the mystical body of Christ. Leadership found in all bishops.
Lutherans	Began with excommunication of Martin Luther in 1521.	Emphasis on authority of scripture. We are saved by faith and grace, not our own good works. Two sacraments: baptism and communion.
Episcopal (Anglican)	Henry VIII of England wished to annul his first marriage; when the pope refused he established himself as the head of the Church of England in 1534.	Very similar to Roman Catholic without allegiance to pope. Focuses on two sacraments: baptism and communion, although other sacramental acts are recognized. "Episcopal" means governed by bishops.
Presbyterian	Founded by John Knox in Scotland, influenced by the teaching of John Calvin (d. 1564).	Little emphasis placed on sacraments or liturgy; focus on living values of faith in the world. Administration of churches by elders.
Methodists	Founded by John Wesley (d. 1791), an Anglican who worked with the poor, Methodism has grown most intensely in the U.S.	Place little importance on doctrines; focus on "lived faith" and social action. Well known for congregational singing, they accept baptism and holy communion and are led by a general conference run by bishops.
Baptists	Began as Anabaptists; adapted by John Smyth in Amsterdam in 1611. Roger Williams founded first Baptist church in North America in 1639.	Importance of individual commitment to Jesus Christ as Lord. Bible is the sole authority, to be interpreted by each person.

from other Christian churches, and they were able to share their thoughts and observations with a special papal representative. In the end, the council issued a **Decree on Ecumenism.** This decree was in some ways revolutionary, for it admitted that **the church was not limited to the Catholic Church and that the reasons for the divisions between Christians came from both sides of the division.** In other words, unity would be restored through an effort on the part of both sides, not a unilateral demand that the other churches rejoin the Catholic Church. This was a major breakthrough which has dramatically changed the nature of the relationship between the Catholic Church and all other Christians. Christian leaders are now likely to work with one another and pray with one another, rather than condemn each other.

For Personal Reflection and Discussion

Ecumenism cannot mean that the churches simply ignore their real differences. But it does ask them to recognize their many similarities and to work and pray together. What are some ways in which the churches can join forces?

NON-CHRISTIAN RELIGIONS

Originally, the *Decree on Ecumenism* was intended to deal with non-Christian religions as well, but the council decided to develop a separate decree for this, *The Decree on the Relationship Between the Church and Non-Christian Religions.* It is a small document which is important as a starting point and for its spirit. In it **the church recognizes the genuine contributions of all religions as they seek to bring men and women closer to God:**

> The Catholic Church rejects nothing which is good and true about these religions. It looks with sincere respect on those ways of conduct and life, those rules and teachings which, though differing in many particulars from what it holds and sets forth, nevertheless often reflect a ray of that truth which enlightens all men (no. 2).

Although the document says little in detail about the religions, **it encourages dialogue with them and respect for their re-**

ligious and cultural values. This is a far cry from a previous mentality which would have simply dismissed them as "false religions." The church is also clear in maintaining the uniqueness and validity of Christian faith while admitting that other religions may share in the truth.

This document is best known for its section on the church's relationship with Judaism. Throughout the history of the church, the Jews had often been portrayed as a people cursed by God and responsible for the death of Jesus. This sad legacy had contributed to the feelings of antisemitism which were at the heart of the holocaust by the Nazis. In this decree the church recognized the many common elements of faith shared by Christians and Jews. More importantly, **it sought to eliminate any mentality among Christians which perpetuated antisemitism.** Although the decree did not explicitly admit and apologize for previous attitudes, it certainly condemned them, and this marked the beginning of a new era in Jewish-Christian relations.

For Personal Reflection and Discussion

The section on relations with the Jews is an example of how the church is called to be a penitent and reforming church and face its own limitations and errors. The irony is that the church is holy yet filled with sinners. What are some of the reasons why people are prejudiced at all against anyone?

THE CHURCH AND THE WORLD

For many years the Catholic Church had perpetuated something of a **fortress mentality:** the church is the fortress guarding its people against the evils of the world. Its attitude toward the world was one of profound mistrust. As we have seen, John XXIII did not share that attitude. He used an Italian word to describe one of the main goals of the council: **aggiornamento.** This means something like updating, or modernizing, getting in touch with the times.

Since this was such an important theme, the council produced a separate document related to it. It had already done one on the church. The new one would be more practical, less theological. It was called the *Pastoral Constitution on the Church in the Modern World,* also known by its Latin name, *Gaudium et Spes.* Its opening sentence has become famous for establishing a new relationship between the church and the world:

> The joys and the hopes, the griefs and the anxieties of the men and women of this age, especially those who are poor or in any way afflicted, these too are the joys and the hopes, the griefs and anxieties of the followers of Christ (*Gaudium et Spes,* no. 1).

The church immediately sought to unite itself with the human race rather than separate itself from them. It was also made clear that the church is a **servant church** that identifies in a special way with the poor and the afflicted. We find in this document much of the basis for the model of the church as servant and for the "preferential option for the poor."

The document emphasizes that the church must exist in the world, "scrutinizing the signs of the times and interpreting them in light of the gospel" (no. 4). The mission of the church then is not to simply continue to repeat the formulas of faith, but to show how that **faith should affect the way that Christians live in the world** and respond to the various situations in the world. It recognized the genuine advances made by society in culture, the arts and science and taught that the church need not be threatened by such advances. It also recognized the importance and dignity of individual conscience. It encouraged a common human solidarity in the search for justice and peace on earth, and recognized that the church must listen to and learn from the world.

The lengthy document also takes the initiative of responding to some of the "signs of the times": marriage and the family, the development of culture, economics and poverty, war and peace. (We will return to these themes in a later section of this book on Christian living.)

For Personal Reflection and Discussion

What are some of the most important issues that the church should be addressing today?

THE CHURCH AND THE BIBLE

In the church before the Second Vatican Council, the Protestants were known as the church of the Bible and the Catholics were known as the church of sacraments and law. Catholics were rarely encouraged to read the Bible on their own for fear that they would misinterpret it. Once again the council changed all this. One of the most important documents of the council was the *Constitution on Divine Revelation (Dei Verbum)*. It recognized the word of God as the source of church teaching and theology, stating that the teaching office of the church is "not above the word of God but serves it, listening to it devoutly" (no. 10). In addition, the council taught that the Bible should not be just in the hands of church authorities, but that **"easy access to sacred scripture should be provided for all the Christian faithful"** (no. 22). It encouraged greater freedom for scripture scholars and accepted the new methods of scholarship. It also recognized the need for the scholars to present their findings to the authority of the church for guidance and approval, for revelation in Christ is not based solely on the scriptures but on the judgment of the believing community as well. In this way, the scriptures are a living word speaking to men and women of various ages and cultures.

The effects of this are just being felt in the Catholic Church. It has done wonders to renew the spirituality of the church and to give it a deeper basis in the teaching and message of Jesus. It has opened the riches of the Bible to millions of Catholics and helped them to interpret their faith more fully and deeply. St. Jerome said, "Ignorance of the Bible is ignorance of Christ," and the council has helped to bring the church more fully in touch with its Lord.

THE LITURGY

The council restored the primary place of the word of God in the life of the church, but it did not eliminate the importance of the sacraments. To the contrary, **the faith of the church is nourished in both word and sacrament.** The council emphasized the importance of the eucharist in the life of faith, describing it as "the summit toward which the activity of the church is directed; at the same time it is the fountain from which all her power flows" (*Constitution on the Sacred Liturgy,* no. 10).

In order to help the church understand and celebrate the sacraments more deeply, the council brought about a renewal in this area as well. For hundreds of years the mass had been said in Latin with exactly the same words and gestures repeated everywhere throughout the world. It was a sign of the universal faith of the church. One could attend mass anywhere in the world and it would be the same experience. The priest said the words alone (aided by altar boys) with his back to the congregation. He was separated from the congregation in the sanctuary surrounded by the altar rail. The mass was clearly the work of the priest, and the people were passive recipients. Although elements of the mass were very beautiful, the council insisted that it involve the entire people of God more fully. It has been in this spirit that the mass has changed in the years following the council (although the essential elements cannot change). It is now celebrated in the language of the people (the vernacular). The laity have a more active role as leaders of song, lectors (readers of the scriptures), and ministers of the eucharist. In addition, the mass is more flexible in meeting the needs of individual groups (teens, children, the elderly, those from other cultures). Today the effects of the council are taken for granted as people celebrate the liturgy with the priest, rather than watch the priest celebrate the liturgy.

For Personal Reflection and Discussion

Talk with some people about the old liturgy in Latin. What were their impressions? Which way do they prefer: the old or the new? What are the advantages of each?

RELIGIOUS FREEDOM

As we have seen in an earlier chapter, much of the church's history involved an inseparable relationship between the church and the state. Christian faith was not only a religious force, it was a social and political one as well. **The church was given special status and privileges. Western Europe was indeed Christendom.**

Heretics were not only a threat to the faith, they were a threat to social stability as well, and they were dealt with harshly. For many, this was the ideal relationship between the church and nations. This status of the church, however, collapsed after the reformation, and many longed for its return.

There was another way of understanding the relationship between church and state, and an example of it could be found in the United States, where there is no privileged religion, but a separation between church and state. Some Catholics strongly believed that this was the ideal situation, not for practical reasons, but because **every person should have the right to follow his or her conscience in matters of faith.** Other Catholics saw these other religions as "false religions" and believed that "error has no rights." Ideally, they believed, the Catholic Church should enjoy a privileged position.

The Second Vatican Council ratified the right to religious freedom, with everyone free in this regard from the coercion of governments. No one should ever be compelled to accept Christian faith, nor should anyone be punished for rejecting it.

For Americans who are born and bred on the notion of freedom, this may seem like an incredibly obvious notion. For the church, however, it was a big step because it abandoned the notion of Christendom as the ideal, and, even more importantly, it revealed that the teaching of the church can indeed grow and develop. The ideas of the council on religious freedom had come a long distance from *The Syllabus of Errors* issued by Pope Pius IX one hundred years before (see chapter 10).

For Personal Reflection and Discussion

Which is the ideal situation: for Christianity to be given special preference by the government or for the government to be neutral? Why?

THE LAITY

The council was a call to freedom and responsibility for those in the church who were not priests or nuns or brothers. The laity were invited to partake in the mission of the church in a deeper way than ever before. In the earlier documents on the church, it was revealed that the church is the entire people of God, and that therefore the laity have a responsibility as the church to do the work of the church. This responsibility is not something to "help the priests" but rather belongs to all Christians by virtue of their baptism. All are called to ministry and service. This ministry and service depends on the individual gifts and talents of persons which are to be used "for the good of mankind and the upbuilding of the church" (*Decree on the Apostolate of the Laity,* no. 3).

The first area of service is in the world where the laity are to bring the values of Christ to all that they do and help to be a "leaven" to society. It is to be hoped that corporations, communications, the arts and sciences will all be influenced by the spirit of the faith of those Christians who are part of their work. Likewise, families will become "mini-churches," small communities of faith where the virtues of love, forgiveness, peace, patience and generosity take root and grow.

The second area is the church itself where there is greater need than ever for the ministry of the laity. Today we can find lay men and women involved intimately in Christian education, and in ministry to the poor, the sick, the elderly, and all those in need. They are also involved more fully in taking part in the liturgy and bringing communion to the sick and homebound. It appears that the church of the future will become increasingly dependent on the ministry and service of the laity.

For Personal Reflection and Discussion

These were some of the great issues facing the church at the Second Vatican Council. What issues do you see facing the church today?

Questions for Review

1. Who was the inspiration behind the Second Vatican Council?
2. Why was the council called? How was it different from past councils?
3. How was the church's self-description different in the Second Vatican Council?

4. What is collegiality?
5. What did the council teach about infallibility?
6. What is ecumenism? How did the Catholic Church change its attitude concerning ecumenism at the council?
7. What did the council teach about other religions of the world?
8. Why is the section on the relationship with Judaism so important?
9. What is meant by a "fortress mentality" in the church? What was *aggiornamento*?
10. How did the council change the church's understanding of its relationship to the world?
11. What changes were made in the liturgy? Why?
12. What were the two different attitudes toward religious freedom which were debated at the council? Which idea won out?
13. What is the role of the laity in both the church and the world?

12

Baptism and Confirmation

THE MEANING OF THE SACRAMENTS

In a number of places throughout this book we have said that God is the infinite mystery. He is not a thing or even a person; he has no body and is not limited to any time, place or even religion. In one sense God is everywhere, but in another sense God is "more" present in some people and events than in others. God seems to be alive in the saints in a powerful way in which he is not alive in the lives of ordinary people. God is more present in the experience of love, forgiveness, service, and compassion than he is in the experience of evil. **So, while we might say that God is everywhere, certain people, places, and events reveal the presence of God more fully and deeply.**

God can only communicate himself to us through his creation (people, events, nature, beauty, etc). This is the idea behind the notion of a sacrament. **A sacrament makes visible the invisible love and grace of God.** Thus, almost anything can be "sacramental" in this sense: the birth of a child, the love of friends, a good book, the beauty of nature, serving the poor, etc. As the theologian/scientist Teilhard de Chardin has said: "All creation is holy for those who have the eyes to see." Yet, in a world that is holy, Christians believe that Jesus Christ is unique in all creation. He is **the sacrament** of God's love. More than anyone or anything else, Jesus has revealed for us, and made present, the love of the Father.

For Personal Reflection and Discussion

Catholics believe very much in the "ordinary." They believe that God can be found in the experiences of family, friends,

188

school, work, etc. All of the ordinary is, in some way, sacramental. In what ordinary ways does God communicate with you?

Christ continues to be present in the community of faith in and through the Spirit. **The Catholic Church celebrates this presence through seven sacraments.** The church believes that through these sacraments Christ continues to offer us his love, continues to be present to us. (We call this presence of God in us "grace.") The sacraments are not magical manipulations of God but celebrations of the ongoing presence of Christ in the community. Of course, Christ is present in our lives outside the sacraments, but these are special avenues of spiritual growth and nourishment.

For Personal Reflection and Discussion

A priest that I know ends the mass by saying, "The mass is ended; now let's go and live it." What do you think it means to live the mass?

In the Catholic Church the sacraments are often divided into three groups. They are the **sacraments of initiation** (baptism, confirmation and eucharist) which bring a person into the church, the **sacraments of healing** (penance and anointing of the sick) which minister to those alienated by sin or oppressed by sickness, and the **sacraments of vocation** (matrimony and holy orders) through which the church is built up by the love of the ordained and the married.

BAPTISM

BAPTISM: SYMBOLS, HISTORY, MEANING

Water. It's the stuff of life. We spend the first nine months of our lives in it. A greater percentage of our bodies is water. Most of the earth is covered with it. We probably take it very much for granted. We go to the sink and turn on the faucet. We go to the pool or the beach; we hop in the shower. It seems as though there is an unlimited supply, and for this thank God, because we cannot live without it. Yet, for millions of people, the water of life is not a dependable fact of life. They live without access to clean drinking water.

Water. It's the stuff of death. Following the ravages of the war in the Persian Gulf, a monsoon swept across Bangladesh killing as many people as the bullets and bombs did in Iraq. A sudden storm can bring a boat and all its passengers under the waters forever. The surprising strength of an undertow at the beach can quickly end a vacation.

In the Bible, water is an extremely important symbol. In the book of Genesis God creates out of the chaos of the waters:

> ... the earth was a formless wasteland and darkness covered the abyss, while a mighty wind swept over the waters.

Soon afterward his creation is under the flood which destroys sinful human beings while offering them a new beginning. In the exodus God creates a covenant people, bringing them through the Red Sea while using the same sea to destroy their enemies. John the Baptist calls the people to repentance, baptizing them in the Jordan River, washing away their sins and preparing them for the coming of the messiah.

It is no wonder that the early Christian community used water as the way in which it brought people into faith in Christ. Water is the perfect symbol for baptism because it is about both life and death. The baptisms were usually performed by immersion into the water. **Going down into the waters symbolized dying to an old life and coming up, being born again in Christ.** In the early church, baptism meant a true choice on the part of the baptized to give up an old way of being and to live in Christ.

As time went on (by the third century), the Christian community developed a more complex way of bringing new members to baptism and faith. It was one that offered previous training in the faith and in the new way of living. When people were interested in becoming Christians, they were presented to the leaders of the community by a friend or "sponsor." Before they would be baptized, however, they would spend two or three years learning about their new faith. They would study the scriptures, pray with the community, perform acts of service and charity and attend

THE SEVEN SACRAMENTS

For Catholics, the sacraments are encounters with the risen Christ. Through the seven sacraments, God's offer of his grace in Christ is made real to us. The sacraments are divided into three categories: initiation, healing and vocation.

Sacraments of Initiation

Baptism: Initiation into the life of grace in the Christian community. "Are you not aware that we who were baptized into Christ were baptized into his death? Through baptism into death we were buried with him, so that just as Christ was raised from the dead by the glory of the Father, we too might live a new life" (Romans 6:3–4).

Confirmation: Celebrating the presence of the Spirit in the life of faith. "All who are led by the Spirit of God are children of God" (Romans 8:14). "The fruit of the spirit is love, joy, peace, patient endurance, kindness, generosity, faith, mildness and charity" (Galatians 5:22).

Eucharist: The source and summit of Christian faith. "Taking bread and giving thanks, he broke it and gave it to them, saying, 'This is my body to be given for you. Do this as a remembrance of me'" (Luke 22:19).

Sacraments of Healing

Penance: A celebration of God's unconditional, forgiving love. "On the evening of the first day of the week, even though the disciples had locked the door of the place where they were for fear of the Jews, Jesus came and stood before them. 'Peace be with you,' he said."

Anointing of the Sick: Celebrating the healing power of Christ in the midst of sickness. "A leper approached him with a request: 'If you will to do so, you can cure me.' Moved with pity, Jesus stretched out his hand, touched him and said, 'I do will it. Be cured'" (Mark 1:40–41).

Sacraments of Vocation

Marriage: Celebrating the human love of two people as a sign of God's love for all. "'For this reason a man shall leave his father and mother, and shall cling to his wife, and the two shall be made into one.' This is a great foreshadowing; I mean that it refers to Christ and the church" (Ephesians 5:31–32).

Holy Orders: Celebrating the call to serve Christ and the community in a unique way: to maintain "holy order" in the church. "He named twelve as his companions whom he would send to preach the good news" (Mark 3:12).

the eucharist, leaving after the readings and the sermon. They were called **"catechumens."** If they were genuinely committed to their new faith, they would prepare for their baptism at the Easter vigil (the evening before Easter) by making a forty-day "retreat" previous to the vigil. (Later the entire community would join them for this special period of prayer, and thus the season of Lent was born.)

On the night of the Easter vigil they would meet in the back of the "church" (or home, since often the community was persecuted and had no building) at a small baptismal pool. With their backs facing the west (representing darkness and sin), they would walk down into the water and be immersed by a deacon or deaconess. The traditional trinitarian formula would be recited: "I baptize you in the name of the Father and of the Son and of the Holy Spirit. Amen." Rising on the eastern side (the sunrise, resurrection, new life), they would come up out of the pool and a new white garment would be placed around them, symbolizing that they were a new creation in Christ. They would be anointed with oil and a prayer would be prayed for the descent of the Spirit into their lives (a practice which would gradually develop into the sacrament of confirmation). They would be invited into the church where they would stay for the mass, this time not leaving after the sermon, but staying and receiving communion for the first time.

As you can see this was a very powerful ritual (sign) which indicated the importance of the baptism for the one being baptized. What had become very clear by this time is that **baptism brought one into the death and resurrection of Jesus, but it also brought one into the community of faith. The two were powerfully connected to each other.**

For Personal Reflection and Discussion

What advantages can you see to the ancient practice of baptizing adults? What advantage is there in being baptized as an infant?

As we have already seen, the conversion of the Roman emperor Constantine dramatically changed the structure of Christianity. Being a Christian soon became "fashionable." The need for a genuine faith and relationship with Christ was being minimized. New Christians were coming into the church faster than they could be prepared. In addition to this political development, there was also a **theological development as well. This was the doctrine of original sin.** It was reasoned that if all men and women needed baptism for salvation, therefore they must be in sin without this baptism. This sin was the "sin of Adam." Humans had been born into a fallen world and condition. Without baptism, it was believed, they could not be saved. If this were the case, then it became essential to baptize infants as soon after their birth as possible. **The theology of baptism shifted away from its earlier meaning and focused on original sin and the baptism of infants.** Now the personal choice was being removed altogether. What once existed as a sign of personal faith in Jesus was now given to infants without a choice.

This has continued to be the main theme of the church's teaching on baptism until recently. Having rediscovered its lost history, the church now places its focus on the baptism of adults into the community. They have readapted the earlier process of the catechumens for those adults preparing for baptism. This places the focus very much on the role of the community in welcoming the new member into the church. The preparation often lasts at least a year and the baptism occurs at the Easter vigil. **This is called the Rite of Christian Initiation of Adults** (or the RCIA as it is often called). This new rite has the wonderful effect of helping all in the church renew the true meaning of their baptism. This meaning can be summarized as the following. Baptism is:

1. a sharing in the death and resurrection of Jesus;
2. a means for the forgiveness of sin;
3. the means of entrance into the Christian community.

For Personal Reflection and Discussion

Let's try to look at the power of original sin as a tendency to selfishness. What are the top ten temptations for young people today?

THE RITE OF BAPTISM FOR CHILDREN

Since most baptisms still involve infants, we look at the rite for the baptism of children. Baptisms are usually celebrated on Sunday. The baptism may be performed by either a priest or a deacon. **The child is presented by parents and godparents** who represent the wider Christian community and who are to help the parents in their task of raising the child in the faith. (Godparents should be people chosen because they are good models of Christian faith.) Throughout the ceremony, the parents speak on behalf of the child and themselves, **renewing their own baptismal vows.**

Celebrant:	Do you reject sin, so as to live in the freedom of God's children?
Parents and godparents:	I do.
Celebrant:	Do you reject the glamor of evil, and refuse to be mastered by sin?
Parents and godparents:	I do.
Celebrant:	Do you reject Satan, father of sin and prince of darkness?
Parents and godparents:	I do.
Celebrant:	Do you believe in God, the Father almighty, creator of heaven and earth?
Parents and godparents:	I do.
Celebrant:	Do you believe in the Holy Spirit, the holy Catholic Church, the communion of saints, the forgiveness of sins, the resurrection of the body, and life everlasting?
Parents and godparents:	I do.
Celebrant:	This is our faith. This is the faith of the Church. We are proud to profess it, in Christ Jesus our Lord.
All:	Amen.

This is followed by the baptism itself as the child is brought to the baptismal font, and as the **water** is poured on the child, the celebrant says, "I baptize you in the name of the Father, and of the Son, and of the Holy Spirit." The child is then anointed with **oil.** Anointing is an ancient practice in the Old Testament, and it means that the person has been chosen for a special task. As we have seen, the title "Christ" means "the anointed one"; thus the child is anointed into Christ with the "chrism of salvation." **A white garment** is placed on the child as a sign that they are a "new creation in Christ." The parents are then given **a candle** which is lit from the large Easter candle. They are to live as "the light of the world" in the light of Christ Jesus. The ceremony is concluded with the Lord's Prayer and a final blessing.

CONFIRMATION

CONFIRMATION AND THE HOLY SPIRIT

The meaning of the sacrament of confirmation is very similar to that of baptism. This sacrament only came into existence in the third century when special prayers and anointings were included for the gift of the Holy Spirit. The roots of the sacrament, however, go back to Jesus' promise of the Spirit to the apostles. The distinct nature of confirmation is to be found in its emphasis on the role of the Holy Spirit in the life of the Christian. **The best way to understand the sacrament is to understand who the Holy Spirit is.**

On the night before his death, Jesus promised his closest disciples that he would not abandon them. He would continue to be present to them in a new way: through the Spirit (the Paraclete).

> I tell you the truth: It is much better for you that I go. If I fail to go, the Paraclete will never come to you, whereas if I go, I will send him to you. . . . When he comes, however, being the Spirit of truth he will guide you to all truth (John 16:7, 11).

Following the death, resurrection and ascension of Jesus, we now live in the age of the Holy Spirit. The same Spirit who led Jesus into the desert, who brought him into prayer and union with his Father, who inspired him to teach and heal, who gave him the courage to face his death, this same Spirit is given to all Christians. **It is the very life of God at work inside us.** It is the life and power of the Spirit at work in the church that we celebrate at confirmation. Yet throughout the history of the church the Holy Spirit has received little attention compared to Christ and the Father.

The Spirit in the Old Testament. In the Old Testament, there is no mention of the Holy Spirit. It speaks, rather, of the Spirit of God or the Spirit of Yahweh. The Hebrew word for God's Spirit is **ruah. This word can mean either wind or breath or spirit.** Like the wind, God's Spirit cannot be seen itself but can only be understood through its effects. Sometimes, like a great wind, the Spirit can act with extraordinary power. In the Hebrew scriptures, this can be seen in the great acts of God: his creation, the exodus, the actions and words of the great leaders of Israel.

Like a breath, the Spirit is a source of life and is an inner principle of life. We rarely pay much attention to the fact that we are breathing, but it is our breath which allows us to live and act. Likewise, the Spirit often goes unnoticed as it is at work quietly, imperceptibly leading us in the ways of God's love. It is this same Spirit that led God's people Israel to a greater and deeper knowledge of him.

In the Old Testament, the Spirit of God is often associated with the themes of creation and re-creation. It is the Spirit of God which hovers over the waters at the dawn of creation. It is the "breath" of God which brings Adam to life. It is also the Spirit of God which promises new life to a people who feel abandoned by God during the exile. Thus, God proclaims to the prophet Ezekiel:

> Then he said to me: Son of Man, these bones are the whole house of Israel. They have been saying, "Our bones are dried up, our hope is lost and we are cut off." ... O my people, I will put my spirit in you that you may live, and I will settle you upon your land; thus you shall know that I am the Lord (Ezekiel 37:11. 14).

The Holy Spirit in the Life of Christians. Christians believe that Jesus is the fulfillment of these promises of the Spirit. He is the one fully anointed in the Spirit of God. Thus, when Jesus begins his ministry in the gospel of Luke, he goes to the synagogue to read and identifies himself with the prophecy from Isaiah:

> When the book of the prophet Isaiah was handed to him, he unrolled the scroll and found the passage where it is written:
>
> > The Spirit of the Lord is upon me;
> > therefore he has anointed me.
> > He has sent me to bring glad tidings to the poor,
> > to proclaim liberty to captives,
> > recovery of sight to the blind and release to prisoners,
> > to announce a year of favor from the Lord.
> >
> > > (Luke 4:17–19)

It is this Spirit of God, the Holy Spirit, that is offered to all Christians in the life of faith. Those who follow Jesus are to make his Spirit their own. St. Paul insists that it is the presence of the Spirit that makes us Christians. **What does the presence of the Spirit do for us?**

1. The Spirit sets us free! The great enemy of love is fear, and the Spirit of God allows us to live in freedom from fear and freedom to love. We have seen how the Spirit freed the apostles from fear on Pentecost. Something extraordinary happened to these very human, very frightened followers of Christ: they were filled with God's Spirit and they were free to love and serve God.

2. The Spirit allows us to see ourselves for who we truly are: sons and daughters of God. It leads us to a true self-knowledge. Thus St. Paul writes:

> All who are led by the Spirit of God are children of God. You did not receive a Spirit of slavery leading you back into fear, but a Spirit of adoption through which we cry out, "Abba" (that is, "Father"). The Spirit himself gives witness with our spirit that we are children of God (Romans 8:14–16).

3. The Spirit enables us to live a new life—to be the new creation. The presence of God's Spirit leads us to holiness. It is the mark of holiness. It leads us along a different path in life. St. Paul describes the life in the Spirit for Christians: **"The fruit of the Spirit is love, joy, peace, patient endurance, kindness, generosity, faith, mildness and chastity" (Galatians 5:22).**

For Personal Reflection and Discussion

Look again at Paul's description of the fruits of the Spirit. In which of these can you see the Spirit at work in your own life? Which ones need the most work?

The Holy Spirit and the Sacrament of Confirmation. The life of the Christian is a life in the Spirit. This Spirit is present throughout a person's life and does not only come for the first time at confirmation. In fact, the **life in God's Spirit is something that usually grows slowly and steadily throughout a person's life as he or she matures in faith.** If you look again at Paul's description of the Spirit, you may realize that few people live fully in the Spirit.

The sacrament of confirmation is a time when we celebrate the life of the Spirit in the church and in those receiving the sacrament. The sacrament has been given at different ages throughout history. Today it is most often received sometime during adolescence. Finally, there is a great deal of irony in the celebration of the sacrament of confirmation today. For many people it signals the end of their religious education and perhaps even their involvement with the church. Ironically, this is a sacrament of initiation. It is meant to be only the beginning of a lifetime of faith.

For Personal Reflection and Discussion

Think back to your confirmation. What did it mean to you at that time? Have you tried to live the sacrament? If so, how?

THE RITE OF CONFIRMATION

The minister of the sacrament of confirmation is the bishop (although priests may give the sacrament under special circumstances). **The connection between baptism and confirmation is very**

clear in the rite of confirmation. The baptismal vows are renewed. The candidate is once again accompanied by a sponsor (who may be their godparent). The **ritual has three main components:**

1. The laying on of hands: This is an ancient practice in the church symbolizing a special call or mission in the church. Confirmation emphasizes the mission of each Christian to spread the good news of Christ in both word and deed.

2. Anointing with oil: As we saw with baptism, the oil is a symbol of being chosen by God for a special vocation. For the Christian, it is the vocation that all Christians share: the life of grace and holiness in God's Spirit.

3. The words "Be sealed with the Holy Spirit": Confirmation does not make the Spirit present for the first time, but it does offer a "seal" of the Holy Spirit. This refers to the ancient practice of kings offering their seal or sign so that a person with that seal is their official representative. Being sealed in the Holy Spirit means that God offers his Spirit to us and the Christian commits himself or herself to living a life in the Spirit.

As you can see from the rite, confirmation places an emphasis on the mission of the Christian. Every Christian is not to be a passive member of the community, but is called to serve the community and the world.

Questions for Review

1. In what way is the world "sacramental"?
2. Could Jesus be considered a sacrament? Why?
3. Define "grace."
4. What is meant by "living the sacraments"?
5. Which are the sacraments of initiation, healing and vocation?
6. How is water a symbol for both life and death?
7. Explain the process of initiation into the church in the third century.
8. What political and theological developments changed the focus of baptism away from adults to infants?
9. What are three key themes to the meaning of the sacrament of baptism?
10. Explain briefly the difference between original sin and personal sin.

11. What four symbols are used in a baptism and what do they mean?
12. Which sacrament is most similar in meaning to the sacrament of confirmation?
13. What does the Hebrew word *ruah* mean? What does it tell us about the spirit?
14. What are three effects of the Spirit on the life of the Christian?
15. What are the fruits of the Holy Spirit?
16. What three components make up the main rite of the sacrament of confirmation?

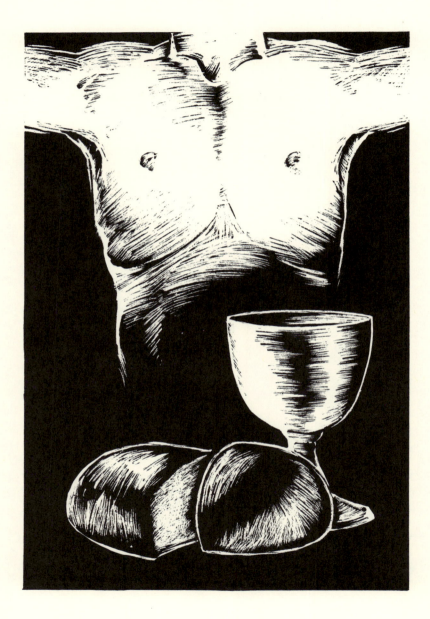

13

The Eucharist

THE LAST SUPPER

> When the hour arrived, he took his place at table, and the apostles with him. He said to them: "I have greatly desired to eat this Passover with you before I suffer. I tell you, I will not eat it again until it is fulfilled in the kingdom of God."
>
> Then taking a cup he offered a blessing in thanks and said: "Take this and divide it among you; I tell you, from now on I will not drink of the fruit of the vine until the coming of the reign of God."
>
> Then taking bread and giving thanks, he broke it and gave it to them, saying, "This is my body to be given for you. Do this in memory of me." He did the same with the cup after eating, saying as he did so: "This cup is the new covenant in my blood, which will be shed for you" (Luke 22:14–20).

On the night before his death, Jesus shared a meal with his closest followers which became the basis for the most important and central sacrament, the eucharist. In order to understand the eucharist, we need to travel back in time to this last supper.

Jesus had gone to Jerusalem as one of thousands of Jews on pilgrimage for the feast of the Passover. Upon entry he had been hailed as a "Messiah," a royal title that would offend the Romans. In Jerusalem he had confronted the leaders of the people. He had gone into the temple and driven out the money changers. He had called the scribes and the Pharisees "blind guides" and "hypocrites." He had challenged the people to love God from the heart, not to use him for profit or to manipulate him for one's own sense of righteousness. He was a challenge to both religious and Roman leaders, and he would not survive the confrontation.

On the night before his death he gathered with his closest friends to share a meal. But this was not just any meal. **Luke (and Matthew and Mark) describe it as the passover meal, the seder— the meal celebrating the Jewish exodus from slavery in Egypt.** It was a meal steeped in profound religious meaning for the Jewish people. For the Jews, the passover meal was meant to recall and relive the exodus from Egypt and their flight from the slavery of Pharaoh. They dressed as people in flight. It included the question from the youngest member of the family, "Why is this day different from all others?" The father would then explain the significance of the exodus for the Jewish people. The food and the meal were highly symbolic.

First, there was the blessing pronounced over **the unleavened bread,** the bread of affliction a sign of the flight from Egypt. They were a people in haste who could not wait for the yeast to work.

The roasted lamb recalled the paschal lamb whose blood was smeared over the doorposts. As the angel of death passed over, they found their salvation in God.

The wine, the cups of blessing, were a reminder of the covenant made between God and his people.

The bitter herbs were a reminder of the bitterness of the desert as the Jews journeyed to the promised land.

It was no ordinary meal that Jesus ate with his friends that evening. It was a meal that expressed the heart of the faith of Israel. **In the midst of the meal, Jesus changed its meaning.** The bread was no longer the bread of the exodus. Instead, Jesus said, **"This is my body."** The wine was no longer meant to recall the old covenant, but now a new covenant would be formed with God, a new way of relating to God, and Jesus would be its mediator. **"This cup is the new covenant in my blood, which will be shed for you."**

Jesus had spent three years with his disciples teaching them. On the night before his death, during this meal, he had the chance to say again who he is: I am bread broken; I am wine poured out. The meal is the culmination of Jesus' entire life of self-surrender. It is also the anticipation of the final act of love. His body will soon be broken like the bread, his blood poured out.

THE FOODS OF THE SEDER MEAL TODAY

The Passover meal that Jesus ate with his disciples on the night before his death continues to be shared by Jews throughout the world. It is a reminder, retelling and reliving of the exodus. Today the following foods are used at the seder meal.

1. *A roasted egg (beytza).* A reminder of the sacrifice offered in the temple in honor of the feast.

2. *A roasted bone (z'roa).* Preferably the shankbone of the lamb, a reminder of the blood of lamb slain in Egypt and offered in sacrifice at the temple.

3. *Bitter herbs (maror).* Often horseradish is used. This is a reminder of the bitterness and hardship of slavery and of the desert.

4. *A green vegetable, usually celery or parsley.* A reminder of springtime, the season of Passover.

5. *Chopped apples, nuts, wine and cinnamon (haroset).* A reminder of the mortar used with the bricks for building Pharaoh's monuments.

6. *Matzot (unleavened bread).* A reminder of the haste in which the Hebrews fled from Egypt.

7. *Wine for each celebrant.* In celebration of the creation and the covenant between God and his people.

He leaves his friends a memorial of his presence to them. It is a meal they celebrate each year but from now on its meaning is new. No longer is the exodus the central event of salvation history. Rather, Jesus says, **"Do this in memory of me."**

This account of the last supper as a seder meal can be found in the gospels of Matthew, Mark and Luke. John, however, tells us none of these details. He simply takes them for granted. Instead, he writes:

> [Jesus] rose from the meal and took off his cloak. He picked up a towel and tied it around himself. Then he poured water into a basin and began to wash his disciples' feet and to dry them with the towel he had around him. . . . After he had washed their feet, he put his cloak back on and reclined at table once more. He said to them, "Do you understand what I just did? You address me as 'Teacher' and 'Lord,' and fittingly enough, for that is what I am. But if I washed your feet— I who am teacher and Lord—so too you must wash each other's feet" (John 13:4-6. 12-14).

At the time of Christ, because the roads were not paved, it was simple hospitality to wash the feet of one's guests when they arrived at your home. This task would be performed by the servant, if there was one. **In the gospel of John, the last supper is associated with Jesus washing the feet of his apostles.** He takes on the role of the servant. It is a ritual we perform but once a year: on Holy Thursday. Yet there is a connection to the eucharist: the eucharist is more than sharing in a ritual meal. It is a lived reality as well. We must live the eucharist, and we do that by placing ourselves at the service of others: by washing feet, by being bread broken and wine poured out. At the last supper, Jesus does more than leave us a ritual to celebrate—he leaves us a way of life, a way of humble service.

For Personal Reflection and Discussion

If you were to go home tonight and offer to wash the feet of one of the members of your family, what do you think that person's reaction would be? Would he or she let you do it?

THE PRESENCE OF CHRIST IN THE EUCHARIST

The Catholic Church has always taught that Jesus is truly present in the consecrated bread and wine at the eucharist. In order to explain this presence, St. Thomas Aquinas used the term **"transubstantiation."** According to this explanation, the material elements do not change: they remain bread and wine. But the substance (the inner essence) changes. The substance is now the body and blood of Christ. Thomas said that the change was not physical but metaphysical and thus could only be grasped with the eyes of faith.

Today, theologians often describe the presence as a sacramental presence. Jesus is truly present, but it is the risen Lord, free from the confines of space and time, who comes to us. **Sacramental presence means that Christ is continuing to offer himself to us in love through the offering of the bread and wine at mass.** God's offer of love to us is the most profound truth of our faith. We celebrate a God who loves us unconditionally and continually wishes to draw us nearer to him. This love and grace is offered in countless ways: in the beauty of creation, in the love of family and friends, in the gifts of intelligence and creativity. For Catholic Christians, it is also offered in a uniquely powerful way in the eucharist. The eucharist was Jesus' personal gift to his followers; through it he would always continue to make himself present to us individually and as a community. **His presence at the eucharist comes through the congregation, the priest, and the word of God, and in a unique way through our communion in bread and wine with the body and blood of Christ.**

For Personal Reflection and Discussion

If you had to explain the presence of Christ in the eucharist to a child about to receive his or her first communion, how would you do so?

THE MASS AS A SACRIFICE

If you have grown up in the Catholic Church, you are probably quite accustomed to hearing the mass referred to as a sacrifice, probably in the expression **"the sacrifice of the mass."** We would now like to turn our attention to this important element of the mass—the notion of sacrifice.

For some, sacrifice means merely a ritual which is intended to somehow appease an angry God. **For Jesus, true sacrifice is that which comes from the heart: it is the gift of oneself to the Father. Sacrifice is not a substitute for love of God, nor is it a way to manipulate God or to appease God.** Sacrifice is the giving of oneself. It is the surrender of one's own self into the joyous, mysterious hands of God. For Jesus, sacrifice, in this sense, is essential to the life of all Christians:

> He who would save his life will lose it, but he who loses his life for my sake will find it.

For Jesus, these words reached their finality on the cross. Jesus' death is sometimes mistakenly described as the sacrifice which opened the gates of heaven, as if the blood of Jesus appeased an angry God. This is a terrible distortion of the meaning of the sacrifice of Jesus. His death on the cross is his final, total and ultimate expression of love for us and his complete trust in the Father.

When we celebrate the mass we do not repeat the death of Jesus. As St. Paul said, "Christ died once for all." **How then is the mass a sacrifice? It is a personal sacrifice, not simply a ritual one.** If we believe simply in the power of ritual, we think to ourselves: "I will sacrifice an hour of my time for God on Sunday and in that way I will be pleasing to him and obey his law." Personal sacrifice, on the other hand, asks us to offer ourselves in love. In this sense, **when we bring the bread and wine up to the altar, we bring our very selves to the altar.** Like wedding vows, we will allow this sacrifice to shape our very being as a people who seek place their lives in the hands of God so that, as the words of the mass proclaim, "we may live no longer for ourselves but for you, O Lord."

Likewise, **the mass celebrates the fact that Jesus' death, his sacrifice, is not something that happened simply in the past without affecting the future.** Jesus continues to offer himself, arms extended, in embracing love for his brothers and sisters. His death contains a universal and timeless truth which is made present in each celebration of the mass. It is the truth of the power of God's love; it is the truth of the cross.

For Personal Reflection and Discussion

The word "sacrifice" comes from the Latin, meaning "to make or do what is holy." Can you think of examples of personal sacrifice which make the world a holier, more Godlike place?

THE MASS AS A MEAL

One of the most striking things about Jesus in the gospels is his love of meals. Throughout the gospels we often find Jesus eating. At one point Jesus reveals that his enemies referred to him as a glutton and a drunkard.

> John appeared neither eating or drinking, and people say, "He is mad!" The Son of Man appeared eating and drinking, and they say, "This one is a glutton and a drunkard, a lover of tax collectors and those outside the law. Yet time will prove where wisdom lies."

For the people of Jesus' time as well as for people today, to share a meal was a sign of friendship and hospitality. Jesus came not with a message of gloom and doom but a proclamation of good news, a message about the love of the Father for all his children. Jesus' table fellowship with public sinners, tax collectors and prostitutes got him into serious trouble with some of the religious leaders of his time. They were scandalized by his association with them, and his joining them for a meal was the ultimate indignity:

> While Jesus was reclining to eat in Levi's house, many tax collectors and those known as sinners joined him and his disciples at dinner. The number of those who followed him was large. When the scribes who belonged to the Pharisee party saw that he was eating with tax collectors and offenders against the law, they complained to his disciples, "Why does he eat with such as these?" Overhearing the remark, Jesus said to them: "People who are healthy do not need a doctor; sick people do. I have come to call sinners, not the self-righteous" (Mark 2:15–17).

THE LITURGICAL YEAR

Throughout the year the church celebrates the mystery of faith in the liturgy of the eucharist. Different seasons focus on various themes of faith.

1. **Advent.** Although Christians believe that the messiah has already come, we continue to await the fulfillment of God's reign. Advent focuses on the waiting and joyful anticipation of the coming of the Lord. It lasts through four Sundays, and purple vestments are worn at mass by the priest, a sign of a penitential season.

2. **Christmas and Christmas Season.** Lasting about two to three weeks, the Christmas season begins as a celebration of the birth of Christ and moves toward the feast of the Epiphany and the manifestation of God's presence to the whole world. The season ends with the feast of the Baptism of the Lord.

3. **Ordinary Time** (1). During ordinary time, there is no special theme. It begins with the Monday after the feast of the Baptism of the Lord and ends at Ash Wednesday.

4. **Lent.** The word "Lent" comes from an old English word meaning springtime. It is a period of preparation for Easter and the renewing of one's baptismal vows. Its main themes are conversion and penance. It begins on Ash Wednesday and concludes with the Easter vigil. The last week of Lent is called Holy Week. It begins with Passion (Palm) Sunday and concludes with the Holy Week triduum: Holy Thursday, Good Friday and Holy Saturday.

5. **Easter and Easter Season.** Easter Sunday is considered the holiest day of the year for Christians. It celebrates the resurrection of Jesus from the dead and the life of the risen Christ in the Christian community. It occurs on the first Sunday following the first full moon of spring. Its date, therefore, fluctuates between March 22 and April 25. The Easter season focuses on the risen Lord and the gift of the Holy Spirit. It begins at the Easter vigil and concludes seven weeks later on the feast of Pentecost, which celebrates the descent of the Holy Spirit and the life of the Spirit in the church.

6. **Ordinary Time** (2). The second season of ordinary time is much longer than the first. It runs from the day after Pentecost through the last Sunday of the year (Christ the King), preceding the first Sunday of Advent.

For Jesus, a meal was more than just a way to fill his stomach. It was a way to teach about the love of God that was being extended to all men and women, especially those most in need of God's mercy. Jesus' meals with the poor, the sinners and outcasts were signs of solidarity with those who were despised and rejected. These meals were signs of the future heavenly banquet.

Within this context, it should come as no surprise that the greatest of the sacraments is derived from the experience of the seder supper. We have already examined its connection to the seder meal, so here we will look at the connections between the mass and the fellowship meals enjoyed by Jesus. It contains many of the important characteristics of the meals that Jesus celebrated. First, **the mass is a sign of community,** friendship, and love. Like Thanksgiving dinner in America, in which families restore the bonds of community, the eucharistic meal draws together and nourishes the Christian community. Second, it is also a meal in which **sinners are invited to participate.** One of the first things that we do at the mass is admit that we have sinned and ask God for his forgiveness. Third, like the meals that Jesus ate with the poor and sinners, the mass is a **sign of the future heavenly banquet.** It foreshadows the day when all will be called to share at the table of the Lord. Finally, it is a **challenge to make God's reign present now.** In a world in which a half billion of our brothers and sisters live in dire malnutrition, the mass is a powerful reminder that all of our brothers and sisters are called to the feast.

For Personal Reflection and Discussion

Meals are sometimes the only chance for families to get together and talk (even if it's just a debate on why you are flunking chemistry). What role do meals play in your family? Do you have to be home for dinner? Are there any special meals each week?

THE STRUCTURE OF THE MASS

People who write plays and novels will always say that their work must have three things: a beginning, a middle and an end. Now that sounds ridiculously simple, but it is the essential structure, and without it the work of literature doesn't work. Well, the same is true for the mass. On one level, the mass is similar to drama. It is not spontaneous prayer but ritual prayer. Like a play, it has a movement and a direction to it. The main two parts or "acts" are the liturgy of the word and the liturgy of the eucharist.

PART ONE: THE LITURGY OF THE WORD

The procession. At the beginning of mass, the priest, the lectors, the eucharistic ministers, the deacon, and the altar servers process into the sanctuary. The procession is similar to a parade. It represents us as a pilgrim people living the journey of faith. Here we journey from our daily lives to the altar of the Lord. The word of God is held aloft in the procession, indicating its special place of reverence and importance in the community of faith.

The penitential rite. After the initial greeting, we begin by recognizing that we are a community of sinners of people who have failed to live up to our faith as fully as possible. We recognize this as we pray: "Lord, have mercy. Christ, have mercy. Lord, have mercy." In addition, we pray a prayer of confession together: "I confess to almighty God and to you, my brothers and sisters, that I have sinned through my own fault, in my thoughts and in my words, in what I have done and what I have failed to do."

The readings and homily. Here we read from the scriptures. We share with each other the stories of our faith that shape our lives and our community. This is the climax of the first part of the mass. Normally the liturgy of the word contains three readings: one from the Old Testament, one from the New Testament epistles, and one from the gospels. The readings are chosen to fit different themes within the liturgical year. The readings rotate over a three year cycle.

In cycle A we read primarily the gospel of Matthew, in cycle B we read primarily the gospel of Mark, and in cycle C we read mostly from the gospel of Luke. During the Easter season, the gospel of John is read each year. The gospel has a special place of prominence among the readings. The sermon or the homily usually is a reflection on the readings. It is the role of the preacher (normally the priest or deacon) to explain the meaning of the readings in light of the situation of the congregation. This is followed by the creed, which is a profession of the basic beliefs of the church coming from the Council of Nicea in the year 325. The liturgy of the word concludes with the prayer of the faithful, at which time we pray for the needs of the church and the world.

PART TWO: THE LITURGY OF THE EUCHARIST

The presentation of the gifts. This used to be called the offertory. It begins with the gifts of bread and wine being delivered to the altar. These gifts represent our very selves being placed on the altar. The priest prays: "Blessed are you, Lord, God of all creation. Through your goodness we have this bread to offer, which earth has given and human hands have made. It will become for us the bread of life."

The eucharistic prayer. The eucharistic prayer is the central prayer of the mass. There are four different prayers which may be read. At the center of each is the recalling of the last supper and the words of consecration: "On the night he was betrayed, he took bread and gave you thanks and praise. He broke the bread, gave it to his disciples and said: 'Take this, all of you, and eat it: for this is my body which will be given up for you.' When supper was ended he took the cup. Again he gave you thanks and praise, gave the cup to his disciples and said: 'Take this, all of you, and drink from it: this is the cup of my blood, the blood of the new and everlasting covenant. It will be shed for you and for all so that sins may be forgiven. Do this in memory of me.'"

The eucharistic prayer is directed to the Father and concludes with the great doxology: "Through him, with him, and in him, in the unity of the Holy Spirit, all glory and honor is yours, almighty Father, forever and ever," after which the entire congregation says: "Amen."

Communion. Having listened to the word of the Lord and brought our prayer to the Father, we now join in communion with Christ and one another. We begin by praying the Lord's

Prayer together. The prayer Jesus taught his apostles unites all believers in faith. We share with each other a sign of peace, emphasizing that communion is not only with God but with each other. We then eat the bread and drink from the cup which have become the living presence of Christ.

Closing prayers and dismissal. We have reached the conclusion of our mass, and we are challenged to go forth and live what we have just celebrated: "Go in peace to love and serve the Lord." The eucharist provides us with the nourishment necessary to live the faith in our families, school, work and world.

The mass calls us together as a people of faith to celebrate that faith, to renew it and enrich it, and sends us forth to live it. We have looked at the drama of the mass in seven parts, but the mass always remains somehow greater than the sum of its parts, for at its center is the mystery of God's love revealed in Christ. The word "eucharist" means thanksgiving or gratitude. And perhaps that says it best. We come to say thank you to the Father for a gift greater than our comprehension: the gift of life, the gift of love, the gift of his Son and Spirit.

For Personal Reflection and Discussion

As is true with almost everything else, you get from the mass what you put into it. It is necessary to come in a spirit of prayer and openness. On the other hand, it certainly helps if the celebration of mass is done well. Have you ever been to a mass that really had an impact on you? If so, why?

Questions for Review

1. How did Jesus change the meaning of the last supper?
2. What was the seder meal? What did the foods used at this meal symbolize?
3. How is John's version of the last supper different from those of the synoptics?
4. How did the earliest church celebrate the mass?
5. How did the liturgy change its focus from a meal to a sacrifice?
6. What do Catholics believe about the presence of Christ in the eucharist?

7. What is the difference between personal and ritual sacrifice? How are they connected in the mass?
8. How is the eucharist as a meal similar to the meals that Jesus ate during his life?
9. What are the two basic parts of the mass? Explain the various parts of the mass and their significance.

14

Penance and Anointing of the Sick

Thus far we have looked at the meaning of the sacraments of initiation: baptism, confirmation and eucharist. These sacraments bring a person into the church, and the eucharist continues to support the followers of Jesus in their faith. We come now to the sacraments of healing: penance and anointing of the sick. These sacraments recognize that **the Christian community is made up of human beings who are imperfect and in need of both forgiveness and healing.** The church is not a community of the perfect, but a community of the wounded and sinful. It is only when we recognize our woundedness and our sinfulness that we become free to be healed and to love again. These sacraments are intended to aid Christians in this process.

PENANCE

JESUS AND FORGIVENESS

Anyone who is even remotely aware of Jesus Christ knows that forgiveness was at the heart of his message. Christ came into a sinful world with a message of God's unconditional love for us. God's love is a love of human beings the way they are: imperfect, sometimes very good, sometimes very weak, capable of both great love and terrible evil. Jesus came to us as we really are: in need of healing and forgiveness. This is one of the great themes of the gospel. Jesus is called the friend of sinners. He claims to have come not for the self-righteous but for sinners.

For Personal Reflection and Discussion

Jesus called sinners to follow him. The biggest enemy of humans may not be sin but fear, which insists that we must be perfect before we can do anything. What are some of the fears that you have at this stage of your life?

If the church is a community of sinners, it is also meant to be a community of forgiveness, for the church is both human and divine, both sinful and holy. Its holiness does not mean its members are perfect, but rather that they are willing to forgive one another. The mission of the church is to be the mission of Jesus. **We are to be a people who reflect God's mercy and compassion to the world.** After the resurrection in the gospel of John, Jesus meets with his disciples and says to them, "As the Father has sent me, so I send you. . . . Receive the Holy Spirit. If you forgive men's sins, they are forgiven them; if you hold them bound, they are held bound" (John 20:21–23).

PENANCE IN THE EARLY CHURCH

There was no sacrament of penance in the earliest church. Baptism was the sacrament for the forgiveness of sin. As we have seen, baptism indicated that one was giving up sin for new life in Christ. However, giving up sin did not mean giving it up altogether. Christians were still imperfect and sinful and in need of forgiveness, but there was no felt need for a sacramental expression of this forgiveness other than baptism. It was believed that God would forgive sins, and, more to the point, Christians were to forgive one another.

After a while, however, the church faced new problems. **What should be done with those Christians who had committed sins so serious that they had, in effect, cut themselves off from the community?** St. Paul deals with this problem in his first letter to the Corinthians. In Corinth there was a Christian living in a sexual relationship with his stepmother. Paul advises the leaders to expel him from the community. His behavior indicates that his baptism is fraudulent. But what of those who commit serious sins and yet seek to be readmitted into the community. What can be done with them?

For Personal Reflection and Discussion

What do you think of Paul's advice? Under what circumstances (if any) should someone be excommunicated from the church? Why would the church excommunicate someone?

By the third century there developed in the church the beginnings of the sacrament of penance. It was only for those who had committed the most **serious sins:** adultery, murder or apostasy (public denial of the faith, which was the most often committed because of the Roman persecutions). The sinner would confess his sin to the bishop and often to the entire community. He would be invited to the mass but would leave after the liturgy of the word. He would often wear sackcloth and ashes or chains to indicate his imprisonment and death by sin. The periods of penance were determined by the local communities, and their lengths varied immensely (from weeks to years). **This sacramental penance could be received only once in a lifetime, for the church feared that more than once would make a mockery of God's mercy.** Most Christians, however, never went through the penance since they never did anything to warrant it. It was a sacrament that very few ever experienced. This began to change when **a custom begun in Ireland by monks was imported to the mainland of Europe.** The monks were in the habit of speaking with a spiritual director about their prayer and their sins. The directors established a book of penances which would be given to the monks to help them grow in the Spirit and away from their sins. **Penances were catalogued** according to offenses. While this was not officially the sacrament of penance, it was a very personal and more private way of growing in faith, and the practice caught on in Europe. At first it was condemned by church leaders, but it proved to be so popular that it was eventually accepted (by the mid-seventh century).

The sacrament of private confession was built on several different ideas: first, the need for sorrow and repentance for sins;

second, the need to do penance for one's sins: third, the sacramental power of the priest to absolve a person from his or her sins. (The priest forgives in the person of Christ and in the person of the church.) It was born of a great idea but was prone to the abuses of legalism. True sorrow was always necessary, but this sometimes got lost in the notion of confessing and doing penance. **The communal elements of sin were often lost in the privacy of priest and penitent.**

In keeping with the spirit of the Second Vatican Council, this sacrament has undergone a recent renewal. Penance now is often celebrated as part of a community celebration of God's forgiveness. It has maintained many of the traditional elements while renewing the understanding of them. Penitents are invited to go to confess their sins to a priest "face to face" rather than in the secrecy of the confessional. **Emphasis is placed on God's unconditional love** and forgiveness and his invitation to grow in faith, hope and love. The power of the priest to forgive is seen in the context of a forgiving community and a forgiving God. Confessions are to be less legalistic (without a preoccupation on "lists of sins"). The penitents should talk about themselves, rather than simply listing sins. Finally, the penance is not a punishment but a practical way of helping the person overcome his or her sins and to grow in God's love. Penances should fit the person and his or her needs (as opposed to the "one penance fits all" mentality: say ten Our Fathers and ten Hail Marys).

For Personal Reflection and Discussion

What is your personal appreciation and use of the sacrament? Do you find it helpful? If so, how?

SPECIAL QUESTIONS

Why do we have to talk to a priest? Can't we talk directly to God? Of course we can. Our **sins can be forgiven through other means than the sacrament of penance.** The church teaches that we **must** go to confession only if we are in a state of serious or mortal sin. **The sacrament does not exempt us from the need to talk with the person whom we have hurt or offended.** This is extremely important. If I am hurting my relationship with someone, I should do more than go to confession. I should tell that person that I am sorry as well.

Even if we are not in mortal sin, it is a good idea to use the sacrament on a regular basis. It forces us to take inventory of our relationship with God and others. It imposes a process of self-examination which can be very helpful to one's growth. Knowing yourself and challenging yourself are important elements in personal as well as spiritual growth. Also, it can be very helpful to speak with another human being about your problems. The priest can offer you forgiveness, assure you that you are not the only one to have the problem, and offer helpful advice.

How often must we celebrate the sacrament? The church teaches that we must go **once a year if we are in serious sin.** Of course, that represents a minimum. It is highly recommended that Christians confess even non-serious sins. Frequency of confessions can depend on the individual and his or her felt need for the sacrament. Every two or three months seems to be a reasonable recommendation offered by spiritual directors.

What is meant by "serious sin"? Serious sins are those that do great damage or threaten to destroy our relationship with God and other people. There is no official list of such sins. Under normal circumstances, the following are seriously wrong:

1. Completely ignoring one's relationship with God, prayer, and the eucharist when the person truly knows better.
2. Performing actions that reflect bigotry and prejudice against another person because of race, religion, sex, etc.
3. Using people sexually.
4. Engaging in physical or verbal violence against others.
5. Abusing drugs or alcohol.

In order for something to be seriously sinful, one must freely chose to do wrong. Thus there is a difference between being a bully and losing your temper and hitting someone. The first is much more freely chosen. The second is still wrong, but comes less from personal choice.

Conclusion. The sacrament of penance should be a sacramental aid in our growth in relationship with God. Christian faith is one of "ongoing conversion." We must continue to grow more deeply into the life of God's love and more fully away from selfishness. Penance is the sacrament of this continuing growth. It is as much a celebration of the future as it is a turning away from the sins of the past. It is rooted in the good news of Christ: we are loved unconditionally by the Father!

ANOINTING OF THE SICK

Sickness comes to everyone. Some are luckier than others and suffer very little from illness. Others are born into a life filled with physical trials and suffering. Sickness can be physical, mental or emotional, and it can be very debilitating to our hearts, bodies, minds and spirit. Into a world filled with sickness, Jesus came as a healer, as someone who brought compassion and love to those in suffering. Yet he also came to us as one who was not immune to suffering, but would come to know suffering's deepest pangs. On the cross he felt the depression and abandonment that comes with suffering. In our worst moments of suffering from illness, we know that Christ too has been there. Jesus has taught us what we may have never known without him: that sickness and suffering can be transformed by faith into a love and trust that somehow brings us closer to God.

JESUS THE HEALER

As we have seen, the miracles most often performed by Jesus were healing miracles. **The power of God present in Christ was very much a healing power.** Jesus not only forgave sins (which was the deepest form of healing), but he healed the sick, the lame, lepers and those possessed by demons. He even raised the dead to life. At the time of Christ, most of the Jews believed that physical deformities were the result of God's punishment for sins committed by the person or by his or her parents. Jesus completely rejects this interpretation. They are not acts of God at all, but run contrary to the will of God. **Sickness is contrary to God's**

reign when all shall be made whole. Thus Jesus does not preach a message of suffering and reward in the next life. Instead, he heals. His healing miracles are signs that the reign of God is at hand.

For Personal Reflection and Discussion

There are "healers" still present in the church. Miracles are said to occur at places like Lourdes in France where there is a shrine to Mary. Have you ever met anyone who has claimed a miraculous cure? Do you think such healings occur? Why might they occur for some and not for others?

...TING OF THE SICK IN THE EARLY CHURCH

e church is to carry on the work and mesnake Christ present in the world. This, of care for the sick and the dying. Healing ed to the apostles, and **Paul mentions mir- be among the gifts given by the Spirit to the** hians 12:28). There is mention in one of the rs about the practice of anointing and pray- an be found in the letter of James:

sick among you? He should ask for the pres- hurch. They are in turn to pray over him, with oil in the name (of the Lord). This prayer uttered in will reclaim the one who is ill, and the Lord will restore him to health. If he has committed any sins, forgiveness will be his (James 5:13–15).

This passage has become the basis for the sacrament of the anointing of the sick. As is often the case in the miracles of Jesus, there is a connection in this passage between healing and the forgiveness of sins.

Throughout the first several centuries of the church, we find indications here and there that the church used anointing of the sick as one of its forms of ministry to the sick. **The actual use and meaning of the oil and anointing varied somewhat.** In some places

A2 THURSDAY, SEPTEMBER 18, 1997

WOMAN INJURED

Sarah E. Starke, 21, received minor injuries at 10 a.m. Wednesday when her car collide a Mid it was interpreted as spiritual healing or forgiveness, in others it was for physical healing. In the early fifth century, Pope Innocent wrote about the practice of anointing as a "kind of sacrament" to be given by either a priest or a layperson to the ill with oil consecrated by a bishop.

In time the sacrament began to be associated less with the sick and more with the dying. It was the custom to give to the dying the eucharist as last rites (called viaticum), and many also requested reconciliation or penance at that time. Gradually priests who performed the last rites began also to anoint the person. At first this may have been done in hopes of restoring them to life; however, before long it was seen as a way of preparing them for death. By the middle ages it was no longer called the sacrament of the sick but the **last anointing or extreme unction.**

THE SACRAMENT OF ANOINTING TODAY

Anointing of the sick remained the sacrament of the dying until it was revised after the Second Vatican Council, when the church sought to restore its primitive connections with the healing ministry. The revised rite was completed in 1974 and includes a number of different forms for different occasions. **When a person is near death it may still be received** with reconciliation and communion. (Communion is now to be **the** final "rite.") **Or it may be received by those with less serious illnesses at home or at the celebration of the mass, which is considered the ideal setting.** Because the person is sick, however, it is often impossible for him or her to attend a public celebration of mass. In such cases, the celebration of the sacrament takes the following form.

First, the priest greets the person, sprinkles him or her with holy water, says a few words about the sacrament, and leads him or her in praying for forgiveness for sins. This is followed by a reading from the scriptures which reflects the power of God over sickness and his call to faith. A brief homily will follow. The priest then includes a series of prayers and lays his hands on the person who is ill. Finally, the priest anoints the person with oil on the forehead and hands and prays:

Through this holy anointing may the Lord in his love and mercy help you with the grace of the Holy Spirit. May the Lord who frees you from sin save you and raise you up.

All present then pray the Lord's Prayer together and (if desired) the sick person receives communion.

Ministering to the Sick. In addition to the change in the celebration of the sacrament, there has come a change in the ministry to the sick. In the past the "last rites" were often approached with a sense of dread and horror as if all hope were lost. The renewal of this sacrament has revived the church's ministry to the sick, the elderly and the dying. However, the sacrament is only a part of this ministry, which should include visiting, praying, counseling, laughing and crying with those in need.

For Personal Reflection and Discussion

A priest is the minister of the sacrament of anointing of the sick. However, the whole church has a responsibility to the sick and the dying in the community. How can you be a part of this ministry?

Questions for Review

1. How would you describe Jesus' attitude toward sin?
2. What does it mean to say that we are all sinners?
3. What was the original sacrament of forgiveness in the early church?
4. How did the sacrament of penance evolve in the early church?
5. How was the early celebration of the sacrament different from today's celebration?
6. How did the sacrament of penance eventually become private rather than public?
7. Why are we given a penance at the sacrament of penance? What is its purpose?
8. What benefit is there to confessing our sins to a priest? Why not just talk to God?
9. How often must a person receive the sacrament of penance?

10. Why was healing an important part of Jesus' ministry? What did his healing miracles signify?
11. How did Jesus' idea of sickness differ from that of his contemporaries?
12. In what passage of the New Testament do we find the basis for the sacrament of the anointing of the sick?
13. How did the meaning of the sacrament change by the middle ages? What was it called?
14. How has the new rite of the sacrament of the anointing of the sick brought together both the ancient practice and the traditional one?
15. Describe the celebration of the sacrament today.

15

Sacraments of Vocation: Marriage and Holy Orders

You may get weary of people asking you what you want to do when you get older. That choice is often based on a variety of needs and concerns: financial, personal, emotional, intellectual and spiritual. Sometimes we do things because we need a job and have to make money in order to eat or go to college. Other times we are following our hearts and souls. We feel "called" to a certain relationship or type of work. A **vocation is literally a "calling."** In a religious sense it is a calling from God. Ideally we should try our best to discern what God wants us to do with our lives and how we should live them. This does not mean, of course, that we will actually hear a voice or get a note in the mail from God. But, in a spirit of prayer, we are to decide where God wants our lives to go. Because we are only human, we try our best to uncover God's wishes for us, but we have to keep open to the possibility that God may be calling us in new directions throughout our lives. However, some of our choices are permanent commitments and vocations. Among these, **the church recognizes two as sacraments: marriage and holy orders. These two vocations, in a special way, are "signs" of God's love to the entire Christian community and to the world.** Like all sacramental signs, they effect or bring about the reality which they signify. God's grace is "made present" through these (and all) sacraments.

For Personal Reflection and Discussion

Do you think that most people think of marriage as a vocation in the religious sense of the word, as a call from God? Do you? Why or why not?

MARRIAGE

Marriage is in a state of siege these days. Nearly one out of two marriages that are entered into today end in divorce. Yet the amazing thing is that the majority of those who divorce get remarried. Even when marriages fail, people come back for more. There is something about marriage that most people simply cannot live without.

JESUS AND MARRIAGE

At the time of Christ, marriage was not the religious affair that it is today for many people. **Marriages were settled and arranged by families.** The social structure was patriarchal, and women were officially the property of men. A marriage included a transferal of property, with the husband's family giving property or services for the wife. (This does not mean that the woman was treated as a slave or merely an object.) The commandment against adultery had very little to do with sexual fidelity due to love. It was related more to a violation of one's property.

Jesus was not married, and he said very little about marriage. His most important statements about marriage were part of a debate within Judaism concerning the married person's right to divorce. **According to the Torah, a man had the right to divorce his wife if she committed adultery and for certain "improprieties."** He had to give her a written bill of dismissal. If she wanted to divorce him, she could only do so if he granted her request.

At the time of Christ there were two different schools of thought concerning the husband's right to divorce. According to the rabbi **Hillel,** divorce was permitted for virtually anything that was displeasing to the husband. According to the rabbi **Shammai,** divorce was only permitted in rare circumstances. **Jesus accepted neither position:**

> Some Pharisees came up and as a test began to ask him whether it was permitted for a husband to divorce his wife. In reply, he said, "What command did Moses give you?" They answered, "Moses permitted divorce and the writing of a decree of divorce." But Jesus told them, "He wrote that

commandment for you because of your stubbornness. At the beginning of creation God made them male and female; for this reason a man shall leave his father and mother and the two shall become as one. They are no longer two but one flesh. Therefore let no man separate what God has joined" (Mark 10:2–9).

Jesus takes the most ideal position as the norm. He believes that the plan of God at the dawn of creation supersedes even the law of Moses. **Like a great deal of Jesus' teaching, his position on marriage is very demanding** and more difficult than the demands of the Jewish law.

In Matthew's gospel, Jesus repeats the same message but includes an exception which would allow for divorce in the case of "lewd conduct" (most likely adultery) on the part of the wife. Even in this case, however, there should be no remarriage. It is very possible that this reflects the actual practice of the church more than the words of Jesus (since the exception is not mentioned anywhere else), but we cannot really know for sure whether Jesus forbade divorce absolutely or included one exception to the rule.

For Personal Reflection and Discussion

Do you think Jesus is realistic in his teaching? Should divorce be allowed? If so, under what circumstances would it be permitted?

SEX AND MARRIAGE

Through the history of the church it was clear to church leaders that the primary purpose of marriage and sex was the procreation and education of children. Some theologians, including the influential **Augustine, believed that sex was intrinsically sinful,** even in marriage. However, it was permissible in marriage since it was for a good reason (children). Other theologians taught that sex had a secondary role which was to enhance the love and unity of the spouses.

In the twentieth century some began to speak of the second

reason as the main reason for sex in marriage. It was primarily an expression of the mutual love of spouses and was meant to build up the love between them. **The Second Vatican Council taught that sex in marriage had two fundamental purposes: as an expression of mutual love and commitment and for the procreation of children. It did not indicate that one was greater than the other. It continued to teach the permanence of marriage and the special role of children in a marriage.** These are commonly referred to as the **unitive and procreative** meanings of sexual intercourse. Here are some of the central teachings from the Second Vatican Council. (If the language sounds a little peculiar, remember that it is a church document translated from Latin. All passages are taken from the *Pastoral Constitution on the Church in the Modern World.*)

"The intimate partnership of married life and love has been established by the creator and qualified by his laws. It is rooted in the conjugal covenant of irrevocable personal consent." (Translation: Marriage is not simply human. It is divine as well, and the church has an important role in marriage. It is called a **"covenant"** rather than a contract in order to emphasize the personal, rather than legal, commitment. Irrevocable consent, of course, means that you can't change your mind. It is a permanent commitment.)

"This love is uniquely expressed and perfected through the marital act. The actions within marriage by which the couple are united intimately and chastely are noble and worthy ones. Expressed in a manner which is truly human, these actions signify and promote that mutual self-giving by which spouses enrich each other with a joyful and thankful will." (Translation: Augustine was wrong. Sex in marriage is good. Augustine was wrong again. One purpose of sex is to help the marriage partners grow in love and unity. Sex is not just for procreation.)

"Marriage and conjugal love are by their very nature ordained toward the begetting and educating of children. Children are really the supreme gift of marriage and contribute very much to the welfare of their parents." (Translation: Children are a very important part of the divine plan of marriage.)

"Marriage persists as a whole manner and communion of life, and maintains its value and indissolubility, even when offspring are lacking—despite, very often, the very intense desire of

the couple." (Translation: Marriage is still a sacrament and profoundly good even when there are no children born of it.)

For Personal Reflection and Discussion

*How important will children be to you when (if) you get
married? Do you have any ideas on how many children you
would like to have? What do you think children add to a
marriage?*

CONTEMPORARY UNDERSTANDING OF MARRIAGE

In order to understand the role of marriage in the life of the
Christian and the church, it is important to recognize an important principle: **genuine human love is a "sacrament" (in the broad
sense) of God's love.** St. John writes:

> Beloved, if God has loved us so, we must have the same love
> for one another. No one has ever seen God, yet if we love one
> another, God dwells in us, and his love is brought to perfec-
> tion in us (1 John 4:11–12).

The best way to ensure the presence of God in our midst is to
love one another. Of all the human loves, one is given a special
place of honor as a sacrament of the church. This is marriage.
Marriage combines all human loves into one. It is a marriage of
friendship. Lovers who are not friends will burn out like a Roman
candle in the night. But it is also more than friendship. Married
partners are also **lovers.** They are "in love." They seek to be
united with each other at the core of their being. This intimacy is
a sexual and personal one. But they are also more than lovers.
The love of a married couple is bound together by more than sexual intimacy and personal friendship. It is also held together by
unconditional love. It is a love not only of the beauty but of the
unattractive. It is for worse as well as better. In other words, the
love that bonds married couples cannot be as fickle as a feeling
of romance or passion. It is a love that mirrors the divine: it is
unconditional and permanent.

Marriage for Christians is a sacrament. It takes place public-
ly in a church, not because churches are pretty, or because your

mother expects it, but because we celebrate not only the love of the couple, but their faith as well. The couple invite the love and grace of God into their lives to enrich them with another dimension of life: spiritual union. Their marriage is more than a passage into the next phase of life. It is truly a "saving event" through which God's grace can grow in their lives, and their love for one another can be a sign of God's love to the broader community.

Earlier we mentioned that sacraments are not just celebrated; they must be lived. This is very true for marriage. The couple must live their sacrament. As a couple, they are a walking, talking, living, breathing, loving sign of the presence of Christ in the community of the church and the world.

For Personal Reflection and Discussion

List ten things that you would look for in a marriage partner.

THE RITE OF MARRIAGE

Most people think that a priest marries two people. In fact, the couple marry themselves. **The couple are the ministers of the sacrament.** The priest (or deacon) is the church's official witness. **The heart of the ceremony is the vows exchanged by the couple (it is not uncommon for couples today to write their own) and the exchange of the rings.** The rings by their circular nature represent the eternal quality of their love. In addition, there are readings from the scriptures (and other sources, if desired). Ideally, the couple will have a very active role in choosing the readings and in the preparation of the ceremony. The ceremony can be part of a mass (called a nuptial mass) or it can be celebrated outside mass.

For Personal Reflection and Discussion

Some people do not see the value of "a piece of paper." They feel as if they should be able to just live with their partner without the complications of marriage. Studies indicate that these relationships fail at a much higher rate than occurs with married couples. Why do you think that is the case?

HOLY ORDERS

As we have seen, a sacrament is a sign of the grace of God and the presence of Christ in the community. Through the sacrament of holy orders, deacons, priests and bishops become such signs of God's love.

JESUS AND THE PRIESTHOOD

At the time of Christ, the Jewish priesthood was one that had authority over the temple in Jerusalem and political authority through the Jewish council called the sanhedrin. **The priests were called Sadducees and their chief functions were connected to the sacrifices of the temple.** Neither Jesus nor his apostles were members of the priestly class.

In the New Testament Jesus is referred to as a great high priest in the book of Hebrews. The author of Hebrews wishes to show that Jesus had offered the ultimate sacrifice: himself. He offered not the blood of goats or bulls or lambs, but his own blood. This sacrifice was the one that would change the entire course of the world. This sacrifice would bring about a new covenant between God and his people.

HOLY ORDERS TODAY

All who receive baptism are baptized into the priesthood of Christ and all are called to ministry in one form or another. However, within the church there are some who are chosen for a unique and special ministry through holy orders. **Holy orders is a three-tiered sacrament. It is received by deacons, priests and bishops.**

The role of the deacon had all but disappeared in the church until recently. There are two types of deacons. Men who are preparing for the priesthood become deacons shortly before they become priests. This is the "transitional" diaconate which has long existed in the church. **The state of the permanent diaconate has been restored by the church since the Second Vatican Council.**

Permanent deacons are those who are not ordained deacons as a step toward the priesthood. They are men who have shown previous commitment and service to the church and are ordained as a sign of service to the Christian community. Deacons must be thirty-five years old. They may be married or single. (If single when ordained, they must remain so.) **They may officiate at weddings and baptisms. At mass they proclaim the gospel and they may preach. The specific ministry that they perform may depend on the needs of the community or their specific talents.** Traditionally deacons have had a special role in serving the poor, but they may also teach, counsel, visit the sick and elderly, etc. Of course these services may be done by the laity as well. Thus, what is most unique about the deacon is his liturgical role. However, his service to the community is also to serve as a sign of the ministry of all the baptized.

Priests have a wide variety of responsibilities within the church, but **at the heart of the priesthood is the mass.** The priest is the chief presider and preacher at the mass. He also celebrates baptisms, hears confessions, and witnesses weddings. Since the eucharist and the other sacraments play a central role in the formation of the Christian community, the role of the priest is more than a sacramental function. He must proclaim the gospel and apply it to the lives of the faithful in the community. **He is often present to the people during some of the most important moments of their lives: births, deaths, marriages.** Likewise, it is his task to provide leadership and direction for the community, seeing to it that all the needs of the community are being served. It is the role of the priest to build up the body of Christ as sacrament and as community. In addition, the service offered by priests will vary according to their individual gifts. Some become involved in education, others in counseling or visiting the sick, etc.

The role of the bishop is primarily to teach and to "govern" the church. The bishop is the head of the local church in each diocese. He is the "overseer," and it is his task to teach in the name of the church. Each bishop is considered a "vicar of Christ" and successor of the apostles. As we have seen in the chapter on models of the church, the universal church is governed by the bishops of the world in union with the head bishop, the bishop of Rome.

Questions for Review

1. What is meant by a vocation?
2. Describe the institution of marriage as it existed at the time of Christ.
3. What was the Jewish position on divorce? What was Jesus' teaching? What was his teaching based upon?
4. What did the church consider to be the primary purpose of sex throughout most of its history?
5. What did the Second Vatican Council teach about the meaning of sexual intercourse?
6. Why did the council refer to marriage as a covenant?
7. What are the key elements to the marriage ceremony?
8. What are three tiers to the sacrament of holy orders?
9. What are the main functions of the deacon, priest and bishop in the church?

16

Christian Principles and Values

THE TEN COMMANDMENTS: YESTERDAY AND TODAY

We have already seen that faith is not simply intellectual beliefs. We must do more than say we believe in God; we must live our faith. This chapter will examine the values and principles that are at the core of Christian discipleship. We will begin at the bottom, at the foundation: the ten commandments. **These commandments do not represent the highest levels of Christian morality, but they do provide a foundation for Christian morality.** They are the basic values and laws upon which Christ builds. These commandments pre-date Christ by more than one thousand years. Their original meanings might not always apply today, but the basic spirit and meaning behind the commandments are eternal. Jesus said that he did not come to abolish the law but to fulfill it. We will look at the classic "ten" commands of Israel and try to apply them to life in the twentieth century.

THE COMMANDMENTS

1. I am the Lord your God; you shall have no gods besides me. Originally this commandment ordered the Jews to make Yahweh first of all gods. They were not to worship the gods of the pagans, but Yahweh alone. **The value of the first commandment is fidelity.** The sin against the first commandment is idolatry.

Today we must ask ourselves as Christians what it means to be faithful to God and what it means to practice idolatry. It would seem that basic fidelity means a commitment to the eucharist, to prayer, and to living lives of love, forgiveness and service. Being faithful to God is like being faithful to a friend or spouse. It is more than a matter of deeds. Fidelity comes from the heart. Therefore we must continue to develop our relationship with God and keep it open to continual growth and development.

Idolatry could involve superstitions or cults, but for most people the temptation of idolatry is to place something as the number one priority in life above God. In our culture there will always be the temptation to regard material success and comfort as our god. Others are committed to power, pleasure or sex. We have to ask ourselves what is most important in our lives. If it has nothing to do with love, then it has nothing to do with God, and it is idolatry.

For Personal Reflection and Discussion

What does it mean to place God as the number one priority in your life? Does it mean becoming a priest or nun? Does it mean spending your free time in prayer? What would it mean for you?

2. You shall not take the name of the Lord your God in vain. Originally this commandment forbade the use of the divine name to invoke curses on one's enemies or for magic. The value associated with the commandment is **the importance of self-control in our words.** The sin associated with it is "cursing" or abusive language.

As followers of Christ we strive to fill our entire lives with care. We care about what we do, think and say. This commandment applies to those things that we say. Words can be very powerful. Our words reveal who we are and what we believe in. Our words shape our relationships to other people. This commandment doesn't teach us to be cautious in expressing our thoughts and feelings as much as it counsels us to be careful with words that have the potential to do harm.

It is very easy to get into bad habits when it comes to our use of language, especially during adolescence. Most people think: "Big deal; it's just words." And for the most part, they are right. Using words that are offensive is more a matter of bad manners than anything else. However, the problem can be deeper than that. Cursing at someone, or using God's name in vain, is more

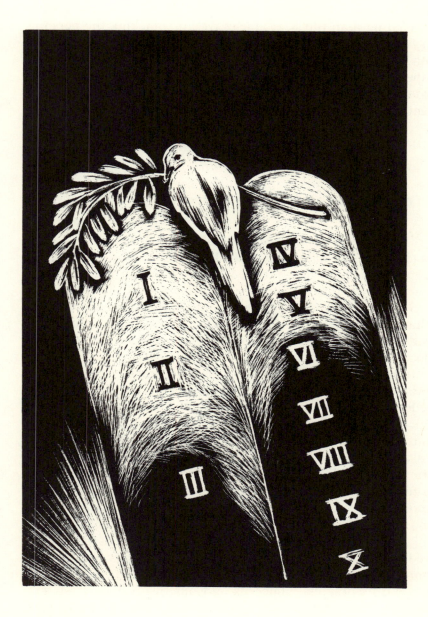

than bad manners. It is a lack of respect for the other person or God. When we verbally abuse people, the effects can be more devastating than physical abuse. We are attacking the person's very dignity and value. If we easily throw about the name of God with expressions like "God damn it" or "Jesus Christ!" it is disrespectful of a very sacred and holy reality. It is probably just a bad habit, without any disrespect intended, but such language creates a careless and disrespectful attitude and mentality.

For Personal Reflection and Discussion

How are you doing with your tongue these days? Do you use it to tear down or to build up? Is there any one person you can think of who could use a kind and loving word from you?

3. Remember to keep holy the sabbath. For the Jews this command meant that Saturdays (actually from sunset Friday to sunset Saturday) were days given to God. The sabbath forbade all forms of work and required time for prayer. It was to show the priority of God in their lives by abandoning all secular concerns. The value of the command is the importance of prayer and giving time to the Lord. The sin against it is attachment to one's own concerns.

Christians do not observe the sabbath in the same way that Jewish people do. Our "sabbath" is Sunday, the day of the resurrection. We are not, however, bound to all the laws of the Torah which prohibit so many types of activity. Christians are to celebrate the eucharist on Sunday and to avoid work on this day if possible. **The important element of this commandment is that we give time to our relationship with God.** All relationships depend on communication and shared life. Our relationship with God is no different. If we have no time for other people or no time for God, we are clearly much too preoccupied with our own interests and concerns. The sabbath command reminds us of the human need for prayer, contemplation of life's joy and goodness, and appreciation of life's beauty. It reminds us that there is more to life than its practical concerns and our own self-interest. The sabbath points to the meaning of the six other days of the week and celebrates the gift of God's creation.

For Personal Reflection and Discussion

Do you set aside any special time for prayer? How do you use your leisure time? Do you think it is well spent? How deep is your commitment to the eucharist?

4. Honor your father and your mother. The Jewish system of authority was based on the respect granted to the elders of the community. They were the ones who shared the tradition with their children and who oversaw the life of the family group. The commandment also implied a responsibility to care for one's parents when they get older.

We live in a culture that idolizes youth. We are told that we should look, feel, think and act young. Our senior citizens are too often neglected and abandoned when they are most in need. This commandment reminds us of our need to care for and respect our parents. In a culture where the elderly are made to feel as if they are a "burden," we are to recall the words of St. Paul that by carrying one another's burdens, we fulfill the law of Christ. Although this commandment is sometimes referred to in terms of obedience, its key point is really honor and respect.

For Personal Reflection and Discussion

Our relationships with our parents often go through a series of transitions. Adolescence is sometimes a difficult time in this relationship. How would you describe your relationship to your father? What are its strengths and weaknesses? Why? If you could change one thing about it, what would it be? How would you describe your relationship to your mother? What are its strengths and weaknesses? Why? What would you change about this relationship if possible? What does it mean for you to "honor" your parents?

5. You shall not kill. This commandment did not forbid all types of killing. Israel was not a pacifist people. They had the death penalty, fought in wars, and believed in the right to self-defense. The commandment forbade murder.

Of course the commandment forbids the same for us today.

Jesus, however, demanded that we interpret this commandment more radically. In Matthew's gospel we hear Jesus say:

> You have heard the commandment imposed on your fore-fathers, "You shall not commit murder; every murderer shall be liable to judgment." What I say to you is: everyone who grows angry with his brother shall be liable to judgment; any man who uses abusive language toward his brother shall be answerable to the Sanhedrin (Matthew 5:21–23).

Jesus' interpretation means that it is not enough to avoid killing someone. We must avoid hatred in the heart as well as in physical deeds. (When Jesus warns against anger, he is not refer-ring to the emotion as much as the hardened heart of hatred.) Likewise, Jesus warns against using "abusive language." In other words, there is more than one way to kill someone. We can kill and crush his or her spirit with our words as well as with our fists.

In addition, Jesus goes beyond this commandment with a spirit of non-violence which includes love of enemies and a will-ingness to be killed rather than kill.

This commandment, then, challenges us to go beyond the basic command not to kill. We are to avoid all forms of killing—those in the heart, body, mind or spirit. Human life is to be valued not just biologically, but spiritually as well. This means an obligation to develop a spirit of non-violence within our-selves, within the church and within the world. Such a spirit goes against the conventional wisdom that "might makes right." It looks for a different vision of life than one based on military power and the "freedom" to abuse others and ourselves. Drug and alcohol abuse, abortion, street gangs and violence, domestic violence, suicide, violence against women, racially motivated violence and the proliferation of nuclear weapons are all forms of the many ways in which this commandment is violated today. This commandment forces us to challenge one of the great lies of history—that killing and violence can be used to achieve good.

For Personal Reflection and Discussion

What are some of the ways that the "kingdom of death" is part of your world? In what ways can you become more sensitive to life and learn to affirm it?

6. You shall not commit adultery. In the Old Testament, adultery had to do with the property rights of the husband over his wife. The wife had no such rights over the husband. Thus he was guilty of adultery only if he had sexual intercourse with a married woman. Both the woman and her partner could be put to death for adultery.

Jesus demands that the command be taken a step further: adultery includes lusting after another woman. Jesus' words are directed to men, and he warns them to go beyond the demands of the law:

> You have heard the commandment, "You shall not commit adultery." What I say to you is: anyone who looks lustfully at a woman has already committed adultery with her in his heart" (Matthew 5:27–28).

This teaching is typical of Jesus, who insisted that we must change not only our behavior but our hearts as well. We must get to the roots of the problem. Jesus reaffirms the traditional teaching but challenges his followers to go deeper into the heart.

What does Jesus mean when he forbids the attitude of lust? He is not talking about sexual attraction. He is referring to the attitude or state of the heart that treats women as objects and uses them for sexual gratification. He is challenging us to examine our relationships with the opposite sex. Are we looking for friendship and true intimacy or are we simply looking for someone to fill our own needs, sexual and emotional?

In the gospel of John a group of men bring a woman caught in adultery to the walls of the city to be stoned to death. Jesus tells them, "Let the man among you who has no sin be the first to cast a stone at her" (John 8:7). Thus while **Jesus is strict when it comes to adultery, he is also compassionate when it comes to dealing with the sinner.** It is important to note that Jesus defends the rights of women in both of these cases. The Jewish laws worked blatantly in favor of men, yet Jesus challenged the prevailing wisdom and stood up for the dignity and worth of women.

For Personal Reflection and Discussion

What do you think about Jesus' command to purify our hearts as well as our behavior? Is this possible or overly idealistic?

Jesus addresses his remarks about lust to men. Are women in need of such teaching as well? Do women have a tendency to use men at all? If so, how? What insights can we bring to the discussion in the light of our twentieth century background?

7. You shall not steal. It would seem to be difficult to get any more obvious than the meaning of this commandment, but scholars believe that it originally referred not only to the theft of possessions but to kidnaping as well.

Seen in its most positive light, this commandment is a challenge to honesty and respect for others' property. It seems that such honesty is easily whittled away with a mentality that "everyone does it." This is often applied to such things as cheating on tests, shoplifting from stores, lifting supplies from work, and cheating on one's income tax. At the heart of the matter is the violation of another's rights or property. In addition, however, a person who steals violates himself or herself. All our actions determine who we are. A person who steals has defined himself or herself by such actions: he or she is a thief.

For Personal Reflection and Discussion

A friend works at a local store and offers to take twenty dollars off the price of your purchases. What do you say and why?

You have an opportunity to purchase a sound system for three hundred dollars rather than five hundred dollars because it is stolen. Do you? Why or why not?

8. You shall not bear false witness against your neighbor. Originally this commandment referred to the Jewish legal system. If two witnesses could be found to testify against someone, then the person was convicted. Bearing false witness could get someone killed. If the perjurer were discovered, he or she would be given the sentence that would have been given to the person whom he or she lied about.

Jesus goes this commandment one better. Instead of being bound to tell the truth under oath, Jesus insists that we tell the truth at all times. Oaths are unnecessary for such people.

You have heard the commandment imposed on your fore-fathers, "Do not take a false oath; rather, make good to the Lord all your pledges." What I tell you is: "Do not swear at all. . . . Say 'Yes' when you mean 'Yes' and 'No' when you mean 'No.' Anything beyond that is from the evil one" (Matthew 5:33–37).

This commandment forbids perjury, but for Christians it also forbids lying at all times. (This assumes, of course, that the person has a legitimate right to know the truth.)

For Personal Reflection and Discussion

Are you a person whose word can be trusted?

9. You shall not covet your neighbor's wife. The key word in this commandment is "covet." The English word means to desire for oneself. The Hebrew word has the same meaning, but it also includes a sense in which it is more than a desire. **It includes a willingness to obtain for oneself.** This command, then, is similar to the one on adultery. It has the effect of looking not only at one's actions but at what is in the heart as well. Thus it takes a look at the root of the sin which is in the human heart and its desires to have what it does not possess.

10. You shall not covet your neighbor's goods. This is similar to the previous commandment in its prohibition against "coveting." However, this one also refers to the seventh commandment and the law against stealing. The final commandment examines the greed and envy that are often at the heart of stealing from others.

If we look at the last two together, we see that the law forbids the "covetousness" that leads to adultery and stealing. These commands make us examine our own attitudes and mentality. Are we constantly envious of the possessions and relationships of others? Do we live our lives comparing ourselves to others, rather than trying to make the most of our own lives, gifts, possessions and relationships?

For Personal Reflection and Discussion

There is a difference between "coveting" and dreaming. Coveting means an attitude of jealousy or envy, wanting something that belongs to another. Dreaming of a better future or a good marriage, etc., is only natural. Coveting fails to recognize, accept or be grateful for all that we have. Have you ever "coveted" something?

JESUS' CALL TO LOVE: THE FOUR LOVES

As we have seen, the ten commandments represent basic laws and values of moral behavior. They provide a foundation for knowing and doing what is right. Yet Jesus called his followers to go beyond the demands of the law to the heart and to the demands of love. Since we have already looked at the basic message and teaching of Jesus in an earlier section of the book, we will focus here on two elements of the message: the call to love and the message of the beatitudes.

At the heart of the message of Jesus is a call to love. Yet oddly this message is easily lost and misunderstood because the word "love" has come to mean so many different things in our culture. We use the same word to describe the way we feel about our family, pets, hobbies and food. Before we look at the understanding of love in the New Testament, let us briefly look at the main ways in which the word is commonly used today. The following are four different types of love:

Affection: This is the love that we experience as a feeling of warmth and closeness. We can feel affection for friends, family, spouses and even pets. Affection is the heart of love, the part that makes it very satisfying and personally rewarding.

Friendship: Friendship is the bond of love between people who are united by common interests, concerns, respect and care. Friendships are often "about" something. That is, there is a common element that brings friends together. Friends then grow to share mutual respect and shared experience. Friendship, by its nature, is open to many. Friendships that are exclusive are not healthy.

Romance: This is the love we refer to when we say that we are "in love." It is a desire to be united with the other person. It is a shared intimacy and openness. This love includes sexual love and union as well. Romance (or "eros" as the Greeks called it) is unlike friendship in that it is exclusive. It is geared to two people.

Agape: This is the word for love used in the New Testament to describe God's love for us. It is unconditional love. It accepts the faults and limitations of the beloved. It includes love of one's enemies. While the other three loves are important, they must somehow be united with agape to become truly fulfilling.

For Personal Reflection and Discussion

Name ten songs that have the word "love" in the title. In which of the four ways above is the word "love" being used?

LOVE IN THE NEW TESTAMENT

What was the notion of love that existed in the teaching of Jesus and in the early church? We will briefly summarize some of its key elements:

1. We are loved. For Jesus, God is the source of all love, and the heart of the good news is that God loves his children unconditionally. Our responsibility to love begins with the insight that we are loved. St. John describes this in one of his letters:

> Love, then, consists in this: not that we have loved God, but that he has loved us and has sent us his Son as an offering for our sins. Beloved, if God has loved us so, we must have the same love for one another (1 John 4:10–11).

Jesus reveals this love in all that he does and especially in his death on the cross.

2. Love of God and love of people are inseparable. When Jesus is asked to describe the greatest of the commandments, he combines two of them:

" 'Hear, O Israel! The Lord our God is Lord alone! Therefore, you shall love the Lord your God with all your heart, with all your soul, with all your mind, and with all your strength.' This is the second: 'You shall love your neighbor as your-self' " (Mark 12:29–31).

The brilliance of Christ is revealed in his unwillingness to divide these two great commands. For Jesus, we simply cannot have one without the other. Christians are to love and serve God. They are to place him first in their lives. They are to pray and to seek God's will for them, but they cannot get lost in their relationship with God. They must allow that relationship to transform the way that they treat people. St. John puts it bluntly:

If anyone says, "My love is fixed on God," yet hates his brother, he is a liar. One who has no love for the brother he has seen cannot love the God he has not seen (1 John 4:20).

3. We are to love as God loves: unconditionally. This is the really hard one. We must love unconditionally, accepting all the limitations of other people, forgiving them their sins. We must even love our enemies.

My command to you is: love your enemies, pray for your persecutors. This will prove that you are children of your heavenly Father, for his sun rises on the just and the unjust. If you love those who love you, what merit is there in that? Do not tax collectors do as much? . . . In a word, you must be made perfect as your heavenly Father is perfect (Matthew 5:41–48).

Jesus does more than talk about love of enemies; he lives it. Ultimately he gave his life for all people, including those who nailed him to the cross, praying, "Father, forgive them; they know not what they are doing" (Luke 23:34).

4. Love is love in action. Jesus consistently makes it clear that pious words are not what God wants from us. He wants us to **do** his will. When asked what it means to love one's neighbor, Jesus tells the parable of the good Samaritan. Real love reaches out to people. It is love in action.

5. Love means reaching out to those most in need. In the ministry and message of Jesus we see God's love offered to those most in need. Perhaps this is said most clearly in Matthew 25, in the scene of the last judgment. The criteria for entering God's kingdom are listed as the following:

> I was hungry and you gave me food, I was thirsty and you gave me drink. I was a stranger and you welcomed me, naked and you clothed me. I was ill and you comforted me, in prison and you came to visit me (Matthew 25:35–36).

For Personal Reflection and Discussion

Which of these five elements of love in the New Testament is your strongest point? Why? Which is your weakest? Why?

THE BEATITUDES

Jesus claimed that he came not to abolish the law and the prophets, but to fulfill them. His teaching is more demanding than the law because it requires inner change of heart. He came not only to change our behavior, but more importantly to change our hearts. The fulfillment of the law and the prophets is proclaimed clearly in the famous sermon on the mount (Matthew 5–7). In these three chapters we find a brilliant summary of what it means to be a follower of Jesus.

The sermon on the mount begins with the beatitudes which describe the attitudes and actions of those who are blessed by God. Each beatitude contains two parts: a present attitude and a future fulfillment. We will analyze these beatitudes and apply them to the task of following Jesus today.

1. Blest are the poor in spirit; the reign of God is theirs. The "poor in spirit" are related to the poor but not necessarily the same. The poor in spirit are the humble: those who realize their complete dependency on God. It is common in our culture to misinterpret humility to mean people who do not think much of themselves. True humility is the truth. Humble people see themselves for what they really are. They realize that their strengths are gifts from God. They realize that they have weaknesses and limitations. Above all they recognize that the world does not revolve around them. They are a creature, not God. The opposite of the humble are the proud and arrogant who have a false and inflated view of themselves, looking down at the rest of God's creatures as if they were somehow God.

For Personal Reflection and Discussion

The humble person knows his or her strengths and weaknesses. Make a list of yours.

2. Blest are the sorrowing; they shall be consoled. Jesus almost seems to be saying that it is good to be sad in this beatitude. That is not the point. Those who are grieving and sad, however, can take hope in God's love. They are not to think of themselves as abandoned by God. Only those who love and care for others will find true sorrow in life. This is a holy sorrow or grief because it is born of love.

3. Blest are the lowly; they shall inherit the land. The lowly here refer to those without land and possessions. They are the poor and the dispossessed. In the Old Testament they are called the "anawim." Jesus reverses the conventional wisdom which saw God's blessing in wealth and instead says the opposite: it is the poor who are especially blessed. Why would he say this? For two reasons: first, Jesus wants to show that the rejection of the poor is wrong; second, being poor can enable people to be more humble and recognize their dependence on God. There is no doubt that in the gospels wealth is seen as an obstacle to entering God's reign.

4. Blest are those who hunger and thirst for holiness, for they shall have their fill. This beatitude challenges us to look at our goals in life. What is it that we are hungering and thirsting for? What do we really want out of life? Jesus says it should be holiness. Not only that, but if we really want it, ultimately we will get it. But who wants to be holy and what does it mean to be holy? Part of the problem is that we tend to see holiness as something boring and cut off from the real world. The picture that Jesus presents in the gospel, however, is one that is very much involved in the world. It is one that is rooted in love.

For Personal Reflection and Discussion

What are you hungering and thirsting for at this stage of your life?

5. Blest are they who show mercy; mercy shall be theirs. At the heart and soul of the message of Jesus is forgiveness, so this beatitude should come as no surprise. Jesus proclaims a God who is merciful and willing to forgive our worst sins. Our love must reflect God's: it must be merciful.

6. Blest are the single-hearted, for they shall see God. This beatitude is much like the great commandment of Israel that Jesus said was the first of all the commandments. Single-hearted means devoted to God. The single-hearted do not give God a place in their lives or a piece of their hearts. The single-hearted give their lives and hearts to God completely. All other loves make sense only in light of their love of God.

7. Blest are the peacemakers; they shall be called sons of God. Christians have a vocation to be peacemakers in a world of violence. One of the great lies of history is that violence and war are valid ways of dealing with conflict. They were not for Jesus who told his followers to put away their swords. Jesus' clear call to non-violent peacemaking is one that has been consistently ignored by Christians throughout history.

8. Blest are those persecuted for holiness' sake; the reign of God is theirs. In this beatitude Jesus destroys the myth of "feel good" religion. For some, religion is a way to feel happy. Jesus says that it may very well bring persecution and rejection. Blessed are those who are not afraid to live their faith in the midst of such rejection and persecution. In the United States, Christians rarely feel the sting of persecution and rejection. Yet throughout the world many still lay down their lives for their faith and the values of the gospel.

For Personal Reflection and Discussion

Which of the beatitudes do you find most challenging? Why?

Questions for Review

1. What role do the commandments play in the value system of a Christian?
2. What did the first commandment forbid for the Jews?
3. What did it mean to take God's name in vain?
4. When was the sabbath and what was its purpose?
5. What was the basis for the commandment to honor one's parents?
6. Did the fifth commandment forbid all forms of killing?
7. How did Jesus comment on the fifth commandment?
8. How did the Jewish adultery laws work? How did Jesus demand that his followers go beyond this law?
9. Why was it so important for the Jews not to "bear false witness"?
10. What did the word "covet" mean for the Jews?
11. Describe each of the four loves.
12. What are five elements of the idea of "love" in the New Testament?
13. Who are the "poor in spirit"?
14. Why does Jesus say: "Blest are the sorrowing"?
15. What is meant by the "single-hearted"?
16. How are the beatitudes different from the commandments?

17

Christian Conscience and Morality

In the previous chapter we examined the fundamental principles and values that are the basis of Christian morality and discipleship. These values provide us with the basic vision of Christian living. Yet these principles do not exist apart from a real world with real people and real decisions. It is the application of these principles that is the true challenge of Christian conscience. In this chapter we will examine the idea of moral values and conscience as the basis for moral decision making for the Christian.

THE HUMAN PERSON

Who are you? What makes you tick? The answer to these questions is determined somewhat by forces beyond your power. You have been born with certain strengths and limitations at a certain point in time into a certain family and culture. All these factors will condition who you are as a person. Yet, to some extent, you choose who you will be. The human capacity for choice is really the ability to decide who we will be, what we will consider important, what we will believe, and how we will live our lives. Perhaps nothing is as important in our lives as our choice of values. They determine to a great extent who we are.

Moral values are those which make us "more human" both as individuals and as a society. We can either choose these values or reject them. When we choose them and we make them a part of our daily lives, they become "virtues." These are attitudes and patterns of behavior which become an ingrained part of who we are as people. Sin is a rejection of these values, and it too can become a part of who we are. For sin is also a choice and a way of defining ourselves.

SIN AND VIRTUE

Since we have already examined the meaning of sin in this book (see chapter 3), we will try here to be more specific by examining the so-called seven deadly sins and the corresponding virtues that they lack.

1. a. **Pride.** The word "pride" often has a positive or virtuous meaning. To take pride in our work, our appearance, etc., is normally seen as a healthy form of self-esteem. Pride, as one of the deadly sins, refers to a different reality. Pride is arrogance and a self-centered view of the world. It is a highly exaggerated sense of one's own importance and a demeaning of the importance of others. Pride is traditionally considered the worst of the deadly sins.

b. **Humility.** This is the virtue that the proud lack. Humility is not a lack of self-respect (as is sometimes thought). To the contrary, humility is self-respect born of the truth. The word "humility" comes from the Latin *humus,* meaning the earth. The humble person realizes that he or she is "of the earth." Human beings, even the greatest, are creatures. They are not God. Thus humble people recognize that all that they have is a gift given to them. They need not deny their talents (which is "false humility"), but they recognize their connection to all God's creation and his creatures.

2. a. **Envy.** Envy is the failure to accept oneself and shows itself in an attitude which begrudges the gifts of others. The envious person feels cheated by life and is often bitter and slanderous.

b. **Faith.** We might not immediately think of faith as the opposite of envy, but the person of faith realizes that life is not a competition and that the basis of one's worth is rooted in the fact that we are sons and daughters of God. Our true value in life is not based on whether we are measured as the richest, prettiest, funniest, smartest, etc. Such a mentality will eventually lead to envy because it is based on comparison and competition. Faith, however, challenges us to love ourselves the way that we are, as God's child.

3. a. **Greed.** This is an inordinate desire for wealth and material possessions. If we measure our worth and humanity by the number of possessions and status that they bring, then greed is

inevitable. This sin flies in the face of Jesus' call to live for God's kingdom. The greedy person is concerned with one kingdom alone: his or her own.

b. **Generosity and Social Justice.** There are two corresponding virtues to be listed here. The first is generosity which is a willingness to share one's own resources with those in need. Unlike greed, it is interested in the welfare of all. However, more than generosity is required to share the earth's resources. Social justice is the virtue which strives to create a society in which all are included and given the opportunity to live a full human life.

4. a. **Lust.** Lust is an attitude of the heart. It views people as sexual objects and intends to use them simply for sexual gratification. Lust reduces people to objects and strips them of their humanity. (It is not the same as erotic feelings or sexual attraction, both of which are normal and can lead to genuine human intimacy.)

b. **Chastity.** The person who lives this virtue is able to direct his or her sexuality toward relationships of love and intimacy. Chastity is not limited to priests, nuns and single people. It is not simply abstaining from sex. It would include this for non-married people. But chastity must be practiced by married people as well. It means fidelity not only in body but in heart and mind as well. In other words, it involves an ongoing commitment to keep love alive in marriage.

5. a. **Anger.** As one of the deadly sins, anger refers not simply to a feeling but to an attitude of the heart. It is more akin to hatred than angry feelings alone. (Some anger is perfectly good. If we don't feel angry in the face of injustice, then something is wrong.)

b. **Patience.** The word "patience" comes from the Latin meaning "to suffer," and the patient person is able to suffer the limitations and weaknesses of others. Patience recognizes that unconditional love requires a great deal of us and is willing to love when love is most difficult. It does not respond to evil with evil, but is able to wait and postpone anger in order to renew a relationship.

6. a. **Gluttony.** This sin is like "greed for the body." It is similar to lust in that it treats the body simply as a pleasure machine, overindulging in food, drink, or drugs. Like all of the

deadly sins, this one places the person's center of attention completely on himself or herself.

b. **Self-control.** Gluttony places few limits or boundaries on our behavior. To be fully human, we must be able to practice self-control. We must be disciplined to doing the good. This includes the way that we treat our body. The effects of such self-control are not only better physical health but an improved spiritual outlook as well.

7. a. **Sloth.** Sloth is laziness, but more specifically it applies to spiritual laziness, an unwillingness to care about what is good. It is a spiritual apathy.

b. **Love.** Love is not just being "nice." It is being creative, passionate, caring and compassionate. It is to be committed to life fully with one's whole heart, mind, soul and strength.

For Personal Reflection and Discussion

Which of the deadly sins seems most alive and well in the society in which you live? Why? Which of these sins is most prevalent among young people? Which of the virtues is most respected in our culture? Which of the virtues is your strongest? Which is your weakest?

CONSCIENCE

The line between sin and virtue is drawn and felt by our conscience. Understanding the Christian notion of conscience is not easy because there are so many different interpretations and misinterpretations associated with it. Let's begin then with a definition:

Conscience is the human drive and ability to discover what is good and to do it. This definition has three different parts to it:

First, conscience is a drive to seek out what is good. In this sense, conscience is "built into" our humanity. Unless a person is mentally or psychologically ill, he or she will have an inborn tendency to seek out what is good. Thus our conscience is part and parcel of our humanity. It is part of the human need to love and to be loved.

Second, conscience is also the ability to understand and learn the difference between good and evil. In other words, **our consciences are "formed" and "informed."** We are not born with a knowledge of what is good. We must learn it. It is on this level that individual consciences may vary quite a bit. Different cultures and religions are more sensitive to some values than others. One person may grow up in a situation where the formation of a healthy conscience is much more possible than it is for another person.

Third, conscience is the actual judgments and decisions that we make. This is what is meant by "following our conscience." Conscience is not an idea. It is a reality, a part of our being, in fact the heart and soul of our being. Conscience is that which enables us to make real decisions in real life. For the most part, of course, we do not refer to the fact that our conscience is at work. It is more like the actions of our hearts and lungs. Conscience usually works automatically. We become aware of it when we are placed in something of a conflict situation, when we are forced to choose and the choice is not immediate and simple.

For Personal Reflection and Discussion

Give an example of how some people are at an advantage in developing a healthy conscience while others are at a disadvantage. Give an example of the most recent time that you could feel your conscience pushing you in a certain direction.

The Second Vatican Council describes these elements of conscience in this way:

> In the depths of his conscience, man detects a law which he does not impose upon himself, but which holds him to obedience. Always summoning him to love good and avoid evil, the voice of conscience can when necessary speak to his heart more specifically: do this, shun that. For man has written in his heart a law written by God. To obey it is the very dignity of man; according to it, he will be judged (*Gaudium et Spes,* n. 16).

The Formation and Growth of Conscience. Newborn babies have within them the potential to develop a conscience, but no one is born with the knowledge of good and evil. We learn it from others. **Our consciences are formed by our families, society and culture, religion, education, and our own capacity for understanding and doing what is right.** Families usually serve as the first and primary training school for values and conscience. The values that exist within our families are taught to us from the first moment of our birth. To a great extent, these values are "caught" as much as taught. By that we mean that we learn values not so much from what people in our family say as from how they act. The "value system" that our families use is communicated to us in the day to day living of our lives.

For Personal Reflection and Discussion

Rank the following values in the order of their importance to you. Ask your parents to rank them. Discuss your findings.

wealth	*being respected by others*
a rewarding career	*religious faith*
a good family	*good looks*
a good marriage	*intelligence*
a good education	*sense of humor*

Values also are communicated through the culture. List your three favorite television shows. What values do these shows communicate? Do you think they are primarily healthy and positive values?

PSYCHOLOGICAL AND DEVELOPMENTAL VIEWS OF CONSCIENCE

Sigmund Freud, the father of modern psychology, tried to describe the development of conscience by dividing the human **personality into three components: the id, the superego and the ego.** The id is the instinctual drive for pleasure and security. It is present from the moment of our birth. The id wants to be held, fed, kept warm and be caressed. Since the id is a pleasure-seeker, it needs a restraint, and this is the task of the superego. The superego is the internalization of the rules and laws of our parents, society and religion. These rules guide our behavior, and when we disobey them, we feel the guilt of the superego. The superego, however, does not really appreciate the values. They are the rules of others. It is the task of the ego to finally decide what I will consider to be important. Although the term "ego" is often used in a negative way, that is not its meaning here. The ego is the self, and the self decides what is valuable and worthwhile and what is not. In terms of conscience, the superego could be called the conscience in its immature form and the ego is the mature conscience. The immature conscience does not recognize **why** something is right or wrong. It simply obeys rules and seeks to stay out of trouble. The mature conscience is much more capable of love and giving of oneself.

For Personal Reflection and Discussion

What are some of the positive effects of the superego? What could be some of its negative effects? How much of your own sense of right and wrong is chosen by you?

More recently, studies of moral behavior have been done by such people as **Jean Piaget and Lawrence Kohlberg.** Piaget distinguished between two stages in moral thinking for children. **The first stage is the "heteronomous" and the second is the "autonomous."** In the first stage, right and wrong is determined simply by the fact that rules have been determined by an authority figure. The rule is what matters and it admits of no exceptions. Motives for behavior are not taken into consideration. In the second stage, the child (often around the ages of seven or eight) begins to develop a greater sense of the reason behind the rules. Rules are understood in the context of the group that they serve, and there is some insight into the motivation for the rules.

Kohlberg expanded Piaget's thinking, working with boys and following their development into adulthood. Kohlberg concluded that individuals go through different stages of moral reasoning. These stages build on each other and are sequential. According to Kohlberg, the six stages of moral reasoning are:

1. Fear of punishment. On this level, right or wrong is determined by whether or not a person will be caught and punished by an authority figure. Thus a person may drive under the speed limit because he or she doesn't want to get a ticket.

2. Desire for reward. At this level the person asks, "What's in it for me?" Good is what is good for me. A person on this level may think, "I will obey the commandments so I will go to heaven when I die."

3. Desire to be liked. The third stage sees more awareness of the expectations of others. At this stage the person wants to fit in, be accepted and liked. It is a conformist stage.

4. Law and order. At this stage it is the rules that determine what is right or wrong. It is not to be confused with the first stage. The person does not act out of fear but out of genuine respect for rules and their importance.

5. Social contract. At this level, the person recognizes that rules must fit the needs of the group and be able to change to meet new insights and understanding. The U.S. Constitution is a stage five document because it can be amended.

6. Universal principles. The person at stage six acts out of universal principles. These are abstract values that are true in all cultures and peoples. These values include love, justice, compassion, the dignity of the individual, etc. Mother Teresa's work with the poor and dying in Calcutta seems to be an example of stage six thinking.

Although the theories of Freud, Piaget and Kohlberg are certainly not infallible, they do help us to see that conscience is something that must grow and develop. They point to an increasing moral sensitivity that we can develop as we mature. In fact, conscience is very much related to our "selves." We are, to a great extent, what we value and consider important in life.

For Personal Reflection and Discussion

Try to give an example of how religious faith at times appeals to each of the six stages of Kohlberg. (There's an example in his second stage.)

SUBJECTIVE AND OBJECTIVE MORALITY:
THE NATURAL LAW

We have seen that according to the teaching of the church, a person is bound to follow his or her conscience. Does this mean that a person's conscience is always correct? That's impossible because one person's conscience may dictate one decision while another person's conscience leads in a different direction. Let's look at an example.

Sally has been raised in a family where she has been taught that a woman has a right to control her own body. Abortion is a part of that right. She lives in a country where abortion is legal, and her religion regards abortion as regrettable but not wrong. She already has four children (one more than she planned) and her family is stretched financially. When she gets pregnant for the fifth time, she decides, in conscience, to have an abortion.

Jennifer has been raised in a family where she has been taught that human life is a sacred gift from God which begins at conception. Abortion, therefore, is wrong. She is also a member of the Catholic Church which opposes abortion. She accepts the sanctity of life in the womb and the teaching of her church. When she gets pregnant for the fifth time (in the same situation as Sally), she decides, in conscience, to have the baby.

Sally and Jennifer have made very different decisions. Neither has broken the law. Both have followed their conscience. Who is right?

In order to answer this question, **we must distinguish between objective and subjective reality.** Subjective truth is the truth as it appears to me. It is the way that I perceive things to be. Objective truth is the way things are in fact, regardless of my perception. For example, if I think that the grass is blue, that may be my real, subjective perception. In fact, however, I am color-blind. It only appears blue to me. In reality it is green. For a person with normal vision, the subjective and objective are the same.

On a moral level it is a bit more complicated. How do we go about determining what is objectively true? Is it all just a matter of opinion? How do we prove something like moral truth? Let's begin with a common-sense observation: It is better to live in peace with each other than to kill each other for no particular reason. What reasonable human being could possibly disagree with that statement? Common-sense wisdom teaches us that it is better to love than to hate, to care than to be apathetic, to use our minds rather than to waste them. In other words, some decisions will be right or wrong **objectively,** based on whether or not they enable us to be better human beings as individuals and as a people. This is what the Second Vatican Council meant when it said that there is a law written in the heart of human beings. This is called the **"natural law."** Natural law means that human beings do not invent what is good—they discover what is good (or they fail to discover it). Discovering what is morally good is the task of all men and women of good will. It requires thought, study, and dialogue. The Second Vatican Council described it this way:

> In fidelity to conscience, Christians are joined with the rest of men in the search for truth and for the genuine solution to the numerous problems that arise in the life of individuals and from social relationships (*Gaudium et Spes,* n. 16).

This brings us back to the notion of the "informed conscience" and to our example of Sally and Jennifer. Their consciences have been informed very differently. Although abortion is a very controversial issue with no consensus at the present moment, its **morality must be determined by applying objective principles.** It is not right or wrong because someone says it is right or wrong. Its morality must have an objective basis to it. We must ask what is the more loving, just and compassionate thing to do. (We will look at the abortion issue more directly in the next chapter.)

For Personal Reflection and Discussion

Many people think that in moral matters one opinion is as good as the next. They believe that you can't argue a person's opinion. But a person's opinion is only as good as the evidence that backs it up. Some opinions are better than others. They come closer to the objective truth. Give an example of how this could be true in a moral issue.

OBSTACLES TO TRUTH

If morality is determined by searching for the truth, as the council said, it must be recognized that we frequently encounter obstacles to such a search. Human beings often resist the truth because it means that they might have to change. The Canadian theologian Bernard Lonergan suggests four different obstacles to the truth. He calls them biases. The first is the bias of egoism. We chose what is good only on the basis of how it affects us directly. What is good for me becomes the basis for what is good. Thus I might cheat on my income taxes and somehow justify it because it benefits me. A woman might get an abortion, not because she believes it is right, but because it is convenient for her.

The second obstacle is the bias of the group. This is sometimes referred to as "tribalism." In this case people make decisions based only on what is good for their group but not good for all. A patriotism that does not value the rights of other people would be guilty of such a distortion.

The third obstacle is the psychological bias. On this level a person blocks out or denies truths that are too difficult for him or her to accept. Alcoholics, for example, very often will deny what is perfectly clear to everyone else: that they have a serious problem.

The last is called the bias of common sense. There is usually nothing wrong with common sense. In this case it refers to short-sightedness. It is a failure to look at long-term effects. Much of the environmental damage inflicted on planet earth has been the result of such thinking.

For Personal Reflection and Discussion

The bias of ego shows itself when we rationalize and make up excuses for selfishness. When are you likely to do so?

The group bias is often the basis for prejudice. Name as many examples of the group bias as you can in American culture.

The psychological bias demands that we have the courage to know ourselves and be willing to take inventory of what makes us tick. How do you examine the direction of your life? Who keeps you honest with yourself?

CATHOLIC CHRISTIAN CONSCIENCE

We have seen that different people can be led in different directions by their conscience depending on how their conscience has been formed. **Christians form their conscience primarily in light of the person, teaching and life of Jesus Christ.** For Christians, Jesus is the "way, the truth, and the life." He holds the primary place in helping Christians understand the way that they are supposed to live. We have examined some of those key values in the last chapter. **The values of Christ should be alive within the Christian community.** It is within this community, especially within the family, that the values of the gospel are communicated to us. However, in some circumstances and situations today it is hard to know what Jesus would have taught. He never said a word about abortion, the nuclear arms race, euthanasia, the environment, medical ethics, a person's right to die, women's rights, racism, etc. **It is the role of the Christian community to apply the teaching of Jesus to issues that are facing people in each age and generation. The pope and the bishops have a special role here as teachers (magisterium).** It is their role to speak on behalf of the community on matters of faith and morals. They do not do this completely on their own. They are served by theologians. Some theologians are scholars trained especially in the area of moral issues. In addition, the pope and the bishops must be sensitive to the general wisdom of the Christian community, the consensus of the faithful, in areas of moral judgment.

Catholics are responsible to know and follow the teaching of the church on moral issues. This is referred to as "assent."

> In matters of faith and morals the bishops speak in the name of Christ and the faithful are to accept their teaching and adhere to it with a religious assent of soul (*Lumen Gentium*, n. 25).

It is not enough to simply obey the teaching of the church. We are human beings, not trained seals. We must understand the church's teaching as well. When the pope and the bishops teach on behalf of the church, we must try our best to understand the wisdom of their teaching. On this point we could distinguish between two levels of knowledge: conceptual knowledge and evaluative knowledge. On the first level I understand what the church teaches intellectually. I understand the concept. On the second level I understand the value not only in my head but in my heart as well. I understand **why** the value is important. Catholics are called to try to have the second level of knowledge. On the first level I may understand that it is wrong to cheat. On the second level I understand why. I know that I must be a person of integrity and that I cannot cheat because it violates who I am.

We not only must understand the teaching but we must obey it. Normally this will not be a problem. If we understand the church's teaching, we should want to obey it, because we will agree with it. It may happen, though, that we do not agree with the teaching of the church. What then? This is a difficult question to answer because the issues are so different and people are also in different situations. The good rule of thumb, however, is that we owe the pope and the bishops obedience unless in our hearts we believe, after serious thought, consultation and prayer, that God wants us to do otherwise. In other words, the teaching of the church should be assumed correct. The Second Vatican Council teaches that "this religious submission of mind and will must be shown in a special way to the Roman pontiff, even if he is not speaking ex cathedra" (that is, infallibly) (*Lumen Gentium,* n. 25). Religious submission of mind and will means that we accept the authority of the pope and the bishops to teach on behalf of the church. If, however, the church's teaching would violate our own conviction of what is good and true, then ultimately we are in a genuine conflict. The church teaches the need to follow our conscience in such a situation. If we were to go this route (it is often referred to as dissent), the following conditions should be respected:

1. We should do everything in our power to know and understand the church's teaching fully.
2. We must be willing to give the magisterium the benefit of the doubt and assume that its position or teaching is true.
3. We should be willing to consult with someone who is knowledgeable in the area.
4. We should see how other Christians in general respond to

the teaching of the church. (If I am the only one who disagrees, this is not a good sign.)
5. Finally, we should keep an open mind on the issue and be willing to rethink our position.

Faith and Morality. Christian morality is not based on a system of laws and rules. Nor is it based on personal opinion. Christian morality has as its heart and soul the person Jesus Christ. Jesus did not become one of us to give us a new set of commandments. Instead he revealed to us the meaning of our humanity, a life lived in love, compassion and service of others. All Christian morality boils down to the art of being a human being as Jesus was and as God's Spirit moves us to be. As a community we are to help each other understand and live that vision.

For Personal Reflection and Discussion

The question of the right to dissent is hotly debated in the church. Where does one draw the line and the limit? Does a Catholic have a right to dissent against any moral teaching? Where would you draw the line?

Questions for Review

1. Define the seven deadly sins and their corresponding virtues.
2. List three levels of conscience.
3. Define id, superego, and ego and relate them to conscience.
4. Describe Piaget's two stages of moral thinking.
5. What are Kohlberg's six stages of moral reasoning?
6. Define the words "subjective" and "objective" and relate them to morality.
7. What is meant by natural law?
8. What are the four biases or obstacles to truth?
9. What is meant by freedom of conscience?
10. Who are the authoritative teachers of morality in the Catholic Church?
11. What is meant by assent and dissent? What is the normal response of a Catholic to church teaching?
12. What factors must be considered if a person should dissent from the teaching of the church?

18

A Consistent Ethic of Life

Since this book is an overview of Christian faith, we cannot delve deeply into a large number of moral issues. We will, however, briefly examine a number of issues that are interrelated. The theme that ties these issues together is that of **life.** In the past decade or so, the Catholic Church has recognized and taught very clearly the need for Christians to affirm life by defending it and promoting it, especially among the most vulnerable in society. Cardinal Joseph Bernardin of Chicago has been a forerunner in an approach which he calls **"a consistent ethic of life"** or "a seamless garment." According to Bernardin, Christians must be concerned with all personal and social issues related to protecting and enhancing the value and dignity of life. We, as a community, must be on the side of life wherever and however it is threatened. In a talk at Fordham University, Bernardin described the connection among different pro-life issues:

> If one contends, as we do, that the right of every fetus to be born should be protected by civil law and supported by civil consensus, then our moral, political and economic responsibilities do not stop at the moment of birth. Those who defend the right to life of the weakest among us must be equally visible in support of the quality of life among the powerless among us: the old and the young, the hungry and the homeless, the undocumented immigrant and the unemployed worker.

In this chapter we will briefly discuss a number of issues that are related to a consistent ethic of life: abortion, social justice, war and peace, euthanasia, drug and alcohol abuse, capital punishment, racism and the environment.

For Personal Reflection and Discussion

What do you think are the most important moral issues facing young people today? Why?

ABORTION

The Catholic Church's position on the immorality of abortion is very well known. Sadly, the church's reasoning is not nearly as well known, nor is the depth of its position on the issue.

The Problem of Legality and Morality. Many of the people reading this book will not be able to recall a time when abortion was not legal in this country. Many people equate morality and legality. If something is legal, then they think that it must be moral. Keep in mind that it was once legal to own slaves in this country and to prevent women from voting. Morality and legality are not the same. When it comes to abortion, its legality has prevented the issue from being debated clearly.

Those who are in favor of a woman's right to have an abortion usually give one of three arguments for their position. The first is that a woman must have the right to control her own body. On this level, it is a question of human rights and freedom, as they see it. A second argument is that the fetus is not yet a person or a human being. A third argument involves the conviction that an unwanted baby is better off not being born. There are other arguments and situations, but these are the three most important ones. In addition to these three, the pro-choice camp often resents the attempts of others to "impose their religious beliefs" on others.

The Catholic Church sees this issue not as a religious one but as primarily a moral issue, and it opposes abortion on moral grounds. The church argues that while a **woman does indeed have a right to control her own body, that right has limits (like all rights). Biologically, the fetus is not a part of her body.** It has its own unique genetic structure, different from that of the mother. It is a new living organism (there is immediate cellular growth and division) genetically distinct from the mother. This is indeed the beginning of a new human life. All lives have a beginning. The moment that a new life begins is when the egg is fertilized by the sperm. If this is not a human life, then what type of life is it? It is human because its parents are human[A woman's right to control her own body ends when she begins to control the body of the unborn life inside of her.]

The church also argues that no child should ever need to feel unwanted. This is part of a cultural problem in which many people have begun to feel as if all decisions must be convenient or fit into pre-arranged plans. Even in cases where a baby would truly be a hardship, the church teaches that **we must change the conditions in society so that poor women can get the help they need in raising their children.** The church also points to the alternative of adoption. In this country thousands of married couples would love to adopt a new-born infant.

The arguments used by the church are not religious ones at all. There is no appeal to faith or to the commandments or to Jesus. However, for a Christian, **abortion becomes even more reprehensible in light of Jesus' compassion for the poor, the oppressed and the voiceless in society. Who is more voiceless than a fetus?**

The Catholic Church not only opposes abortion but strongly **opposes the conditions that lead to the need for abortion:** discrimination against women in the workplace, poverty, lack of adequate health care and child care. The church cannot take a stand against abortion unless it is also willing to take a stand against the conditions that lead to it.

For Personal Reflection and Discussion

What do you think are the most important issues in the abortion debate? Why?

WAR AND PEACE

Earlier we saw that the church developed a theory which recognized the possibility of a war being morally justifiable. This tradition in the church, known as the just war theory, states that war is always a tragic circumstance to be avoided at all costs. The bishops of the United States issued a pastoral letter in 1983 called *The Challenge of Peace*. In it they reiterated that a decision for war, "especially today, requires extraordinarily strong reasons for overriding the presumption in favor of peace." They then outlined the criteria used for a just war.

First, there must be a just cause. War is only permissible if there is a clear danger and threat to innocent human lives or to values that are essential for a decent human existence.

Second, war must be declared by a competent authority.

Third, there must be "comparative justice." That is, the causes of the war must be sufficient to take on the damages. This is particularly difficult to determine because the actual causes of war are almost never recognized at the onset of the war.

Fourth, war must always be a last resort. All peaceful alternatives must be exhausted before war is declared.

Fifth, there must be some probability of success which would make the war worth fighting.

Last is the "principle of proportionality" which states that the damage done by war should not outstrip the good which is achieved. Of course, one can only take an educated guess at what the damage will be before a war is fought.

In addition to these principles, there is also the principle that once a war has begun, it must be fought by armies and not directed against civilians.

The U.S. bishops also recognized a different tradition in the church which emphasized non-violence as an approach to solving conflict. They taught that both traditions are to be respected as genuine means of seeking peace. It must be noted that non-violence is not an option for Christians. It is essential to the message of Jesus and the gospel. Even those who are in favor of the just war theory must be firmly committed to principles of non-violence, in which war is always a last resort.

In light of these teachings, the bishops concluded that Christians may indeed join the armed services and consider themselves peacemakers. On the other hand, the rights of those who refuse to bear arms for religious or moral reasons (conscientious objectors) must also be respected.

For Personal Reflection and Discussion

Pope John Paul II has emphasized the immorality of war in an age of weapons of mass destruction. Do you think Christians should serve in the armed services? Why or why not?

NUCLEAR ARMS RACE

The Catholic Church has consistently spoken out against the arms race as a "theft of the poor." The stockpiling of nuclear weapons by the superpowers has led to an insane position in which civilization itself can be destroyed. In addition, the pursuit of more and better nuclear weapons diverts money, creativity and intelligence in directions in which they are not needed. In a world in which countless millions go hungry, the arms race is an affront to the poor. As the Second Vatican Council stated: **"The arms race is an utterly treacherous trap for humanity, and one which injures the poor to an intolerable degree"** (*Gaudium et Spes,* n. 81).

The U.S. Catholic bishops called for a freeze by the superpowers in the building of nuclear weapons and an eventual disarming on both sides. The possession of nuclear weapons for the sake of deterrence (to scare the other side from using theirs) is only provisionally acceptable. Ultimately they must be eliminated as weapons of mass destruction.

The actual use of nuclear weapons would be immoral because the damage done would never be proportionate to the good achieved. In addition, nuclear weapons do not discriminate between armies and non-combatants. They kill all within their radius of power. Again we listen to the fathers of the Second Vatican Council: "Any act of war aimed indiscriminately at the destruction of entire cities or at extensive areas along with their population is a crime against God and man himself. It merits unequivocal and unhesitating condemnation" (*Gaudium et Spes,* n. 80).

In *The Challenge of Peace* the U.S. bishops stated that Pope John Paul II captured the essence of the problem during his pilgrimage to Hiroshima when he said:

In the past it was possible to destroy a village, a town, a region, even a country. Now it is the whole planet that has come under threat. . . . We live today, therefore, in the midst of a cosmic drama; we possess a power which should never be used, but which might be used if we do not reverse our direction. We live with nuclear weapons knowing that we cannot afford to make one serious mistake. This fact dramatizes the precariousness of our position, politically, morally, and spiritually.

SOCIAL JUSTICE

Closely related to the question of war and peace is that of social justice. As Pope Paul VI reminded the church and the world, **"If you want peace, work for justice."** It is the lack of social justice that often leads to conflict and war in the world today.

The topic of social justice is extremely broad and includes a wide variety of issues. Social justice in general refers to the creation of social conditions which are fair to all and allow for all to attain the highest development possible of their human potential. Thus issues of social justice will include the right of the poor to housing, jobs and medical care, and care for the elderly, the handicapped and the mentally and emotionally disturbed. Social justice examines the economic structures of countries and judges how they affect all within their influence. It seeks to eliminate racism and prejudice and to establish equal opportunity.

Economically, the Catholic tradition has not blessed either capitalism or socialism as the ideal ways in which justice is to be found. Instead, the popes have pointed out that each of these systems brings with them both blessings and dangers. There is no doubt that the Catholic tradition has more strongly endorsed capitalism than socialism, but it has criticized capitalism's tendency to produce huge gaps between rich and poor and for the strongly developed capitalist countries to exploit the poorer, undeveloped or developing countries. **The U.S. Catholic bishops have emphasized the importance of weighing economic decisions in light of how they impact all people, especially the poor and the powerless.**

In the U.S. bishops' pastoral letter *Economic Justice for All* they state:

Every perspective on economic life that is human, moral and Christian must be shaped by three questions: What does the economy do for people? What does it do to people? And how do people participate in it? . . . No one can claim the name Christian and be comfortable in the face of hunger, homelessness, insecurity and injustice found in this country and in the world.

For Personal Reflection and Discussion

Every culture has its "sins." One of the glaring North American sins is consumerism. We have a strong tendency to measure our value in terms of what we own and to buy what we want rather than what we need. What are some ways that you could change your lifestyle in order to learn to live more simply? Are you interested in doing so?

In *Homelessness and Housing: A Human Tragedy, a Moral Challenge* from the U.S. Catholic Conference in March 1988 it states:

The church has traditionally viewed housing, not as a commodity, but as a basic human right. This conviction is grounded in our view of the human person and the responsibility of society to protect the life and dignity of every person by providing the conditions where human life and human dignity are not undermined but enhanced. As Pope John Paul II said . . . "A house is much more than a roof over one's head. It is a place where a person creates and lives out his or her life."

For Personal Reflection and Discussion

One of the great myths of our society is that the poor are poor because they are lazy, that all poor people have a chance to raise themselves up by the bootstraps. Admittedly some people are lazy. But most of the poor are born into poverty, poor education and lack of opportunity. Their self-esteem is damaged early in life and poverty becomes a pervasive, depressing fact of their existence. The large majority of the poor in the United States are women and children. What do you think are some of the main causes of poverty in America?

OFFICIAL CATHOLIC SOCIAL TEACHING: THE LAST 100 YEARS

Title—Latin, English	Author, Date	Context	Main Points
Rerum Novarum *On the Condition of Workers*	Pope Leo XIII May 15, 1891	the industrial revolution; exploitation of the worker by the owner; poor are unprotected by the laws	1. the need for respect of human dignity of all persons 2. workers have the right to receive a just wage and to form trade associations 3. right to private property 4. right of the church to speak out on social issues
Quadragesimo Anno *Reconstructing the Social Order*	Pope Pius XI May 15, 1931	response to the great Depression throughout the world and the rise of European dictators	1. criticizes capitalism's terrible excesses 2. denounces the communist solution 3. the state has a responsibility in economic affairs
Mater et Magister *Christianity and Social Progress*	Pope John XXIII May 15, 1961	growing gap between the developed and undeveloped nations; the cold war and the nuclear arms race	1. examines the international economic scene 2. duty of advanced nations to aid undeveloped nations 3. arms race adds to poverty 4. all Catholics must have social commitment
Pacem in Terris *Peace on Earth*	Pope John XXIII April 11, 1963	deepening problem in cold war and third world	1. clarion call to human rights and dignity as the foundation of peace in the world

Document	Author / Date	Context	Key Points
Populorum Progressio *On Promoting the Development of Peoples*	Pope Paul VI March 26, 1967	Vietnam War; African wars of independence; disparity of rich and poor nations	1. the goods of the earth belong to all 2. development of the third world is essential to peace ("development is a new word for peace")
Evangelii Nuntiandi *Evangelization in the Modern World*	Pope Paul VI Dec. 8, 1975	atheism communism hedonism poverty	1. evangelization proclaims (like Jesus) liberation from all oppression 2. teaching of church must challenge all injustice
Laborem Exercens *On Human Work*	Pope John Paul II Sept. 14, 1981	90th anniversary of *Rerum Novarum*	1. developed themes from *Rerum Novarum* 2. work should be a humanizing force in life 3. rights of the worker to just pay, health care, working environment, vacation
Sollicitudo Rei Socialis *On Social Concerns*	Pope John Paul II Dec. 30, 1987	continuing gap between the north–south caused by east–west cold war	1. condemnation of east–west cold war and the imperialism and militarism they engender 2. criticizes both socialism and capitalism for its excesses 3. injustices built into the very structures of economic policy ("structures of sin")
Centesimus Annus	Pope John Paul II May 15, 1991	100th anniversary of *Rerum Novarum*; end of cold war	1. reiteration of previous social teaching 2. continues to critique capitalism, but more optimistic about its possibilities 3. includes environmental concerns with others of social justice

In their pastoral letter on handicapped people in November 1978, the U.S. Catholic bishops stated:

> All too often, abortion and post-natal neglect are prompted by arguing that the handicapped infant will survive only to suffer a life of pain and deprivation. We find this reasoning appalling. Society's frequent indifference to the plight of handicapped citizens is a problem that cries aloud for solutions based on justice and conscience, not violence.

For Personal Reflection and Discussion

Jean Vanier has worked with the mentally retarded for years. His L'Arche community is a model of how some Christians do more than care about the handicapped. They live with them and share their lives with them. They develop a sense of solidarity with them. How do you feel when you are around handicapped people? Why?

HUMAN RIGHTS

One of the grave misconceptions that people have is that we do the poor and handicapped a favor when we help them. The fact is, however, that all human beings have dignity and all must enjoy the benefits of essential human rights. One of the great encyclicals of this century was Pope John XXIII's *Pacem in Terris*. In it he described many of the basic human rights to which all men and women should be entitled. These include the following: the basic needs of life, food, clothing and shelter; the right to medical care and social services, education, a job with humane working conditions and a just wage; the right to private property; the right to take part in a union; the right to travel freely; the right to protection under the law; the right of freedom of conscience in following one's own religion. It is the responsibility of society to create conditions which allow for these rights to be respected. The right to private property has been a consistent part of the teaching of the church, yet that right has always been a limited one. **The general principle is that the goods of the earth are intended for all, and that no one is entitled to unlimited wealth and property while others do not have their most basic needs.**

For Personal Reflection and Discussion

In the light of American culture, what do you think of the principle that wealth is to be limited according to the needs of all?

RACISM AND PREJUDICE

At the heart of the teaching of the church concerning human rights is the conviction that all persons must have human rights and are due those rights because of their inherent dignity as persons. Racism is both an individual and a social attitude which excludes a certain group from full inclusion in the rights of a society based solely on their race. The South African system of apartheid, now being dismantled, is based on racist premises which allows discrimination and refuses certain rights to the majority of the people based on their race. The United States of America has its roots in a system which allowed blacks to be enslaved and not counted as persons under the Constitution.

Racism is not limited to a person's individual prejudices. Society develops racially discriminatory structures which are often hidden and officially rejected. For example, while the law does not permit discrimination in housing against persons because of their race or ethnic origin, such discrimination is often practiced. The same can be said for job discrimination. Such practices perpetuate racist mentalities and keep certain groups from fully participating in the economic life of the country. Poverty breeds hopelessness, more poverty, and often leads to the breakdown of family and community supports. The result is a system which is biased in favor of the wealthy and middle class.

The position of the church is that racism must be erased from human hearts as an attitude which is thoroughly repulsive to the gospel of Jesus Christ. But this is not enough. Society must structure itself in such a way that racist practices are eliminated and all are given a fair share in the life of the society and culture. In the 1950s and 1960s Martin Luther King, Jr., motivated by his faith in Jesus Christ, led a civil rights movement which sought not only to change the hearts of the prejudiced but also to change the unjust laws which kept blacks oppressed. In his famous

"Christmas Sermon on Peace," Dr. King described the basis for the elimination of racism:

> Now let me suggest that if we are to have peace on earth, our loyalties must become ecumenical rather than sectional. Our loyalties must transcend our race, our tribe, our class, and our nation; and this means we must develop a world perspective. No individual can live alone, no nation can live alone, and as long as we try, the more we are going to have war in this world. Now the judgment of God is upon us, and we must either learn to live together as brothers or we are all going to perish together as fools.

What has been said about racism applies to all forms of prejudice. Globally speaking, women represent the largest group of those often denied their basic human rights due to prejudice. In our country, known for its freedom and democratic ideals, women have only gained the right to vote in this century, and they remain victims of economic systems that lead them into poverty much more than men (e.g. divorce laws, salaries, opportunity). Throughout the world the system is often dramatically much worse.

For Personal Reflection and Discussion

What prejudices have you been exposed to in your family and culture? In what ways are you prejudiced? What can you do to help overcome these prejudices?

EUTHANASIA

Euthanasia literally means "a good death," and it refers to a wide variety of issues related to death and dying. One could distinguish four categories of euthanasia: voluntary or involuntary, passive or active. Voluntary euthanasia refers to a person's free choice to take actions which will end his or her life. Involuntary euthanasia is when someone else chooses for us. Passive euthanasia refers to a process of allowing someone to die; active euthanasia actively takes his or her life. As you can see, euthanasia is very much related to "right to die" issues.

The position of the Catholic Church has always been that a person has the right to die with dignity if nothing within ordinary means can be done to keep him or her alive. Thus a person who is hopelessly comatose would have the right to have the respirator removed which is keeping him or her alive. People have a right to refuse "extraordinary means." The difficult part of the issue has been defining what constitutes ordinary and extraordinary means. Is hydration (being fed water through a tube) extraordinary or ordinary? Thus, while the principle is firmly established, the church will continue to be involved in the debate within society.

On the other hand, **the church has absolutely prohibited any and all forms of active or involuntary euthanasia.** It has taught that God is the author of life and that any attempt to decide for ourselves what the moment of death shall be violates the gift of God. The church's teaching also protects against horrific scenarios in which the elderly and the handicapped are given a "good death."

In its *Declaration on Euthanasia* in 1980, the Congregation for the Doctrine of the Faith declared:

> No one can in any way permit the killing of an innocent human being, whether a fetus or an embryo, an infant or an adult, an old person or one suffering from an incurable disease, or a person who is dying. Furthermore, no one is permitted to ask for this act of killing. . . . Nor can any authority legitimately recommend or permit such an action.

For Personal Reflection and Discussion

If you were in a permanent comatose state, would you want to be removed from extraordinary means of being kept alive? Why or why not? Do you agree that a person does not have a right to actively end his or her own life? Why or why not?

THE ENVIRONMENT

St. Francis used to call the animals his brothers and sisters. He had a wonderful sense of how all creation is interconnected. The book of Genesis tells us that God looked at his creation and saw how good it was. He then gave human beings responsibility over the creation. More than ever before, we are well aware of the fragility of mother earth. This is a critically important moral issue because it underlies all others. It involves the very survival of the planet as the place where human and all other forms of life can exist. Some of the damage done to the earth is the result of ignorance. We simply were unaware of the results of some technological advances. But much of the damage done to the planet is the result of human greed and stupidity. If there was ever time to add an eleventh commandment, the time seems upon us now: "Love thy mother, the earth."

For Personal Reflection and Discussion

What personal habit can you change to be more ecologically responsible?

CAPITAL PUNISHMENT

In theory, the Catholic Church has defended the right of the state to execute prisoners. In reality, however, this teaching can no longer find any approval among popes and bishops. In 1980 the U.S. Catholic bishops released a statement in which they opposed the death penalty as a just or moral solution to the problem of crime. They cited the following reasons for their opposition:

First, the death penalty gives up all hope in the person. There is no chance for rehabilitation or change of heart.

Second, there is no evidence that shows the death penalty to be a deterrent to crime. It has had no impact on the rate of murders or other violent crime.

Third, revenge is not the same as justice and is morally unjustifiable.

Fourth, human life is a sacred gift from God. The death penalty does not increase an appreciation for the value of life, but diminishes such an appreciation.

Finally, the death penalty always includes the possibility that an innocent person may be executed.

For Personal Reflection and Discussion

How would you respond to the bishops' arguments opposing the death penalty? Do you think it can be justified from the perspective of Christian morality? If so, how?

DRUG AND ALCOHOL ABUSE

Drug and alcohol abuse are also related to the consistent ethic of life. The use of drugs in our society accounts for thousands of deaths to both users and those on the street who suffer from related crime. Drug abuse is not only destructive of oneself but has had extraordinary social consequences as well. Many of the cities of the United States have been turned into battlegrounds in which no one is safe. Drugs usually defeat the most vulnerable in society: the poor, the homeless, the unemployed.

Alcohol remains, by far, the drug of choice in the United States. Nearly every two years we lose as many lives on our highways due to alcohol-related accidents as we did in the entire Vietnam war. Alcoholism is the most devastating disease in the country with nearly one in ten adults afflicted. It destroys not only individuals but entire families.

For Personal Reflection and Discussion

Alcoholism can begin in adolescence, and alcohol abuse among young people is widespread. If you had a friend who was a serious alcohol abuser, would you tell him or her your opinion? If that friend didn't change his or her habits, would you inform a parent, counselor or teacher? Why or why not?

Questions for Review

1. Explain what is meant by a "consistent ethic of life."
2. What arguments are used by those in favor of a woman's right to abortion?
3. Explain the church's position on abortion thoroughly. Why does it teach what it does?
4. What criteria are necessary for a "just war"?

5. What is the position of the United States bishops concerning the arms race and the use of nuclear weapons?
6. What is meant by "social justice"?
7. What are some of the human rights that all humans are entitled to according to *Pacem in Terris*?
8. What are the personal and social elements of racism?
9. What is euthanasia? What does the church teach about a person's right to die? What does the church teach about active euthanasia?
10. What are some reasons why the U.S. bishops oppose capital punishment?

19

Saints and Heroes

The history of the church is more than the history of its leaders, teachings and turmoil. At the heart of the history of the church are those who have lived the message of Christianity most faithfully: its saints. In this chapter we will examine the heart of the church by looking at those men and women who have lived as models of faith and who challenge each generation to place Christ and his mission at the center of the church.

One of the most striking things about the saints is the variety of their personalities and individual gifts. Saints are anything but conformists. They do not even conform to each other. Each of them brings something unique to the concept of sanctity. The choice of the saints we mention here is extremely limited (due to lack of space) and somewhat arbitrary. They have been chosen because each represents a unique font of holiness, a different way of being a saint. In addition to the six different saints, we will also look at a number of contemporary "heroes" of faith: men and women of the twentieth century who have continued the Christian call to holiness.

Catholics also believe that we live within a "communion of saints." As believers in the resurrection, we are convinced that the saints are still somehow mysteriously present to us. Different saints are remembered on each day throughout the year, to remind us of the unique ways in which the grace of God has been present to us and to challenge us to recognize why we were created in the first place: to be saints, channels of God's grace and love in the world.

MARY: THE MOTHER OF GOD,
THE MOTHER OF THE CRUCIFIED

At the head of the list of the saints in the church is Mary, the mother of Jesus. Mary is considered the greatest of saints and the mother of the church. Above we have referred to her through two different titles. The first, mother of God, emphasizes Mary's unique role in the history of salvation and her continuing role as the greatest of saints. The second, mother of the crucified, emphasizes the historical figure who was a human being, a mother, and who watched her only son be killed.

Very little is said about Mary in the New Testament. The key passages are found in the gospels of Luke and John. In Luke's version of the birth of Jesus, Mary is portrayed as the ideal disciple who opens her heart to the word of God and says yes to it. These attitudes are revealed in Luke's famous description of the annunciation.

In the sixth month, the angel Gabriel was sent from God to a town in Galilee to a virgin betrothed to a man named Joseph of the house of David. The virgin's name was Mary. Upon arriving, the angel said to her: "Rejoice, O highly favored daughter! The Lord is with you. Blessed are you among women." She was deeply troubled by his words, and wondered what the greeting meant. The angel went on to say to her: "Do not fear, Mary. You have found favor with God. You shall conceive and bear a son and give him the name Jesus. Great will be his dignity and he will be called Son of the Most High. The Lord God will give him the throne of David his father. He will rule over the house of Jacob forever and his reign will be without end."

Mary said to the angel, "How can this be since I do not know man?" The angel answered her: "The Holy Spirit will come upon you; hence the holy offspring to be born will be called Son of God. Know that Elizabeth your kinswoman has conceived a son in her old age; she who was thought to be sterile is now in her sixth month, for nothing is impossible with God."

Mary said, "I am the servant of the Lord. Let it be done to me as you say." With that the angel left her (Luke 1:26–38).

Mary says yes to the strange and mysterious request. It is important that we not interpret the story in an overly literal fashion. The conversation between Mary and the angel Gabriel is not on the same level as human conversations. Mary is open to God's message to her (the angel). We may think that we too would respond to the message of an angel, but this misses the point. Can we hear the voices of "angels" in our lives? Are we open to God's will for us? Is our heart free to respond whole-heartedly to God? Mary is favored by God not at random but because of her openness and love of God. This faith of Mary is described in the first part of the famous prayer that she prays, the Magnificat:

> My being proclaims the greatness of the Lord,
>   my spirit finds joy in God my savior.

Mary is chosen by God because she represents God's favorites: those who are humbly dependent on him. Again, we find this theme in the Magnificat:

> He has deposed the mighty from their thrones
>   and raised the lowly to high places.
> The hungry he has given every good thing,
>   while the rich he has sent away empty.

She is the poor young girl who gives birth in a stable, who must flee from the powers who seek to kill her baby, and whose "heart is pierced with a sword" (Luke 2:35) as she endures the death of her son.

In Luke's gospel, Mary is the model of all disciples because of her openness to God's word. It is not her biological motherhood that is as important as her spiritual motherhood. This is made clear later in the ministry of Jesus when someone cries out, "Blest is the womb that bore you and the breasts that nursed you!" Jesus replies, "Rather, blest are they who hear the word of God and keep it." All who hear the word of God and keep it can be like Mary. They too can "give birth" to God's love in the world.

THE ROSARY

Catholics believe that the communion of saints is made up of those who have died but live on in God's love. They remain present to us still. Mary, the mother of Jesus, has a special place in this communion. Catholics have traditionally prayed for her intercession. The rosary has been the most popular form of devotion for the past six hundred years. It is prayed as a meditation on the life of Christ and divided into three sets of mysteries: the joyful, the sorrowful and the glorious. Each mystery contains five decades or groups of ten "Hail Marys" which are prayed and act as a meditative guide. The rosary begins with a recitation of the Apostles' Creed, the Lord's Prayer and a doxology. Each decade is also preceded by the Lord's Prayer and a doxology. The prayers are counted on rosary beads.

The Joyful Mysteries
1. The Annunciation
2. The Visitation
3. The Birth of Jesus
4. The Presentation
5. The Finding of Our Lord in the Temple

The Sorrowful Mysteries
1. The Agony in the Garden
2. The Scourging at the Pillar
3. The Crowning with Thorns
4. The Carrying of the Cross
5. The Crucifixion and Death of Jesus

The Glorious Mysteries
1. The Resurrection
2. The Ascension
3. The Descent of the Holy Spirit
4. The Assumption of Mary into Heaven
5. The Coronation of Mary as Queen of Heaven and Earth

It is in the gospel of John that we find Mary at the foot of the cross. She who brought God's love into the world will remain faithful to the end:

> Near the cross of Jesus there stood his mother, his mother's sister, Mary the wife of Cleopas, and Mary Magdalene. Seeing his mother there with the disciple whom he loved, Jesus said to his mother, "Woman, there is your son." In turn he said to the disciple, "There is your mother." From that hour onward, the disciple took her into his care.

The church has traditionally interpreted this passage to mean that Mary becomes the mother of the church, a new Eve. Through her the human race has gone through a second birth.

The official teaching of the church regards Mary as a unique figure in the history of salvation. She is the greatest of all saints, and even more. At the Second Vatican Council, the church wanted to make sure that Mary was recognized and honored, yet they wanted to avoid the past excesses which almost seemed to turn her into the fourth person of the Trinity. Thus they wrote:

> She is the favorite daughter of the Father and the temple of the Holy Spirit. Because of this gift of sublime grace she far surpasses all other creatures, both in heaven and on earth. At the same time, however, because she belongs to the offspring of Adam, she is one with all human beings in their need for salvation (*Lumen Gentium,* n. 53).

Although she is truly one of us, Mary is also unique. The church teaches that she was conceived free from original sin. From the moment of her conception, she was especially blessed and favored by God. She also was assumed into heaven and exalted as queen of heaven and earth.

Throughout its history the church has encouraged devotion to Mary and prayer to her. This does not mean that she replaces Christ, but that, like all the saints, she is part of the mystical body of Christ through whom we have solidarity in faith. Mary's role is always to bring Christians closer to Christ and the Father through the Spirit.

Perhaps the most important and enduring devotion to Mary has been the praying of the rosary. The full rosary consists of fifteen "decades" (a series of ten Hail Marys comprises a single decade). Each decade focuses on a different mystery of faith. The prayers are said as a form of "centering" one's attention while the mind meditates on the different mysteries of faith. There are five joyful, five glorious, and five sorrowful mysteries.

Finally, devotion to Mary continues throughout the church, aided by a series of "appearances" made by Mary to certain visionaries. Some of these include Lourdes in France, Fatima in Portugal, Guadalupe in Mexico, and Czestochowa in Poland. These and other Marian shrines continue to draw millions of pilgrims each year.

For Personal Reflection and Discussion

What role does Mary play in your faith? How can you enhance that relationship?

PAUL OF TARSUS

It is very possible that no one has had as much influence on the church as Paul. He was born in Tarsus in Cilicia about ten years after the birth of Jesus. He was born into a Jewish family, but in a Roman province and city. Thus he was both a Roman citizen and a Jew. He had both a Roman name (Paulus) and a Jewish one (Saul).

Paul studied in Jerusalem under the learned rabbi Gamaliel. He belonged to the Pharisees, the most devout of all Jews, who believed in a strict interpretation of both the oral and the written law. When he first heart of the new sect of Christians, he opposed them wholeheartedly. The Acts of the Apostles tells us that he was present at the death of the first Christian martyr Stephen, and that he zealously persecuted the church.

God, however, had other plans for Paul. As he was traveling to Damascus, his life took a dramatic turn:

Saul, still breathing murderous threats against the Lord's disciples, went to the high priest and asked him for letters to the synagogues in Damascus which would empower him to arrest and bring to Jerusalem anyone he might find, man or woman, living according to the new way. As he was traveling along and approaching Damascus, a light from the sky suddenly flashed about him. He fell to the ground and at the same time heard a voice saying, "Saul, Saul, why do you persecute me?" "Who are you, sir?" he asked. The voice answered, "I am Jesus, the one you are persecuting. Get up and go into the city, where you will be told what to do."

This experience would completely change Paul's life. It was this "conversion" on the road to Damascus that became the basis of everything else that he did. He went on to be baptized, spent three years learning about the "new way," and became one of the church's greatest missionaries. The leaders of the early church were skeptical about accepting Paul because of his previous attacks on the church, but he eventually gained their approval. Paul made three great missionary journeys and established churches throughout the regions of Greece and Asia Minor. Wherever he traveled, he taught first to the Jews, then to the Gentiles. He had a great deal more success with the non-Jews, and is known as the apostle to the Gentiles. Paul defended the importance of freedom for Christians. The Gentile Christians were not to be shackled with the burdens of the law of Moses. He was not in the least afraid to stand up for his beliefs. In his letter to the Galatians, he describes an argument that he had with Peter concerning foods forbidden by the Jews but allowed for the Gentiles.

> When Cephas [Peter] came to Antioch I directly withstood him, because he was clearly in the wrong. He had been taking his meals with the Gentiles before others came who were from James. But when they arrived he drew back to avoid trouble with those who were circumcised (Galatians 2:11–12).

Perhaps even more important than his missions was the fact that Paul gave the church what it desperately needed: a brilliant thinker. He was able to explain the meaning of Christ's life, death and resurrection in a manner which has been the standard for the last two thousand years. His letters to the various churches have become part of the New Testament.

Paul did more than speak and write about Christ: he imitated him. Paul suffered greatly for his faith, being imprisoned a number of times, even for years, and ultimately being martyred by Nero in Rome.

For Personal Reflection and Discussion

Paul reminds us that we don't have to give up our brains in order to be a Christian. We can use them to serve God. A mind is a terrible thing to waste. What are you doing to exercise your brain? What more can you do?

ST. AUGUSTINE

Saints are men and women of their time. They reflect the concerns and needs of a specific period of history. Yet, in another way, they transcend their time. They touch upon the eternal. Augustine is truly a saint for all ages. He represents the yearning and hungering of the human heart for true fulfillment and meaning. He is a symbol of God's grace at work in the most restless of souls.

Augustine was born in present-day Algeria in a city called Tagaste. His mother Monica was a devout Christian (and a saint as well). His father Patricius was not baptized until he was on his deathbed. Augustine was a brilliant student, but a lazy one. His parents worked hard to offer him the best education, and were harsh in their punishment when he did not work at his studies. When he was sixteen, they could not afford to send him to school and the boy spent the year in a wild series of sexual escapades. Fortunately, a friend of the family offered to pay for Augustine's education and he went off to the great city of Carthage to study. There he took a mistress, who bore him a son, Adeodatus. He lived with her for fourteen years, and then dismissed her and took another mistress.

In 372, Augustine became a Manichaean. This was a religious sect led by a man named Mani who taught a religion based on dualism: the forces of evil fighting against the forces of light in the world. He went off to Rome where he taught and wrote his first book. From there he went to Milan where he was a professor of rhetoric. He became disillusioned with his faith as a Manicha-ean and went to listen to the preaching of the bishop Ambrose. One day he went into a garden with the letters of St. Paul and heard a child singing, "Take and read! Take and read!" He opened the letters of Paul and turned to Romans 13:13: "Let us walk honestly, as in the day; not in rioting and drunkenness, not in chambering and wantoness, not in strife and envy. But put on the Lord Jesus Christ, and make not provision for the flesh, to fulfill the lusts thereof" (*Confessions* VIII, xii, 28–30).

His life would never be the same. He felt these words sear into his heart, and he was able to put behind him all his former lusts and desires. He quit his job, entered the church, and re-turned to Africa. His first impulse was to live a monastic life in-fluenced by the followers of St. Antony. When the local bishop Valerius asked the people to help him find an assistant, the peo-ple seized Augustine and, ignoring his protests, insisted that he be ordained. Five years later he became an auxiliary bishop, and shortly after that, when Valerius died, he was made bishop of the city of Hippo. He remained a monk at heart and continued to live as one. He also founded a number of monasteries through-out northern Africa, including one for women.

Augustine went on to become one of the greatest thinkers and writers in the history of Christianity, with an intellectual influence rivaled only by Paul and Thomas Aquinas. As a saint, however, it is Augustine's restless soul that has spoken to so many over the years. Augustine learned that the only true way to know and understand himself was to know and understand God, for it is God who is our true source and goal in life. After much struggle, searching and many sins, Augustine was able to write: "You have made us for yourself, O Lord, and our hearts are rest-less until they rest in you."

For Personal Reflection and Discussion

Like Augustine we often look in the wrong places for fulfill-ment. In America, alcohol, drugs, and wealth are meant to fill the hole that can only be filled by faith, hope and love. Augustine also shows us that we are never beyond hope. What do you look for in your life for fulfillment?

ST. FRANCIS OF ASSISI

Born in Assisi in 1182, Francis was the son of a wealthy cloth merchant. His mother was a young woman from Provencal; thus even though he was baptized John Baptist, he was called Francesco, the little Frenchman. Francis worked with his father and was known as a quick-witted, spontaneous young man who loved parties and was sensitive to the cries of beggars. When a war broke out between two rival cities, Francis fought on behalf of Assisi and was taken prisoner for a year. Shortly after his release he became ill and more reflective. He decided to leave behind his former life and went to live alone. One day, as he was traveling by horseback to his cave, he saw a leper approach. Although he was repulsed by his condition, he got down and kissed the leper. The next day he volunteered to help at the leper hospital and found great joy in this service.

Francis, like Paul and Augustine, also experienced a profound conversion in his life when he heard a voice tell him: "Repair my house." The voice seemed to be coming from the crucifix in the church of San Damiano in Assisi. Francis took the call of the Lord literally and began to repair the church, using some of his father's funds and begging for others. He gave the money to the local priest. His father was furious and locked Francis in the basement of the house on a diet of bread and water. Eventually, he had him arrested. When the case was taken to the ecclesiastical authorities, Francis was told to return the money to its rightful owner. Francis then returned not only the money but took off all his clothes in the middle of the court and left them at his father's feet. He renounced all things that belonged to his earthly father, and became intent on marrying himself to Lady Poverty, freeing himself to be a true son to his heavenly Father.

Francis then began to live the life of a beggar and hermit, dressed in rags, preaching that poverty is the true way to Christ. He was soon joined by others who were attracted to his message. Their lives were ones of simplicity and service, embracing all creation in love. Although poor and often suffering greatly, Francis and his followers loved to sing and praise God in all ways. Francis had an extraordinary sense of God's presence in all things and referred to all created life as his brother and sister. He and his followers were officially recognized by the church as a religious order in 1215. Unlike the monks, the Franciscan friars were primarily missionary in their vocation. Francis' followers have been an important part of the history of the church, with sixteen saints and five popes coming from their ranks.

Francis is a model of true happiness for men and women today. We live in an age which constantly tells us that happiness lies in comfort, security and wealth. Francis challenges us to go beyond the happiness of comfort to the deep joy of the gospel.

For Personal Reflection and Discussion

Francis challenges us to simplify our lives in the belief that we will be freer and happier. How can you simplify your life? Is it filled with too much garbage time and too many possessions? Do you think those possessions really make you a better person?

ST. CATHERINE OF SIENA (1347–1380)

Many saints seem to begin by seeking to flee from the world in order to find God, only to be drawn back into the world in ways which they might never have guessed.

Catherine of Siena certainly fits this description. She was born of Jacobo and Lapa Benincasa, an upper middle class family who had twenty-two children (twelve of whom survived). Unlike the saints we have seen thus far, Catherine seems to have been chosen for sanctity early in life. At the age of six she had a vision of Christ and vowed to serve him alone. She refused to marry, which horrified her mother, but eventually her saintly father gave in and recognized that she was called to a different life. At the age of nineteen she joined the Dominican Sisters of Penitence. She continued to live in her home, but in the solitude of her room, living a life of prayer and fasting. She enjoyed a deep spiritual sense of God's presence and reported having "visions" of Christ. However, she went through a period of intense temptation, many of them sexual in nature, and she was deeply confused by them. Finally she offered them up as part of the cross she must carry, and they left her as quickly as they had first come. She gained an extraordinary reputation for holiness, and many miracles were attributed to her prayers. Sinners came to repentance upon meeting her.

Meanwhile the church was in one of its worst periods. The papacy had moved to Avignon and there was corruption everywhere. Catherine wrote to the papal legate and was finally given a meeting with Gregory XI. He was taken by her obvious sincerity and holiness. She left the pope on September 11 and on September 13 he left for Rome, never to return to Avignon again. He was succeeded by Urban VI who asked her to come to Rome to speak to the cardinals. The odd little mystic girl who sought to live in solitary prayer spent her last years counseling popes and preaching to cardinals.

Catherine is truly a story of God's grace. She was willing to trust in the call that she heard and to follow that call to places about which she had never even dreamt. As a woman she was constantly told to return to her proper place, but she was able to convince many of her strongest skeptics because of her obvious holiness. Catherine is also a sign of the fact that God can work in whomever he choses. She was no Paul or Augustine when it came to intelligence. She had none of the natural charm or wit of Francis. But she did have courage to spare, and that allowed God's grace to channel through her and to change the course of the history of the church.

For Personal Reflection and Discussion

Catherine refused to allow typical conventions to keep her from doing what she believed was right. She spoke her mind bravely to those in power. If you were to write a letter to the pope with suggestions for improving the church, what would it say?

ST. THOMAS MORE (1477–1535)

It would be difficult to find a saint more different from the other-worldly Catherine than Thomas More. He enjoyed no great visions of youth or desires to flee the world. He was born the son of a lawyer and was given an excellent education in England, where he also became a lawyer (after giving some thought to being a priest). He was one of the great minds of Europe at a time when Europe was in the midst of great upheaval and the church in need of great reform. England, however, was enjoying a great intellectual renewal. He wrote a classic work entitled *Utopia* which is still read and studied. He was a close friend to Erasmus who describes him as a man of quick wit, great humor, a true friend whose company was greatly enjoyed by all. As a young man, Thomas had earned the enmity of the king by opposing him on a financial issue while a member of parliament. Later, however, he became a great favorite of his son, Henry VIII.

Thomas was married and had four children by his first wife, Jane, when she died. He remarried an older woman named Alice who irritated many of his friends. Thomas believed in a good education for women as well as men and offered his three daughters and stepdaughter the best education. His eldest daughter Margaret was his favorite and seemed to share much of his brilliance.

The king constantly sought the companionship of Thomas and would keep him for days on end at his palace or come to visit him at his home. Eventually he appointed Thomas as chancellor of England, the highest position in the land next to the king. Friendship turned to tragedy, however, when the king sought to divorce his wife Catherine in order to marry Anne Boleyn. When the pope would not grant the necessary dispensation, the king declared himself head of the church of England and required all to swear an Oath of Supremacy. More resigned his office of chancellor when he saw the crisis coming, but it was not enough to save him. He refused to take the oath and was placed in the tower and eventually tried and convicted of treason. His last words to the people were: "I call you to witness, brothers, that I die in and for the faith of the Catholic Church, the king's loyal servant, but God's first."

Thomas More was not an apostle like Paul or a great sinner like the young Augustine. He did not give up all possessions like Francis, nor was he a mystic like Catherine. He was a "man for all seasons" whose mind belonged to the world, but whose heart belonged to God.

For Personal Reflection and Discussion

Thomas More is a great example of someone who lives in the world without becoming "of" the world. Is there anyone today who reminds you at all of Thomas More? Can you think of any politicians who are "holy"?

Thomas Merton, Dorothy Day and Oscar Romero are not officially canonized saints. It is possible that they never will be. Each of them, however, represents a profound way of living one's faith in the twentieth century. They are very different people with very different backgrounds. Yet they share in common a passion for God and a passion for peace. They represent just a few of many people who could be held up as models of Christian faith in the twentieth century.

THOMAS MERTON

Thomas Merton was born in Prades, France on January 31, 1915 to Ruth and Owen Merton. His mother was an American and his father was from New Zealand. His parents were artists who could not make enough to support themselves in France, so they moved to Douglaston on Long Island where Thomas' maternal grandparents lived. They had another son, John Paul, and a few years later Ruth died of cancer. Owen stayed briefly with Ruth's parents and left again for Europe and his career in painting. Thomas went with him, and they traveled throughout Europe, eventually landing in England where Thomas attended a fine prep school. His father died of a brain tumor when Thomas was sixteen, after a long and painful illness.

Thomas then went to live with a close friend of the family. He traveled about Europe and visited his brother and grandparents in America in the summers. He enrolled in Cambridge after high school where he spent more time drinking and going to parties than studying. Eventually it was decided that he would be better off under the guidance of his grandparents, and so he left again for America.

Merton's restless life and the loss of his parents were also shaping the state of his soul. He was disgusted with his life, and he longed for a purpose and direction. He slowly began to find this direction while at Columbia University. Although he was still the life of the party, he was also reading a great deal about Catholicism and making friends with men who would help to give him a deeper sense of direction. Finally he went for instructions and was welcomed into the Catholic Church. He lived the life of a pious new convert, praying daily and trying to change his old habits. When he told his friend, Bob Lax, that he wanted to be a "good Catholic," Lax told him he was aiming for the wrong thing. He should want to be a saint. This became his consuming passion. He tried to join the Franciscans but was rejected when they heard of his past. Instead he wound up joining the Trappists, and offered his life to God in the monastery.

Merton believed that he was leaving the world behind to lose himself in love of God. Finally he had a place where he belonged. But once again God had different ideas. While in the monastery, he wrote the story of his life, entitled *Seven Storey Mountain.* The book described his life and conversion and was a monumental best-seller. It touched a nerve deeply rooted in the American psyche, and Merton was now a well-known personality. He continued to write and he poured out books at a rate that seemed almost impossible. He became the best known, most widely read and influential spiritual thinker of his time, perhaps of the entire twentieth century. His thoughts and spirit were always growing, and the later years of his life were devoted to writings related to peace and justice in the world. In these areas he also proved a prophetic voice. Oddly enough, he died in an accident in Bangkok, Thailand, having been given permission to leave the monastery to participate in an international conference.

Merton's life was a constant paradox. His childhood was rooted in tragedy and insecurity. His adult life was a search for a God who alone could fill the emptiness he experienced as a young man. He was a monk whose voice was heard throughout the world. He had a vow of silence and yet influenced the church profoundly. He was a man of the spirit who always loved a good laugh and a cold beer. He was, and continues to be for many, a sign of hope and faith in the midst of life's absurdities.

For Personal Reflection and Discussion

It is said that God can write straight with crooked lines. He can take the events of our lives, even when tragic, and give them a new direction in light of his love. This was certainly true for Merton whose emptiness and lack of direction opened him up to God's fullness.

Can you think of any occasions when you learned something very important through mistakes or tragedy?

DOROTHY DAY

Many people believe that Dorothy Day was a saint, yet, unlike Thomas Merton, Dorothy desired not so much to be a saint as simply to place herself at the service of God by calling for a new order in society based on love and community. Like Merton, she was an unlikely instrument for God's use. She was born on November 8, 1897 into a family where religion was barely tolerated. Her father was a racetrack reporter who went from job to job and led his family around the country with him. Her mother was a docile, submissive woman of her times.

Dorothy was exceptionally bright and loved to read. She was a bit of a loner as a child and lost herself in books and ideas. When she attended the University of Illinois in Chicago she made friends with men and women who exposed her to the ideas of communism and revolution. The communist revolution was occurring in Russia, and Dorothy and her friends believed that this was the dawn of a new age of freedom and equality for the masses of common people. She moved back to New York and got a job as a reporter for a radical newspaper. The next ten years were ones of turmoil for her. She fell madly in love, only to have her heart broken. She married a man who made a mockery of their marriage, and she left him in Europe to return to America. She was broken-hearted, lonely and depressed, but she wrote a novel which did well enough for her to buy a home on Staten Island. She lived with a man who fathered her child, Tamara, but he was not interested in the child or in Dorothy's new interest in religion.

Dorothy decided to have her baby baptized into the Catholic faith, and she too entered the church in December 1927. She immersed herself in the faith, reading theology and spirituality, and also continued her social activism. The direction of her life took its most radical change when she met Peter Maurin. She believed that Peter was both a genius and a saint. He taught a philosophy of "personalism" and emphasized the dignity of all persons and the need to get to the roots of life's meaning. Inspired by Peter, she moved to the Bowery in New York City and began to work with the poor and to publish a newspaper called *The Catholic Worker*. She opened a house of hospitality where the homeless could live and be fed. Soon they opened a larger one, and others began to be attracted to their work. Volunteers began to arrive, and the work expanded. People who read the newspaper sent in donations, and by the time World War II began there were some forty houses of hospitality around the country.

Like Merton, Dorothy was led to God by a deep intellect and a continual restlessness which could not be filled by her political commitments and activism alone. She discovered for herself what Augustine had said so long ago, "You have made us for yourself, O God, and our hearts are restless until they rest in you." Dorothy's influence continues today as Catholic Worker houses throughout the country continue to minister to the poor and the homeless.

For Personal Reflection and Discussion

What passage in the gospel comes to mind when you hear of the life of Dorothy Day? How is she similar to and different from Merton?

OSCAR ROMERO

It has been said that some people are born to greatness while others have it thrust upon them. Oscar Romero probably belongs to the latter group. In order to understand Romero, it is necessary to understand the country and time in which he lived and died.

The church in Central and South America had often been associated with the wealthy and those in power since the development of these new world nations. To the poor multitudes it proclaimed a message of God's love and his ultimate reward in heaven. In the latter part of this century, all this began to change. The enormous gap between rich and poor, and the severe deprivation suffered by the poor, forced the church to face the fact that these injustices cried out to heaven for help. Rather than exhorting the poor to accept their lot, the church began to help the poor to recognize their dignity and human rights. Many church leaders began to live among the poor and organize them into small "base communities." These communities would read and reflect on the word of God in light of their situation of poverty. Often this would lead them to organize for their own rights.

Oscar Romero was born in El Salvador, a tiny country in Central America which experienced some of the severest poverty and injustice in the western hemisphere. Romero came from a "middle class" family and was given the traditional training for the priesthood. He was more inclined to theological ideas than he was to social justice. He was bright and was raised to the rank of auxiliary bishop and then, to the surprise of many, was appointed archbishop of El Salvador.

Meanwhile, human rights abuses in the country became more intense. The military "death squads" often tortured and killed anyone associated with the base communities and accused them of being communists. Although Romero spoke out in favor of justice, he failed to see the extent and depth of the persecutions suffered by the poor.

In 1977, the Jesuit priest Rutilio Grande was killed while on his way to say mass, and Oscar Romero's eyes were opened. He began to speak out harshly against the abuses of the military and became identified as the voice of the poor in El Salvador. He moved out of his home and lived among the poor and ministered to them. The church was now seen by many as a threat to the power of the military and the country itself. They were portrayed as communists, and pamphlets were spread with the slogan: "Be a patriot. Kill a priest."

Romero himself was a marked man. Yet he continued to speak out against the military which was slaughtering its own people. On March 24, 1980, Romero was shot through the heart while he celebrated mass. The words that he spoke in the homily that day, seconds before his death, reveal the meaning of his life united with the sacrifice of Christ.

> May this body immolated and this blood sacrificed for humans nourish us also, so that we may give our body and blood to suffering and to pain—like Christ, not for self, but to bring about justice and peace for our people.

For Personal Reflection and Discussion

Much of Romero's sanctity is rooted in a profound courage: a willingness to suffer even unto death for the sake of the poor and the message of the gospel. Can you think of a time when you were called upon to really stand up for what you believe in?

Questions for Review

1. What role does Mary play in our faith as the mother of God and the mother of the crucified?
2. What incident brought about Saul's conversion to Christianity? How had he lived previous to that conversion? What contributions did he make to the future of the church?
3. What type of person was Augustine before his conversion to Christianity? What was Augustine's great contribution to the church?
4. Who was Catherine of Siena and how did she dramatically affect the history of the church?
5. What was the inspiration of St. Francis of Assisi in serving the church? What brought about his conversion? How did his life change?
6. How was Thomas More different from Francis in the way that he lived his faith. What events led to More's eventual martyrdom?
7. How did the events of Thomas Merton's life help to shape his personality and his relationship to God?
8. Dorothy Day was a radical socialist. How did her political views influence the work that she did as a Christian?
9. Who was Oscar Romero and why is he a great hero of Christian faith?

Index

BEVERLY CLEARY

HENRY AND THE CLUBHOUSE

Illustrated by LOUIS DARLING

SCHOLASTIC INC.

New York Toronto London Auckland Sydney
Mexico City New Delhi Hong Kong Buenos Aires

ISBN 0-439-38596-2

12 11   4 5 6 /0

Printed in the U.S.A.   40

First Scholastic printing, November 2001

Table
of
Contents

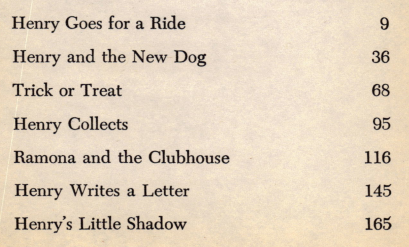

HENRY AND THE CLUBHOUSE

CHAPTER ONE

Henry Goes for a Ride

HENRY HUGGINS had a lot of good ideas that fall
when he first had his paper route, but somehow
his ideas had a way of not turning out as he had
planned. Something always went wrong.

There was, for example, that Saturday afternoon in October, when Henry found himself with
nothing to do until it was time to start delivering
Journals. Naturally he wandered into the kitchen

and opened the refrigerator to see what he could find. At the sound of the door opening, his dog Ribsy and his cat Nosy came running in case he should be planning to feed them.

"Henry, you just ate lunch," said Mrs. Huggins, who had washed her son's slacks and was now struggling to shove metal stretchers into the legs. "Can't you find something to do instead of opening the refrigerator every five minutes?"

"I'm thinking, Mom," answered Henry. He was thinking that he would like to build something, some kind of a house. A doghouse, a tree house or a clubhouse. A tree house would be pretty hard, but he was sure he could build a doghouse or a clubhouse. All he needed was lumber and nails.

"Well, think with the refrigerator door shut," suggested Mrs. Huggins with a smile. She had succeeded in stretching Henry's slacks and now she leaned them, tight on their frames, against the sink. "And *please* find something to do."

"O.K., Mom," said Henry, and walked out the
back door in search of something to keep him
busy. He considered. He could go over to the
Quimbys' house and play checkers with Beezus, a
girl whose real name was Beatrice, but her pesty
little sister Ramona would probably spoil the
game. He could go see if his friend Murph, who
was the smartest boy in the whole school, was
building anything interesting in his garage. Or he
could try to sell subscriptions to the *Journal.* That
was what he should do, but somehow Henry was
not anxious to start ringing strange doorbells. No,
what he really wanted to do was build something.
He decided to scout around Klickitat Street and
see if he could find enough boards for a doghouse.
That would be the easiest to build and would not
take much lumber.

As Henry walked around the side of his house,
he noticed his next-door neighbor's car parked on
the driveway with a U-Haul-It trailer attached.

Now that was interesting, thought Henry. What was Hector Grumbie going to haul?

The front door of the Grumbies' house opened, and Mr. Grumbie appeared to be coming out backwards. This was even more interesting. Why didn't Mr. Grumbie walk out frontwards? Bit by bit more of his neighbor appeared, and Henry saw that he was tugging at something.

Henry decided he had better investigate. From the Grumbies' front walk he discovered that Mr. Grumbie was pulling and Mrs. Grumbie was pushing a bathtub out of the house. They were sliding it across the floor on an old blanket.

Mr. Grumbie paused to wipe his forehead. "Whew!" he exclaimed. "These old bathtubs were built like battleships."

"May I help?" Henry asked eagerly. After all, his mother wanted him to find something to do.

"Sure," said Mr. Grumbie. "You can get on the other end and help push."

Henry ran up the steps, and because the bathtub was blocking the door, he climbed into it, out the other side, and joined Mrs. Grumbie in pushing.

Henry was secretly wondering, but was too polite to ask, if the Grumbies were planning to give up bathing. Instead he inquired, "What are you going to do with it?"

"Take it to the dump," answered Mr. Grumbie, "unless you would like to have it. We are remodeling the bathroom and have to get rid of it to make room for the new tub, which will be delivered Monday."

Henry thought it over. There were all sorts of interesting things he could do with a bathtub in his back yard. Wash his dog Ribsy in it, cool off in it himself on a hot day, bob for apples at Halloween. Build a clubhouse around it if he had that much lumber. All sorts of things. A bathtub in the yard would be much more fun than a tub in the bathroom, but Henry was sure his mother would not feel the same way about it.

"No, thank you, Mr. Grumbie," Henry said with regret and then he had a better idea. The new bathtub would come in a crate and perhaps Mr. Grumbie would let him have the boards to build a doghouse.

By that time several neighbors had come over to the Grumbies' to watch. Even Ribsy had taken an interest and had come down from the Huggins' doormat where he had been napping. Mr. Grumbie tied a rope around the tub and with the help of Henry and the bystanders who hung onto the rope, eased the tub, bump-bump-bump, down the front steps, slid it across the lawn, and then boosted it onto the trailer, where Mr. Grumbie tied it securely.

"Want to go for a ride to the dump?" Mr. Grumbie asked Henry.

The dump! Immediately Henry pictured a fascinating jumble of old bathtubs, washing machines, tires, and baby buggies. There was no telling what he might find at the dump. There might even be some old boards he could bring home.

"Can I ride in the bathtub?" he asked eagerly.

"Sure." Mr. Grumbie was agreeable. "Go ask your mother."

Henry ran to the open kitchen window. "Hey, Mom! Mr. Grumbie wants me to ride to the dump with him. Can I go?"

"All right, Henry." Mrs. Huggins' voice came through the window.

"Come on, Ribsy!" Henry bounded across the lawn and climbed into the bathtub. Ribsy scrambled in behind him.

"All set?" asked Mr. Grumbie, opening the door of his car.

"All set," answered Henry, and Mr. Grumbie maneuvered the car and trailer down the driveway and into the street.

Riding in a bathtub, which of course had no springs or upholstery, was bumpy, but Henry did not care. No one else in the neighborhood had ever gone for a ride in a bathtub. He shouted and waved to his friends Scooter and Robert, who were playing catch on the sidewalk. They stared after him in surprise. Ribsy put his paws on the edge of the tub and barked.

When Mr. Grumbie stopped at the first stop sign, Henry saw his friend Beezus and her little sister Ramona, who had a lot of string stuck to her chin with Scotch tape. Henry guessed she was trying to copy one of the many disguises of Sheriff Bud on television. Ramona never missed the Sheriff Bud program.

"Hi!" called Henry.

"Hello, Henry." Beezus looked with admiration

at Henry in the bathtub. He could tell she wished she could go for a ride in a bathtub too.

Ramona scowled ferociously and pointed straight at Henry. "Remember—only *you* can prevent forest fires."

Henry ignored Ramona. He knew she was only repeating what she had heard Smokey Bear say on television all summer. "So long!" he called to Beezus as Mr. Grumbie drove on.

Ribsy, tired of barking over the edge of the tub, curled up and tried to go to sleep, but whenever the trailer went over a bump, he lifted his head and looked annoyed. In the bathtub little bumps felt like big bumps. They rumbled and bumped down Klickitat Street to a main thoroughfare, and then Henry had an idea. He was the president of the United States riding in a parade! He sat up straight in the bathtub, nodding and waving and doffing an imaginary hat. Mr. Grumbie's car became a column of tanks preceding him down the

avenue, and one airplane in the sky became a formation of fighter planes overhead. Henry could practically hear the cheers of the throngs crowded along the curbs to watch his journey to the White House.

Henry did in fact hear a few real cheers, or perhaps jeers was a better word, mostly from boys along the way.

"Hey! Don't forget to wash your back!"

"Be careful! Don't step on the soap!"

With great dignity Henry nodded and waved. A great man on his way to the White House could afford to ignore such people, especially when he was surrounded by Secret Service men.

Henry was having too much fun to act dignified very long. He saw several boys standing in front of a bicycle shop and could not resist waving and shouting, "Hats off! The flag is passing by!"

"Boo!" yelled the boys. "Boo! Boo!" They held their noses and waved Henry on down the street.

Ribsy scrambled to his feet and barked over the edge of the tub. Henry, who was the kind of man who *would* take his dog to the White House, folded his arms and grinned in a superior manner, because he was riding in the bathtub and the boys were standing on the sidewalk. The afternoon had turned out better than he had expected, and he still had the dump to look forward to.

And then Henry passed a *Journal* truck heading in the opposite direction. Suddenly he was no longer president of the United States. He was no longer interested in lumber for a doghouse. He was plain Henry Huggins, a boy who had completely forgotten that he had forty-three papers to deliver this afternoon. This was terrible! If he did not get those papers delivered, his route might be taken away from him before he had had it a month. Then, because he was the youngest *Journal*

carrier in the neighborhood, Mr. Capper, who was
the district manager, and everyone else, would say
he was not old enough to handle a route. And that
would be about the worst thing that could possibly
happen. He would never live it down.

"Mr. Grumbie! Mr. Grumbie!" yelled Henry,
but Mr. Grumbie drove on down the street unaware that he was carrying his passenger farther
and farther from his paper route.

"Mr. Grumbie! Mr. Grumbie!" There was no
response but the bump and rattle of the trailer.
Henry was trapped in a bathtub in the middle of
Lombard Street. "Mr. Grumbie! Mr. Grumbie!"

At the next stop sign Henry stood up in the
bathtub and frantically waved both hands, hoping
to attract Mr. Grumbie's attention in the rear view
mirror.

It worked, because Mr. Grumbie stuck his head
out the window and called, "Something wrong
back there?"

"My route!" yelled Henry. "I forgot my paper route!"

The signal changed and cars and trucks began to honk. Mr. Grumbie, in the center lane of traffic, had to drive on.

Henry sat down with a bump. The Saturday afternoon traffic was heavy and it would be difficult for Mr. Grumbie to change lanes while pulling a trailer. They were still in the center lane when they came to the next stop sign.

"I'll pull over as soon as I can," Mr. Grumbie called back to Henry.

Henry now felt ridiculous sitting in the bathtub in the middle of a heavily traveled street. He wondered why he had thought riding in a tub would be fun in the first place. A boy who was old enough to have a paper route was too old to do such a silly thing. Cross street after cross street went by and Henry was carried farther and farther from his route. By this time the other boys were counting and folding their papers and Mr. Capper was probably wondering what had happened to Henry, the youngest carrier. Maybe Mr. Capper was already wondering what boy could take over Henry's route. Maybe he was saying to Scooter and the other boys, "I'm afraid Henry isn't old enough to handle a route. Do you know any older boy who could take his place?" It was not a happy prospect.

A gap appeared in the right-hand lane of traffic and Mr. Grumbie eased his car and the trailer into it. There was a solid line of cars parked along the curb, and no place to stop. Another block went by. Still there was no place where Mr. Grumbie could stop. Henry caught a glimpse of a clock inside a dry-cleaning shop. Four thirty-five. He would never get to the district manager's garage and get his papers folded and delivered by six o'clock.

Mr. Grumbie signaled and made a right turn into a service station. Henry, followed by Ribsy, scrambled out of the bathtub as Mr. Grumbie got out of his car.

"I'm sure sorry I forgot about my route," Henry apologized.

"What are we going to do about it?" asked Mr. Grumbie. "I can't turn around and take you home now, because the dump closes at five and I've got to get rid of this tub this week end. Besides, I am renting the trailer by the hour and I want to get it back as soon as I can."

"That's all right," said Henry. "I have enough money for bus fare."

"Do you know the way home?" asked Mr. Grumbie.

"Sure. I can catch the bus across the street and I know where to transfer to the other bus." Henry was eager to be on his way.

"O.K.," agreed Mr. Grumbie, and climbed back into his car.

"Wait!" yelled Henry as Mr. Grumbie started to drive off. "Ribsy! Can you take Ribsy with you? I can't take him on the bus."

Across the street a bus pulled up to the stop,

discharged a passenger and departed with a puff of exhaust.

"I guess so. Come on, pooch." Mr. Grumbie opened the rear door of his car and Henry shoved Ribsy inside and slammed the door. He knew from past experience that a dog was not allowed on a bus unless it was in a box tied shut. Henry had enough problems without searching for a box.

When Mr. Grumbie drove off, Henry waited for the traffic light to change from red to green before he crossed the street to the bus stop. He had just missed a bus, he knew, and as he wondered how long he would have to wait for the next bus, he fingered the change in the pocket of his jeans. Bus fare and a dime left over. Enough for one telephone call. Probably he should call one of the boys and ask him to go over to Mr. Capper's garage and start folding his papers for him. But which boy? He had only one dime. What if he called Robert's house and Robert's mother answered and said he wasn't home? His dime would be gone.

Henry decided to telephone his own house and ask his mother to call Robert or Murph for him. Once more Henry waited for the traffic signal to change, ran back across the street and into the glass telephone booth in the corner of the service station. He pushed his dime into the smallest hole, dialed, and counted four rings.

"Hello?" It was Mrs. Huggins.

"Say, Mom," began Henry, his eye on the bus stop, "my paper route sort of slipped my mind and I wondered if you would phone Robert or Murph or one of the fellows and ask them to fold my papers for me. I'll get there as soon as I can."

"Henry, where are you?" asked Mrs. Huggins.

"In a filling station out on Lombard Street," answered Henry.

"It is twenty minutes to five now." Mrs. Huggins sounded exasperated. "You'll never get your papers delivered on time."

"Mom, I can't stand here all day arguing,"

Henry pointed out as a bus pulled up to the curb. "Here's my bus now!"

"Honestly, Henry, sometimes I wonder—"

Henry had to cut his mother off.

The traffic signal changed to red just as Henry reached the curb. "Hey, Mr. Bus Driver!" Henry called frantically. The bus driver glanced at him and pulled out into the stream of traffic. He had a schedule to follow and could not wait for one boy. Henry groaned and then he discovered it was not even his bus.

When the signal changed to green Henry walked across the street. He had done all he could do to get his route started and there was no use worrying about it. But Henry did worry. He wondered if his mother was able to find a boy to fold his papers and what Mr. Capper would say when the boy folded Henry's *Journals*. Henry worried when the bus finally came. He worried while he rode on what seemed to be the slowest bus in the world. He worried when he got off and waited for the second bus. He worried when he had transferred to the second bus, which seemed even slower. If there was ever a contest to find the slowest bus in the world, this bus would win. A snail could beat it any day.

And then as the bus finally reached Henry's neighborhood and drove down one of the streets on which Henry should have been delivering papers that very minute, Henry saw a car exactly like the Huggins' car. In fact, it was the Huggins' car. Henry could tell, because he saw his mother get out and throw a folded *Journal* toward a house. She threw awkwardly. The paper did not go far enough so she picked it up and threw again. Henry was horrified. A boy did not want to see his mother delivering papers, especially when she was such a terrible thrower. It was awful. He did not see how anybody could grow up and throw that way.

Hastily Henry jerked the cord that stopped the

bus at the next corner. He bounded out of the door and ran back to Mrs. Huggins, who was consulting his route book to see where to throw the next paper. Henry could not help feeling that he had reached her in the nick of time. He did not want

the passengers on the bus to see her throw again.

"Hey, Mom," he panted. "How come you're delivering my papers?"

"There wasn't anyone else to do it," answered his mother. "I couldn't reach Robert or Murph so I drove over to Mr. Capper's and found the other carriers were leaving with their papers. I've delivered twenty-eight of them."

"Gee, Mom, did you *fold* my papers?" asked Henry. If she had she was better at folding than throwing.

"The other boys had already folded them for you," answered his mother. "They must have known you were going to be late."

Henry opened the car door and pulled out his bag of *Journals*. "I'll take over, Mom," he said, as he slipped the bag over his shoulders. "Thanks a lot. You saved my life."

"You're welcome," answered Mrs. Huggins and then added, "I guess," as she climbed into the car.

Henry had to know something. "What did Mr. Capper say?" he called after his mother.

"He just laughed and wanted to know if I was taking over your route," answered Mrs. Huggins.

Henry wished he had his bicycle. He could actually cover his route almost as fast on foot, but it was more fun to deliver papers on his bicycle. Because he was short for his age the bag of papers bumped against his legs when he went on foot. He walked up one driveway and down the next, remembering which customer wanted his paper left on the doormat and which one had warned him against breaking the geraniums in the flower box on the porch.

Henry walked as fast as he could and soon covered his route. He was late, he knew, but with luck no one would complain—and so far he had been lucky. There was no reason why he should not continue to be. He was tired and sweaty when he reached home, but he was cheerful. The papers were delivered, weren't they? That was all that mattered.

When Henry opened the front door he was surprised to see his father wearing a white shirt and a necktie. Mr. Huggins always wore a sport shirt around home. "Hi, Dad. How come you're all dressed up?" he asked.

"Because your mother had quite a day with one thing or another around here, and we are going to take her out to dinner for a change," said Mr. Huggins.

"Oh—maybe I had better get cleaned up." Henry was surprised at this change in routine. He hoped they would not go to a fancy place with cloth napkins and a long menu. When he went out to dinner he liked to order a hamburger and pie.

"Well, Henry!" Mr. Huggins sounded stern. "Don't you have anything to say for yourself?"

"Why . . . uh . . . I finally got the papers delivered," answered Henry, not quite certain what his father expected of him.

"It seems to me your mother also delivered quite a few papers," said Mr. Huggins.

"Yeah, and golly, Dad, you should see her throw," confided Henry, demonstrating to his father the way his mother delivered papers. "It is pretty awful."

"Henry, I want one thing clearly understood," said Mr. Huggins, ignoring his son's remark. "That paper route is yours. It is not your mother's route and it is not my route. You are to deliver the papers and collect the money and do all the work yourself, and if you can't do it without any help from us, you will have to give the route to someone else. Do you understand?"

Henry looked at the carpet. His father did not often speak to him this way, and he felt terrible. He wanted his father to be proud of him because he was the youngest paper carrier in the neighborhood. "Yes, Dad," he answered. He felt he should offer some explanation for forgetting his route. "I was planning to get some old boards to build a doghouse."

Mr. Huggins grinned. "You don't need to build a doghouse. You're in a doghouse with your mother already."

Mrs. Huggins came clicking into the room on high heels. Henry caught a whiff of perfume and noticed she was wearing one of her best dresses, which meant a restaurant with cloth napkins. She looked so nice Henry felt ashamed of himself for criticizing the way she threw and for wanting a hamburger for dinner. "Gee, Mom, I'm sorry I caused you so much trouble," he said. "It just seemed like such a good chance to go for a ride in a bathtub that I just—well, I forgot all about my route."

"In a bathtub!" exclaimed Mrs. Huggins.

"Sure. Didn't you know? Mr. Grumbie had this old bathtub he was hauling to the dump on a trailer."

"A bathtub! I had no idea—" Mrs. Huggins sat down and began to laugh. "You mean you were riding down Lombard Street in a bathtub?"

"You told me to find something to do," Henry pointed out.

"Yes, I know I did," admitted Mrs. Huggins, "but riding around town in a bathtub wasn't exactly what I had in mind. Honestly, Henry, sometimes I wonder how you get into these things."

"I don't know, Mom, I just do," said Henry thinking with regret of the good idea that had somehow gone wrong. He knew one thing for sure. If he was going to keep his paper route he had better not get into things. He had better keep out of things—especially late in the afternoon.

CHAPTER TWO

Henry and the New Dog

HENRY soon found that there was not enough wood in a bathtub crate to build a really good doghouse. As he rode around the neighborhood delivering papers, he kept his eye out for any old boxes or packing cases that he could use. There was one empty house in the neighborhood which he passed every day hoping he would get some packing cases from the new owners, but the house remained empty. Wood was so scarce that he was about to give up the idea of a house for Ribsy when he had an unexpected piece of luck.

Most of the houses in Henry's neighborhood had been built way back in the nineteen-twenties when cars were shorter and narrower than they are today. Now many people were finding their new cars too long for their old garages and so they built box-like additions onto the ends of their garages to make them long enough for their cars.

One neighbor, Mr. Bingham, was not so fortunate. When he proudly drove his new car into his garage he found there was no way for him to get out of it. His garage was so narrow he could not open the door of his car. So poor Mr. Bingham backed out and parked his car on the driveway. All the neighbors on Klickitat Street had a good laugh over this, and Mr. Bingham announced that he was going to tear down his old garage and build a larger one.

As soon as Mr. Bingham began to tear down the garage, Henry rode his bicycle over to his house to ask if he could have some of the old lumber.

"Sure, Henry, help yourself," said Mr. Bingham, who was prying at a board with a crowbar. "Take all you want but get it out of here before Saturday, when the truck comes to haul it away."

"O.K., Mr. Bingham," agreed Henry. "Do you want to get rid of the windows, too?"

"Take anything you want," said Mr. Bingham. Doghouse! Why, there would be enough lumber for a clubhouse, a clubhouse with windows and a good one, too. He would save up his paperroute money and buy one of those down-filled sleeping bags he had seen in the window of the sporting goods store and sleep out in the clubhouse he would build out of all the secondhand lumber.

Now Henry found himself with more to do than he had time for. He could not neglect his paper

route, so he saw that he would have to have help.
He told his friends Robert and Murph about the
free lumber and they saw the point at once.

"Sure, we'll help," they both said. The boys bor-
rowed wagons and every afternoon between
school and paper-route time they hauled lumber
from Mr. Bingham's driveway to the Huggins'
back yard. When Henry left to fold his papers,
Robert and Murph went on hauling. By Saturday
the boys were sure they had enough lumber for a
clubhouse.

"Let's start building," said Henry eagerly.

"Nope," said Murph. "When you build a house,
you've got to have a plan. You can't build it any
old way."

"Aw, Murph," said Robert. "Where are we
going to get a plan?"

Henry, too, was skeptical. He thought that any
old way was the only way to build a clubhouse.
"Yes, where are we going to get a plan?"

"I can draw one," said Murph. "I'll do it this week end. But remember, when we get the clubhouse built, no girls allowed."

"No girls allowed," vowed Henry and Robert.

"And when we get it built, we can sleep in it in our sleeping bags," added Henry, thinking to himself, when I get a sleeping bag. The boys agreed this was the thing to do with a clubhouse.

Mrs. Huggins looked at the old lumber in her yard and said, "My goodness, Henry, isn't that a lot of lumber?"

"Don't worry, Mom," Henry assured her. "The clubhouse will be real neat when we get it finished and I'll saw up the leftover boards for kindling."

Mr. Huggins looked at the old lumber. "I don't know about this, Henry. It looks to me as if you have taken on a pretty big job."

"The three of us can do it, Dad," said Henry, eager for his father's approval. "And I won't let it interfere with my paper route. Cross my heart."

"See that you don't," said Mr. Huggins. "If you can't handle them both you'll either have to give up your route or tear down the clubhouse."

That week end Murph, who was the smartest boy in the whole school and practically a genius, did draw a plan. He drew it on squared paper, each square equaling one foot. Henry was pretty impressed when he saw it and realized that Murph had been right. It would not do to build a clubhouse any old way.

Murph would not hear of building the clubhouse directly on the ground. "We don't want termites eating our clubhouse," he said.

Henry agreed that it would not do to have bugs chewing away at their clubhouse. This meant the boys had to buy some Kwik-Mix concrete and make four cement blocks for their clubhouse to rest on. It was soon plain to Henry that there was more to building a clubhouse than he had realized and that it was going to take a lot of time—time that he was not sure he had to spare because of his paper route. However, he could not back out now that Robert and Murph had already worked so hard on their new project.

Then one afternoon when Henry was folding his *Journals* on Mr. Capper's driveway with the other paper carriers, Scooter McCarthy spoke. "Say, Mr. Capper, I will be needing one more paper after this," he said.

"Is that so?" Mr. Capper sounded interested. "A new subscriber?"

"That's right, Mr. Capper." Scooter quite plainly was pleased with himself for having sold a subscription.

Henry suddenly pretended to be interested in a headline in the paper he was folding, because he hoped that if he did not look at Mr. Capper, Mr. Capper might not look at him. Henry was ashamed, because it was already October and he had not sold a single *Journal* subscription. Not that

he hadn't tried—a little bit. He really had rung
several strange doorbells before he became interested in the clubhouse, and had tried to sell subscriptions, but the results were discouraging.
Strangers had a way of listening to his sales talk
about the *Journal's* easy-to-read type with amused
smiles and then saying, "No thank you." One man
interrupted with a brusque "Not today" and closed
the door in Henry's face. A lady embarrassed him
by telling him what a splendid little salesman he
was and then saying she couldn't afford to take
another paper. Splendid *little* salesman! That was
the last straw. After that Henry found it easy to
think up excuses for not trying to sell new
subscriptions.

Now Mr. Capper was saying, "Good for you,
Scooter. Suppose you tell us how you went about
selling the subscription."

"Aw, it was easy," boasted Scooter, stuffing his
folded papers into his canvas bag. "I just told this

man what a good paper the *Journal* was and he said he didn't have time to read it, because he went fishing every Sunday and I said, 'You could use it to wrap your fish eggs in,' and he laughed and said O.K., put him down for a subscription, so I did."

"I call that quick thinking on your part, Scooter," said Mr. Capper. "The rest of the boys could take a lesson from you."

Out of the corner of his eye Henry could see Mr. Capper looking around the group of boys. "What about you, Henry?" asked Mr. Capper. "You haven't turned in any subscriptions since you have had your route."

"Well . . . I—I have been trying," Henry said, admitting to himself that he really had not tried very hard. He had been much too busy with the clubhouse.

"I know it's hard to get started sometimes," said Mr. Capper sympathetically. "I'll tell you what you do. The other day I saw a *Sold* sign on a house on your route. When the new owners move in, you march right up to that front door, ring the doorbell, and sell them a subscription to the paper."

"Yes, sir." Mr. Capper made it sound so easy— march right up and sell them a subscription, just like that. "I'll try, Mr. Capper," said Henry, who knew the house the district manager was referring to. It was the house where he had once hoped to get enough old boxes to build a doghouse. It seemed a long time ago.

And so each day, as Henry delivered his papers, he watched for the new owners to move into the empty house. When he finally did see packing crates and empty cartons stacked on the driveway he decided he should give the people a little time, say about a week, to get settled before he marched right up and rang that doorbell.

The next afternoon Mr. Capper said, "Well, Henry, I see the new owners have moved into the empty house."

"I am going over today as soon as I finish my route," promised Henry, knowing he could not put off the task any longer.

When Henry had delivered his last paper he hung his canvas bag in the garage, washed his hands, combed his hair and, followed by Ribsy, walked the two blocks to call on the new neighbors. He did not ride his bicycle, because it seemed more businesslike to go on foot. Fuller Brush men did not ride bicycles.

As he approached the house he whispered to himself some of the things he planned to say. "Good afternoon. I am Henry Huggins, your *Journal* newsboy. I deliver the *Journal* to a lot of your neighbors." That much he was sure of, but he did not know what to say next. Find a selling point, Mr. Capper always said. Talk about some part of

the paper that would interest a new subscriber.

Henry walked more and more slowly. Ribsy finally had to sit down and wait for him to catch up. The *Journal* had a good sports section . . . a good church section. . . . How was Henry supposed to know what would interest a new subscriber? What if he told someone about the church section when all he wanted was to read the funny papers?

But before Henry could decide what to say, he met Beezus and her little sister Ramona. Ramona

was wearing a loop of string around her neck. The
ends of the string were fastened with Scotch tape
to a cardboard tube.

"Hi," said Henry to Beezus. "What are you
doing?"

"Keeping Ramona away from the television set,"
answered Beezus. "Mother says she spends too
much time in front of it."

"Ask me my name," Ramona ordered Henry.

Henry could feel no enthusiasm at all for this
new game of Ramona's. "What's your name?" he
asked in a bored voice rather than risk Ramona's
having a tantrum because he would not play.

Ramona held the paper tube in front of her
mouth. "My name is Danny Fitzsimmons," she
answered, looking down at the sidewalk and smiling in a self-conscious way that was not at all like
Ramona.

"It is not," contradicted Henry. "You aren't even
a boy."

"She's just pretending she's being interviewed
on the Sheriff Bud program," explained Beezus.
"That's her microphone she's holding."

"Oh," was all Henry could find to say.

"My name is Danny Fitzsimmons," repeated
Ramona, smiling shyly in an un-Ramona-like way,
"and I want to say hello to my mommy and my
daddy and my sister Vicki, who is having a birthday, and Mrs. Richards, who is my kindergarten
teacher, and Lisa Kelly, who is my best friend, and
Gloria Lofton, whose cat just had kittens and she
might give me one, and her dog Skipper and all the
boys and girls in my kindergarten class and all the
boys and girls at Glenwood Primary School and
Georgie Bacon's sister Angela, but I won't say
hello to Georgie, because I don't like him, and . . ."

"Oh, for Pete's sake." Henry was disgusted with
Ramona's new game. "Why don't you just say
hello to the whole world and be done with it?" He
had no time for this sort of thing. He was on his

ay to sell a *Journal* subscription and get back to the clubhouse. "So long, Beezus," he said.

". . . and Bobby Brogden who has a loose tooth . . ." Ramona was saying as Henry went on down the street.

When Henry came to the house that was his destination, he turned to Ribsy and said, "Sit," not because he expected Ribsy to sit, but because he wanted to put off ringing that doorbell a little longer. He had not decided what to use as a selling point, because he could not even guess what might interest a new neighbor.

Ribsy sat a moment and then got up and sniffed at the shrubbery.

"I said 'Sit,' " Henry told his dog, deciding that it would be a good idea if Ribsy really did sit. Some people were very particular about dogs running through their flowers and he was anxious to make a good impression.

Like the good dog he was, part of the time, Ribsy sat once more, but he did not stay seated. He stood up and wagged his tail.

"Sit!" ordered Henry sternly, as he started up the steps.

Ribsy appeared to think it over.

"Sit!" Henry raised his voice.

Ribsy waved his tail as if to say, Do I really have to?

A strange dog, a Dalmatian, came trotting around the house and began to investigate Ribsy. The dogs sidled around one another, sniffing. Henry did not pay much attention. Dogs who were strangers to one another always did this.

Next a woman who was wearing an apron, and had a smudge of dust on her cheek, appeared on the driveway at the side of the house. She was older than Henry's mother. Probably she was old enough to be a grandmother. Before Henry had a chance to speak, the Dalmatian left Ribsy and frolicked over to his owner. Ribsy, an agreeable dog who was ready to play, followed.

That was Ribsy's mistake. Now he was trespassing on the Dalmatian's territory. The Dalmatian began to growl deep in his throat and to hold his whiplike tail stiff and straight.

Ribsy stopped short. This was his neighborhood. He was here first. It was the Dalmatian who was trespassing. Each dog began to resent the other's looks, sound, and smell.

"Ribsy!" Henry spoke sharply.

"Ranger!" The woman spoke sharply, too.

The dogs paid no attention to their owners. Each was too intent on letting the other know exactly what he thought of him. The growls grew louder and deeper and they raised their lips and bared their teeth as if they were sneering at each other. And just who do you think you are, Ribsy's growl seemed to say.

I have just as much right here as you have, Ranger's growl answered.

No, you don't, said Ribsy. I was here first.

I'm bigger, growled Ranger.

You're a bully, growled Ribsy.

Get off my property, Ranger told Ribsy.

You make me, Ribsy told Ranger.

"Cut it out, both of you," ordered Henry.

Planning to grab Ribsy's collar and drag him away, Henry jumped down from the steps to the lawn just as the growls erupted into snarls and the dogs went for each other's throat.

"Ranger!" shrieked the woman.

"Ribsy!" shouted Henry. The dogs were on one another in a twisting, tumbling tangle that seemed to be made up of feet, fangs, and tails.

Henry ran over to the snarling, yelping pair and just as he was about to grab Ribsy's collar, he found the other dog's mouth in front of his hand. Quickly he drew back. He saw that he could not stop the fight and since he could not, he wanted Ribsy to win. If it had not been so important for him to sell a *Journal* subscription he would have yelled, "Go get 'im, Ribsy."

"Look out!" shouted the woman. "Don't let him bite you!"

Neighbors began to gather on the sidewalk to watch the excitement. "Dog fight! Dog fight!" a boy yelled.

"The hose!" shouted someone. "Turn the hose on them!"

"I can't," cried the new neighbor. "I don't know where it is!"

"Hey, look at old Ribsy," said Scooter, who had ridden over on his bicycle to see what all the noise was about. "Go get him, Ribsy!"

"You keep quiet!" ordered Henry, even though he wanted to cheer his own dog on.

"Aw, your old mutt couldn't lick a Chihuahua," scoffed Scooter.

"He could, too," said Henry hotly. He wasn't at

all sure Ribsy could lick a Dalmatian, but he could lick a Chihuahua. Henry was positive of that.

"Who's winning?" asked Robert, who had just arrived, along with Beezus and her little sister Ramona.

"The new dog," answered Scooter, and rode on down the street as if the fight was already over.

Half-afraid that Scooter might be right, because the new dog was both bigger and younger than Ribsy, Henry tried once more to reach into the snarling, rolling mass of dog to grab Ribsy's collar. He did not have a chance.

A man grabbed Henry by the arm and pulled him away. "Don't you know that's a foolish thing to do?" he demanded. "Those dogs might bite you."

"Yes, but he's my dog," Henry tried to explain. "I don't want him to get hurt."

The next-door neighbor was screwing the garden hose to the faucet. He turned on the water and advanced toward the dogs with the gushing nozzle in hand. "Stand back, everybody!" he yelled and turned the full force of the hose on the dogs.

Water sprayed in all directions. Still the dogs snarled and snapped. The man with the hose moved closer, so that the force of the hose was stronger. The stream of water caught Ribsy right

in the face and blinded him for the moment. This gave Ranger the advantage. He seized Ribsy by the scruff of the neck, and though Ribsy was a medium-sized dog, Ranger began to shake him. The man turned the hose in Ranger's face.

Ribsy wrenched free and ran dripping down the

street with his tail between his legs, *ki-yi*-ing all the way. The Dalmatian was after him in a flash of black and white.

Henry did not know what to do—whether to run after Ribsy and try to rescue him, or to stay and tell the woman he was sorry his dog got into a fight with her dog, even though it was her dog that started it all. He also wondered what Mr. Capper would think of all this. A fine job of marching right up and ringing that doorbell this had turned out to be.

Before Henry had a chance to decide what to do, Ranger came trotting back down the street looking much pleased with himself. In the next block Ribsy could be heard *ki-yi*-ing toward home.

"Bad dog!" said Ranger's owner, shaking her finger at her pet.

Ranger shook himself with a great clatter of license tags. He did not look one bit sorry. Instead, he looked disapprovingly at Henry, who felt it was wise to retreat to the sidewalk. Ranger walked to the foot of the steps, flopped down, and looked around as if to say, I am monarch of all I survey.

Henry was still trying to collect his thoughts and say something. How had he planned to begin his sales talk? I am Henry Huggins, your *Journal* carrier, but what came next? Ribsy's *ki-yi*-ing in the distance did not help Henry to think.

Before Henry said anything, Ramona passed him and walked right up to Ranger's owner. "Are you the new lady?" asked Ramona.

"Why yes, I am, dear," answered the woman, pleased to have a little girl making friends with her so soon after she had moved into a strange neighborhood.

For once Henry was glad to see Ramona. If she talked to the lady a minute he would have a chance to think of his sales talk once more.

Ramona looked straight at the new neighbor. "Remember," she said with a ferocious frown as

she pointed her finger, "only *you* can prevent forest fires!"

Henry groaned to himself.

The lady looked startled. She had no answer for Ramona.

Beezus ran up to Ramona and grabbed her by the hand. "Don't pay any attention to her," she said apologetically. "She says that to everybody because she hears it on T.V. so much. You know,

Smokey Bear comes on and says it between commercials."

"Oh . . . yes." The lady did not look as if she understood at all. Perhaps she did not own a television set.

"Come on, Ramona." Beezus tugged at her sister's hand.

This was too much. Henry felt the only thing he could do was leave. First his dog got into a fight with the lady's dog and now the little sister of a friend of his practically accused the woman of going around setting forest fires. This was no time to sell a subscription. "I'm sorry about the fight," he blurted and left quickly, followed by Beezus, who was pulling Ramona along by her hand.

"Remember—only *you* can prevent forest fires!" Ramona shouted back to the lady.

That Ramona, thought Henry crossly. She was only five years old but she was the biggest pest in the neighborhood. At the corner Henry paused to glance back. The woman was nowhere in sight but Ranger was sitting on the front porch as if he was standing guard. It seemed to Henry that the dog was challenging him to set foot on his property. Just go ahead and try it, he seemed to say. Go on, I dare you.

To Henry's surprise Mr. Capper did not ask the next day if Henry had sold a newspaper subscription to the new neighbors, and Henry suspected Mr. Capper wanted him to bring up the matter. He didn't see how he could come right out and say, "I didn't get that subscription, because the new neighbor's dog didn't like my dog." Henry made up his mind that since he left Ribsy at home while he delivered papers, he would stop on his route this very afternoon and sell that subscription. By that time Ramona would be home watching television, so she could not spoil his sale a second time.

When all his papers were folded and stuffed

into the canvas bag, Henry mounted his bicycle and zigzagged down the street pitching *Journals* right and left. He was wearing a different T shirt today and he hoped the new lady might have been so busy watching the dog fight that perhaps she hadn't noticed what he looked like. "Good afternoon," he whispered to himself. "I am Henry Huggins, your *Journal* carrier. . . ."

When Henry came to the house he saw Ranger resting on the front porch, his nose on his paws, his eyes watchful. "Hi, Ranger," said Henry, in his most friendly manner.

Ranger's answer was to jump to his feet, barking furiously and leap down the steps after Henry.

There was nothing for Henry to do but pedal down the street as fast as he could go, with the dog snarling and snapping at his right foot every time he pushed down on the pedal. Never had Henry ridden a bicycle so fast. By the time he reached the corner he could no longer breathe in all the air he really needed to keep him going, and each time he bore down on the pedal he expected to lose a piece of his jeans or maybe even a piece of his foot.

By the middle of the next block Ranger suddenly stopped chasing Henry, turned around, and trotted toward home with an air of having done his duty. It seemed to Henry that the dog was not even out of breath.

Henry came to a stop, sat on his bicycle, and panted. Boy! That was close, but the worst of it was that Henry still had to deliver the papers in Ranger's block. When he had caught his breath he parked his bicycle against a tree and returned on foot very, very quietly, being careful to keep out of Ranger's sight. He did not throw the papers. He laid them silently on the lawns and tiptoed away so that he would not disturb Ranger. He had cured Ribsy from running off with newspapers by squirting a water pistol at him every time he went near a paper, but Ribsy was a good-natured dog. Henry did not think he would care to pause long enough to aim at Ranger. He might lose a leg while he aimed. He would like to see Mr. Capper march right up and ring that doorbell. He would have to wear a suit of armor. Or maybe even ride in a tank.

And each time Henry silently laid a paper on a lawn he became a little more angry. He had just as much right around here as that old Ranger. More, because he had lived here longer. And he was a human being, not a dog. By the time Henry had finished delivering the papers in Ranger's block he was just plain mad. He wasn't going to be pushed around by any old dog. No, sir! He was going to get that subscription if it was the last thing he did.

And remembering Ranger's speed and his sharp white teeth, Henry felt that getting that subscription might very well be the last thing he did.

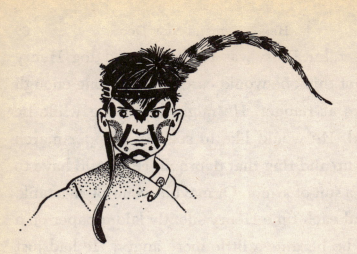

CHAPTER THREE

Trick or Treat

HENRY HUGGINS was sure that this year he had thought up a better Halloween costume than anyone else in his neighborhood. No tramp or clown suit—not for Henry. He had thought up something different, something that no one else would think of in a million years.

There was just one flaw in Henry's anticipation of Halloween. He still had not sold the new neighbor a *Journal* subscription and although Mr. Capper had not mentioned the matter, Henry knew the district manager was waiting for him to say something about it. But what could Henry say? Every time he tried to approach the house Ranger chased him away. How the other *Journal* carriers, especially those in the eighth grade and high school, would laugh at that!

Henry was particularly worried because his father knew Mr. Capper, and if the two men happened to run into each other, Mr. Huggins would probably say, "How's Henry getting along with his route?" and Mr. Capper would answer, "He delivers the papers all right, but he's a terrible salesman." Mr. Capper always said there were three parts to a carrier's job: delivering, collecting, and selling. Then his father would say, "No more work on the clubhouse." He might even tell the boys to tear down the frame which they had so carefully built.

After supper on Halloween Henry tried to shove all this to the back of his mind. It was time to get ready to go trick-or-treating, a time for fun, not a time to think about his troubles. Henry went to his room and shut the door. He got out a bottle of ink (washable, it said on the label and he hoped the label knew what it was talking about) and an old lipstick of his mother's. He went to work and applied war paint to his face. When he finished he did not need a Halloween mask from the dime store like the ones the rest of the boys and girls would wear. No one would guess it was Henry Huggins under the lines and circles he had drawn on his face. Then he fastened an old belt around his head and through it stuck a feather from one of his mother's old hats. Next he draped an Indian blanket around his shoulders and fastened it with safety pins—lots of them. He needed his hands free to carry the paper bag for all the treats he would collect that evening.

Henry studied himself in the mirror and was pleased with what he saw—a fierce Indian that no one would ever guess was really Henry Huggins. But the best part of his costume was still to come. Henry opened his bedroom door. "Here, Ribsy," he called. "Come on, boy!"

Obediently Ribsy trotted down the hall and into Henry's bedroom. Henry opened a bureau drawer and took out a rubber wolf mask which he slipped over Ribsy's head. There! His costume was complete. He was now an Indian accompanied by a wolf, a funny-looking black-and-white-and-brown spotted wolf, it was true, but from the neck up Ribsy was a wolfish-looking wolf with long white fangs and a bright red tongue.

It would certainly be lucky for Henry if he and Ribsy happened to meet Ranger. Boy, old Ranger would take one look at Ribsy-the-wolf and practically turn a backward somersault he would be so surprised and scared. Then he would tuck his tail between his legs and run for home as fast as he could go with Ribsy-the-wolf right after him. By the time Ribsy got through with him, old Ranger would have learned which dog was boss around this neighborhood.

Unfortunately, as was so often the case, this good idea of Henry's had a flaw. With a rubber mask over his head Ribsy would not have a chance

if he got into a dog-fight because he would not be able to bite back. With Ranger he probably would not have a chance *without* a mask. It would be wisest for Henry to stay away from the new neighbor's house that evening. He did not mind. Halloween was no time to sell a newspaper subscription.

Ribsy sat down and scratched.

"Hey, cut that out!" ordered Henry. "You'll tear the mask."

Henry went out to show off his costume to his mother and father. Mr. Huggins laughed and Mrs. Huggins pretended to be frightened at seeing an Indian and a wolf in the house. Nosy, the cat, was really frightened. He fluffed up his tail and jumped to the back of the couch, where he arched his back and kept a wary eye on the wolf.

"Do you think Ribsy is going to stand for that mask very long?" asked Mr. Huggins.

"I think so," said Henry as he opened the front

door. "We've practiced in my room every day this week. When I finished my route I came home and put the mask on him. He seemed sort of puzzled at first, but he's used to it now. I held him up so he could see himself in the mirror, and I think he likes it."

It was a perfect night for Halloween. The stars were bright and a north wind sent leaves skittering along the pavement. Jack-o'-lanterns grinned in front windows. Bands of boys and girls, some of them wearing costumes that glowed in the dark, trooped from door to door. Mothers of small children lurked in the shrubbery, while their little rabbits or ghosts climbed steps and rang doorbells. Henry felt so good he did a war dance in the middle of his front lawn before he started down the street.

Before Henry had had time to ring a doorbell, he met a boy wearing a green cardboard head intended to look like the head of a man from outer space. Suddenly the outer space man's eyes lit up in a fiendish and scary way that made Henry suspect his friend Murph must be inside. Murph was the only boy in the neighborhood who knew enough about electricity to think up such a costume.

Henry raised his hand in an Indian salute. "How," he said, carefully disguising his voice.

Silently the space man held out his hand. Henry grasped it. "Yipe!" he yelled, in his own voice, because he was grasping a buzzer that Murph held in the palm of his hand.

Murph laughed. "I thought it was you under that war paint." He leaned over and patted Ribsy. "Hiya, wolf," he said. "I knew who you were by your spots."

Together the boys proceeded down Klickitat Street ringing doorbells and shouting, "Trick or treat!" Everyone laughed at Ribsy's costume and gave Henry an extra treat for his wolf. Gradually

their bags grew fat with candy, peanuts, popcorn balls, individual boxes of raisins, apples, and
bubble gum. The boys no longer stopped at every
house. They compared notes with other trick-or-
treaters and soon learned which people gave jelly
beans or all-day suckers. These houses they
skipped. They did not like jelly beans and Henry
felt that a boy who had a paper route was too
grown-up to lick a sucker.

At one house which was completely dark, Henry
and Murph hesitated. "Should we bother?" asked
Henry. "It doesn't look as if the Morgans are
home."

"We might as well skip it," said Murph, and just
then a car turned into the driveway and drove into
the garage. The headlights revealed a garage clut-
tered with tools and boxes, and decorated with a
collection of old license plates. On a shelf at the
back a stuffed owl with wings outstretched and

claws poised for attack stared glassily into the night.

"Come on," said Henry, as Mrs. Morgan got out of the car. "She's got a lot of bags in back. Maybe she just bought something good at the market."

The two boys and Ribsy walked up the driveway. "Trick or treat!" shouted Henry and Murph. Murph pressed the button that lit up his outer space head.

"Oh, my goodness!" Mrs. Morgan exclaimed, turning around. "An Indian and a man from space. And a wolf! You certainly startled me." Then she hesitated. "Well . . . I'm afraid you will have to go ahead and play a trick." She peered into the paper bags in the back seat. "I've just come from the market, but all I bought was detergent and coffee and cat food and some things for breakfast. I don't have a thing to treat you with."

This was awkward. Henry could not recall a

Halloween when he had not been treated by everyone. Why, some of the younger children in the neighborhood did not know that trick or treat meant they were supposed to play a trick if they were not given a treat. Neither Henry nor Murph was prepared to play a trick. They had not even brought a piece of soap for soaping windows.

"Aw, that's all right, Mrs. Morgan," said Henry. After all, she was a very nice lady, and one of his *Journal* customers.

"Why, it's Henry Huggins!" exclaimed Mrs. Morgan. "I didn't recognize you in all that war paint."

Naturally Henry was pleased that his neighbor had not penetrated his disguise. "That's a keen owl you have there," he remarked. "It's real fierce-looking, as if it was about to catch an animal or something."

"It's a great horned owl," said Murph, whose

head was full of information like this. "Those license plates go all the way back to 1929."

"Mr. Morgan always nails the old plates on the wall every time he gets a new one." Mrs. Morgan followed Henry's eyes to the owl. "Henry—since I don't have a treat for you, how would you like to have the owl?" she asked, as if she had just had an inspiration.

"Gee, Mrs. Morgan . . ." Henry was almost speechless, he was so busy considering the possibilities of a stuffed owl. In his room on his chest of drawers . . . or in the clubhouse. That was it! In the clubhouse. A stuffed owl was exactly what they needed for a finishing touch. "Gee, could I really have it?"

"Certainly," said Mrs. Morgan. "You boys just climb up on that apple box and lift it down."

The boys quickly obeyed before Mrs. Morgan could change her mind. Henry could scarcely believe his good fortune. The owl was at least five feet from wing tip to wing tip. Why, this was better than all the peanuts and popcorn balls in the world. "Thanks, Mrs. Morgan," said Henry. "Thanks a lot."

"Oh, don't thank me," said Mrs. Morgan. "I've been looking for a way to get rid of that thing for years. It's too big to go into the garbage can, and the Goodwill refused to take it."

"Are you going to put it in the clubhouse?" asked Murph, when the boys had left Mrs. Morgan's garage.

"Sure," said Henry. "Then we can call it a hunting lodge."

"Nobody hunts owls," Murph pointed out.

Henry could see no reason for continuing the rounds of the neighborhood. Nothing he would get could possibly be as good as a stuffed owl. Besides, carrying his paper bag and lugging his owl, which was an awkward size and shape, did not leave him a free hand for ringing doorbells.

On their way home Henry and Murph met a gypsy and a small red devil who turned out to be Beezus and—appropriately, Henry felt—Ramona. They were carrying a jack-o'-lantern that had been carved too long before Halloween. Now its lips were shriveled and there was a smell of cooking pumpkin in the air.

"A stuffed owl!" exclaimed Beezus. "How spooky! What are you going to do with it?"

"Put it in the clubhouse," said Henry, "but no girls are allowed." Henry really would not have minded Beezus' visiting the clubhouse, but Murph had been firm from the beginning. No girls allowed. And perhaps Murph was right. A boy who was in the business of delivering papers was too old to play with girls.

Before Beezus could answer, Ramona held up

her paper bag. "We each got a Nutsie," she said
and began to recite. "Nutsies give both children
and adults quick energy. Avoid that mid-afternoon
slump with a Nutsie, chock-full of protein-rich
nuts!"

"Jeepers," said Henry. "What does she do? Memorize commercials?"

"Oh, Ramona," said Beezus impatiently, "stop reciting commercials. You don't have to believe things just because you hear them on T.V." Then she turned to Henry and Murph. "Stay away from that house on the corner," she advised. "When we said, 'Trick or treat' they said they would like to see us do a trick for them and why didn't we sing a little song. I guess they don't understand about Halloween."

"I sang a little song," boasted Ramona, twitching her red devil's tail. "I sang 'Crispy Potato Chips are the best, North or South, East or West, Crispy Chips, hooray, hooray! Get your Crispy Chips today.'"

"And the people thought it was cute," said Beezus crossly. "They asked her to do it again each time."

"It's a nice song," said Ramona. "I like it."

While they were standing under the street light, Scooter McCarthy appeared out of the darkness. He was wearing his father's old Marine uniform, without even a mask, and was licking a candy apple. "Hey, where did you get the owl?" he asked.

"Mrs. Morgan," answered Henry, who suspected Scooter of wanting to let everyone know that his father had been a Marine.

Scooter looked closer. "Sort of beat-up, but not bad," he conceded.

"Where did you get the candy apple?" asked Murph.

"That house where the people moved in last week."

"What are we waiting for?" Murph asked Henry. "Come on, let's get some candy apples."

"Oh . . . I don't know." Henry did not think he cared to meet Ranger when he was wearing an Indian blanket and carrying a stuffed owl. He might trip if he tried to run. There was Ribsy to think of, too. Henry did not want his dog to get in another fight with Ranger.

"Henry is scared of their dog," said Scooter.

"I am not!" said Henry indignantly.

"Then why do you let him chase you every day?" asked Scooter.

Henry wondered how Scooter knew about this. "Come on, Murph, let's go ring the new lady's doorbell." Henry spoke with more assurance than he felt. He only hoped that the dog would feel more friendly toward him when he was not delivering papers and perhaps would not even recognize him in his war paint. Ranger would probably be in the house and, anyway, Henry was not going to be pushed around by a dog. If his owner was giving out candy apples, Henry was going to have a candy apple. If the worst came to the worst he could use the owl to fend off Ranger. He also had the happy thought that it might be pretty hard for Ranger to bite him through the folds of a blanket.

"Sit, Ribsy," Henry ordered, when they were in front of the house. To be on the safe side he pulled off the rubber wolf mask. "Sit!" he said again.

For once Ribsy sat. Probably he was no more eager to meet Ranger than Henry was. As the boys advanced toward the front steps Henry noted that the wind was blowing his scent away from the house. He also thought that since he was disguised with war paint the lady would not recognize him as the boy whose friend had told her that only she could prevent forest fires. That was a good thing. "You ring," he said to Murph, as he rested his bag of treats in front of his feet and held the owl in his left hand. This left his right hand free to accept the candy apple.

Murph turned on his outer-space eyes and rang the doorbell while Henry braced himself. The door opened and the new neighbor, the one to whom Henry was so anxious to sell the *Journal,* appeared.

"Oh!" She clapped her hands to her chest and stepped back, pretending great fright.

"Trick or treat!" shouted Henry and Murph, who could not help being pleased by her performance. Henry was glad that the lady could not possibly recognize him.

Ranger, who was trotting toward the door, saw the owl with its outstretched wings, sharp claws and glittering eyes, looking as if it were about to attack. He skidded to a stop on the hardwood floor, turned, and tried to run, but his claws could not dig into the slippery wood. He slipped and skidded to the edge of the carpet, where his claws could take hold. He slunk under the chair, whimpering with fright.

Old Ranger wasn't so brave after all, Henry thought, as he heard a growl behind him in the

dark. Now that Ranger had turned tail, Ribsy was ready to protect his master.

"Go home!" Henry ordered even though he could not see Ribsy.

The lady bent over and looked under the chair. "What's the matter with Ranger?" she asked. "What's the matter with the boy? Come on out, baby. It's just a stuffed owl. It can't hurt you."

Baby! The lady called that ferocious animal "Baby!" Henry heard the jingle of license tags behind him. He noticed that Ranger had heard them too. Henry wished he had not bothered with a candy apple when he already had a whole bag full of things his mother would not want him to eat.

At that moment Ribsy poked his head around the door.

"Why, it's that dog that got into the fight with Ranger," exclaimed the lady, holding out a tray of candy apples to Henry, "and you must be the paper boy."

Henry accepted an apple. "Uh . . . yes," he admitted now that his disguise had been penetrated. He used his foot to give Ribsy a shove down the steps. "I—I'm sorry about the fight and what Ramona said about not causing forest fires."

"Oh, children and pets!" said the lady, with an airy laugh. "You never can tell what little children are going to say, and I have had a lot of pets and they are always into something. Don't worry about the little girl and please don't worry about Ranger. He'll get over it."

Suddenly a word the woman had spoken repeated itself in Henry's mind. Pets. She was interested in pets! He looked at Ranger whimpering under the chair, steadied his owl, and decided to speak up. Now that the lady knew who he was he had nothing to lose, and somehow he had a feeling it would be easier when he was disguised as an Indian. It was almost as if someone else was speaking instead of Henry. "My name is Henry Huggins," he began. "I am your *Journal* carrier. I deliver the *Journal* to many of your neighbors. The Sunday supplement has a good column about pets you might enjoy reading. . . ." Here he paused to catch his breath, and try to think what to say next.

"Well, it's about time," said the lady with a smile. "I am Mrs. Peabody, and I have been waiting for you to come and sell me a subscription."

"You have?" This possibility had never occurred to Henry.

"Yes, I thought you might want to get credit for selling a subscription," answered Mrs. Peabody.

"Oh, he does," Murph assured her earnestly.

"It took you so long I was about to give up and phone the paper myself," Mrs. Peabody continued.

"Please don't do that," said Henry, lest the lady change her mind about the subscription.

"I won't," Mrs. Peabody assured him. "I have a grown son who used to deliver papers when he was your age and I know all about it."

Henry wondered if she really did know everything about a paper route—things like dogs who chased paper boys. Ranger, it seemed to him, was getting over his scare. He had poked his nose out from under the couch.

"Now don't you worry about my dog," said the lady a second time. "He felt he had to defend his property against intruders, but now that he sees we are friends, he will be all right." She leaned over and spoke to her dog. "Won't you, Ranger, baby?"

Ranger peered out from under the couch and thumped his whiplike tail.

"He's really just a lamb," said Ranger's owner.

Some lamb, thought Henry, but he felt that he should try to make friends with Ranger, so he gave Ribsy another shove with his foot and said, "Hiya, Ranger? How's the fellow?"

Ranger did not growl or bare his teeth. That was progress.

"Well . . . uh . . . thanks a lot for the subscription and the candy apple," said Henry. "I'll start leaving the paper tomorrow."

"Good!" said Mrs. Peabody. "I've missed the crossword puzzle."

She did not say one word about having the paper left in some special place, not a word about being careful not to hit the shrubs or the windows.

Henry could tell this lady was going to be a good customer. Probably she would always be home when he came to collect and would always have the exact change ready.

"Good night, Harry," the lady called after him. She was such a nice lady Henry did not want to tell her his name was Henry, not Harry.

"Well, what do you know," Henry remarked to Murph when they were out on the sidewalk once more. "Two treats—a candy apple and a *Journal* subscription." He felt as if a burden had been taken from him. He had actually sold a subscription, and now that he had sold one, he was sure he could sell others. From now on it would be easy.

Murph laughed. "The way that old Ranger dived under that couch! He sure thought something was after him, but he didn't know what."

Henry laughed too. He laughed at the thought of Ranger skidding on the floor. He laughed because he felt good.

"I've had enough," said Murph. "Let's go home."

"Not yet," said Henry, who no longer felt like going home. "Just one more house."

"What for?" asked Murph. "We have more junk than we can eat now."

"Aw, come on, Murph," coaxed Henry. "Let's stop at Mr. Capper's. I'll bet he's giving something good."

"You just want to tell him about the subscription," said Murph.

"Yup," answered Henry. It was true. News like this could not wait until tomorrow. Now it would be safe for his father to talk to Mr. Capper, who would tell him Henry was a good salesman. There was no danger of his father's telling him to tear down the clubhouse now.

"O.K.," agreed Murph, and the boys started toward Mr. Capper's house with the good news.

CHAPTER FOUR

Henry Collects

THE day after Halloween was the first of November. Henry regretfully had to leave the building of the clubhouse to Robert and Murph, while he called on his subscribers to collect for the *Journal*.

Beezus visited the Huggins' back yard and offered to pound nails in Henry's place. "Ramona is playing over at Lisa's house," she said, "so she won't get in the way."

Murph scowled. "No girls allowed."

"Oh, all right," said Beezus, and flounced down the driveway.

"It won't take me long to collect," said Henry cheerfully, but it was not long before his cheerfulness faded. First of all, he started out to collect without taking any money along. He had to go home and rob his piggy bank so he would have change to give his customers. That took time.

As usual, Henry found that not everyone was home when he rang the doorbell. Sometimes he had to go back a second and even a third time. That took more time. One man who was home had only a twenty-dollar bill. Henry did not have that much change, so he had to make a second trip. And all the time he was eager to get back to the clubhouse.

Henry did have one customer who was just about perfect to collect from. That was Mrs. Peabody. She not only had the exact change ready, she had it waiting on a table by the front door so that Henry was not delayed while she went to get her purse. She also had some cookies wrapped in a paper napkin for him. Ranger behaved himself, too. He watched Henry, but he did not move.

There was only one thing wrong with Mrs. Peabody. She opened the door and said, "Well, here is Harry Higgins to collect for the paper!"

Naturally, since she was such a good customer to collect from, Henry did not like to speak up and say, "Excuse me, my name is Henry Huggins." He just gave her the receipt and thanked her for the cookies.

"You're welcome, Harry," said Mrs. Peabody.

Harry Higgins! Henry wondered how Mrs. Peabody would feel if he started calling her Mrs. Beanbody, not that he intended to. Now that Ranger behaved himself, Mrs. Peabody was his nicest customer, and he would never hurt her feelings.

Then in contrast to Mrs. Peabody there was

Mrs. Kelly, who was Henry's most difficult customer when it came to collecting. The first time Henry walked up the Kellys' walk, which was strewn with tricycles, kiddie cars, and battered kitchen utensils, and rang the doorbell, a little voice inside screamed, "Doorbell, Mommy!"

Mrs. Kelly called from an upstairs window, "Who is it?"

"It's me, Henry Huggins," Henry answered. "I'm collecting for the *Journal*."

"You'll have to come back some other time," Mrs. Kelly called down. "I'm giving the baby a bath."

The second time Henry rang the doorbell, Mrs. Kelly answered. She wore pedal pushers and an old blouse, and her hair was bound up in a faded scarf. Two small children followed her to the door, and another was crying somewhere in the house. Behind Mrs. Kelly, Henry caught a glimpse of Ramona playing with a little girl her own age.

"Oh, it's you again," said Mrs. Kelly, before Henry had a chance to speak. "I'm sorry. I don't have a cent in the house. You'll have to come back after payday."

Henry realized as he tripped over an old muffin tin on his way down the front steps that he had forgotten to ask Mrs. Kelly when payday was.

Henry was able to drive quite a few nails into the clubhouse before he got up his courage to go back to the Kellys'. The building, under Murph's direction, was going along smoothly when it was not interrupted by Ramona, who was sometimes accompanied by Lisa, her little friend from kindergarten. They wanted to know if they could have nails to take home. They also asked the same riddles over and over.

"How is a dog different from a flea?" Ramona would ask.

"I don't know." Henry was the only boy who bothered to answer.

"Because a dog can have fleas, but a flea can't have dogs," Ramona would answer, and no matter how many times she asked the riddle, she and Lisa screamed with laughter at the answer.

"What is black and white and red all over?" Ramona always asked next.

"No girls allowed!" Murph yelled at this point. Then Ramona and Lisa would walk down the driveway, scuffing the toes of their shoes on the cement to show they were angry. The next day they would be back.

"Can't you find a way to get rid of those pesty girls?" Murph asked.

Henry could only shrug. There was no easy way to get rid of Ramona.

Finally Henry decided he had to get up his courage to go back to the Kellys', or Mr. Capper would start asking him why he had not finished collecting.

This time Mrs. Kelly met him at the door with a baby balanced on her hip. "Oh, it's you again," she said for a second time, glancing over her shoulder toward the kitchen, where Henry could hear an automatic washing machine running. "Come in while I find my purse."

Henry stepped into the living room, which was scattered with toys, children's clothing, and crumpled pages torn from magazines. There was a bowl of soggy breakfast food on the coffee table.

A little boy who was sucking his thumb and holding an egg beater looked out of the kitchen door.

"Don't pinch your fingers in the egg beater, Kermit," said Mrs. Kelly. She looked wearily at Henry. "Would you mind keeping an eye on the children while I go find my purse? They are all in the kitchen. Kermit, Bobby, Lisa, and her little friend."

"Sure." What else could Henry say? Anything to collect and get back to his clubhouse. He stepped into the kitchen where the washing machine was busily swish-swashing. Lisa and her little friend, who turned out to be Ramona, were kneeling on chairs at the kitchen table, cutting circles out of Play-Doh with cookie cutters.

"I know him," said Ramona to Kermit and Bobby. "That's Henry Huggins."

"Let's cross him out," suggested Lisa. Laughing wildly, the two little girls made big crisscross motions in the air in front of Henry.

"There," said Ramona. "I guess we crossed him out."

Henry did not know what to make of this and did not have time to give the matter much thought, because Bobby started to crawl out of the kitchen. Henry did not know how old Bobby was, but he knew he couldn't be very old, because he was wearing diapers, plastic pants, and a T shirt. In one hand he carried a piece of toast. Henry had never seen a baby drool as much as Bobby. As he crawled he left little puddles on the floor.

Henry heard Mrs. Kelly's footsteps going up the stairs. Bobby dropped his toast on the floor. Lisa and Ramona giggled over some private girl joke. Kermit spun the egg beater and made a noise like machinery with his mouth. The washing machine churned. A dog walked into the kitchen, picked up Bobby's toast, and dropped it again. It did not look as if anyone would get into trouble, but just the same Henry hoped their mother would hurry back. He was a paper carrier, not a baby sitter.

Bobby picked up the soggy toast the dog had dropped and began to chew it. "Hey," said Henry feebly. He was pretty sure babies were not supposed to eat toast that had been in a dog's mouth. Gently he tried to take the toast from Bob, who clung to his crust and uttered a piercing scream. Henry backed away. Bobby put the toast back in his mouth and gnawed contentedly. Oh well, thought Henry, it looks like a pretty clean dog.

Then Henry discovered Kermit was missing. He stepped into the living room where Kermit was twirling the egg beater in time to see the dog lap up the soggy breakfast food in the bowl on the coffee table. "Cut that out," said Henry even though it was too late to do any good.

The washing machine stopped swish-swashing and was silent as if it was resting up before starting to spin.

Mrs. Kelly called down from upstairs, "Kermit, what did you do with my purse?"

"I put it under the bed so Bobby wouldn't get it," answered Kermit.

Henry heard a chair being dragged across the kitchen floor. Followed by Kermit and the dog he went back to investigate. Ramona was standing on a chair in front of the washing machine. She was not actually doing anything wrong, but knowing her, Henry was not taking any chances. "You better get down from there," he said.

"Pooh," said Ramona.

The washing machine gave a loud click and started to spin. Ramona reached toward the lid.

"What do you think you're doing?" Henry spoke more forcefully this time.

"I don't have to mind you," Ramona informed him. "You're just an old boy." She lifted the lid of the washing machine to peek inside. Instantly dirty water and detergent spun out of the machine with a great *whoosh,* hitting Henry right in the face, drenching Ramona and spraying the whole kitchen.

"Cut that out!" yelled Henry, snatching Ramona off the chair and slamming down the lid of the washing machine, but not until the jet of dirty water had circled the kitchen several more times.

All the children were howling with fright and Ramona howled the loudest. The dog shook himself and began to bark. Henry mopped his face with his damp sleeve and looked around at the rivulets of dirty water trickling down the walls and cupboard doors onto the floor. It was a wet, sloppy mess, and there was no time to clean it up. "What did you have to go do that for?" he demanded of Ramona, as Mrs. Kelly's feet came thumping down the stairs.

Ramona who was dripping with dirty water

stopped howling and looked sulky. "I just wanted to see what it looked like inside when it was spinning," she said.

Disgusted as he was, Henry felt a small flash, a very small flash, of understanding for Ramona. He had always been curious to see a load of spinning clothes, too.

"Oh, my goodness!" exclaimed Mrs. Kelly from the doorway as she looked at the wet children and dripping walls. The children's howls subsided when they saw their mother. "What on earth happened?"

"I'm awfully sorry," Henry apologized. "I tried to stop Ramona, but she lifted the lid of the washing machine before I could get to her." He glared at Ramona, who made a face right back at him.

"Tattletale," said Ramona.

Maybe he was a tattletale, but Henry didn't know what else he could have told Mrs. Kelly. She would know the washing machine did not open itself. "I'll help wipe it up," he offered, feeling this was the least he could do.

Mrs. Kelly looked around her dripping kitchen. "Oh well," she said with a sigh. "I suppose I should wash down the walls sometime. No, don't bother to help. You just take Ramona home so she can get cleaned up and into some dry clothes."

"O.K. . . . ." Henry tried to sound willing. "I'm sure sorry, Mrs. Kelly. I'd be glad to come back and help clean up."

Mrs. Kelly managed a smile. "No thank you, Henry. You've done enough already."

Henry was not at all sure how she meant this remark. "Come on, Ramona," he said, anxious to get away.

Outside, Ramona pushed her wet hair back from her forehead so it wouldn't drip into her eyes and said, "I can go home by my own self."

"That's all right with me," said Henry crossly.

He knew that now that Ramona went to kindergarten, she was allowed to cross all but the busiest streets alone.

Ramona went her way and Henry went his. When he came to Klickitat Street he found Mrs. Peabody out raking up leaves from her lawn. Ranger, who was lying on the porch, looked suspiciously at Henry, but did not move.

"Why, Harry Higgins!" she exclaimed. "You're all wet."

"Yeah, I know," said Henry sheepishly. He was trying to find a polite way to let Mrs. Peabody know his name was not Harry Higgins. Then his thoughts began to leap. Mrs. Peabody. His paper route. The money for the *Journal*. He had forgotten to get the money from Mrs. Kelly!

Henry's thoughts were in a turmoil as he walked down the street. He could not go back and ask Mrs. Kelly for the money after what had happened. He would just skip the whole thing and pay for the Kellys' papers himself. Nobody would ever know the difference. No, he wouldn't either. He would never save enough for a sleeping bag if he did that. Yes, he would, too. He could never, never bring himself to ring that doorbell again. Yes, he could. No, he could not. That Ramona! She was the cause of all this. A little old kindergartner.

That settled the matter for Henry. He was not going to let a girl in kindergarten keep him from getting the money he had coming to him. Henry turned around and started back toward the Kellys' house.

"Well, Harry, did you forget something?" asked Mrs. Peabody.

"Yes, I did," answered Henry, managing to sound polite. He was so disgusted with Ramona that he felt like snapping at the whole world. First she had told Mrs. Peabody only she could prevent forest fires, and now this. If she ever caused him any more trouble on his paper route he would . . .

he would . . . do something. What he would do he did not know.

Henry marched straight up the steps and rang the Kellys' doorbell.

Lisa looked out of the window smeared with little fingerprints and screamed, "Mommy, it's that boy again!"

When the door opened, Henry was the first to speak. "Mrs. Kelly, I am sorry to bother you again, but I didn't get the money for the paper when I was here before." He was still so disgusted with Ramona he forgot to be embarrassed.

"I thought you would be back." Mrs. Kelly laid down the cellulose sponge in her hand and picked up her purse, which was lying on a chair near the door.

Henry accepted the money and gave Mrs. Kelly a receipt. Whew, he thought, I hope I never have to go through this again. And he decided he had better make sure that he did not. "Uh . . . Mrs.

Kelly," he ventured, "what day would be best for me to collect?"

"The first Saturday of the month," answered Mrs. Kelly. "That is payday."

Henry pulled his route book out of his hip pocket and made a note after the Kellys' name. "Collect 1st Sat." There. That ought to show Mrs. Kelly he could be businesslike. "Thank you," he said, and once more started for home. Now he did not care if he was damp and dirty. He had actually collected from every single one of the forty-three customers on his route. The job was finished until the first of next month and now he could go back to working on the clubhouse.

"Did you get what you went after, Harry?" asked Mrs. Peabody as Henry passed her house for the third time that afternoon.

"I sure did." Henry was now feeling so confident that he was certain someday he would be able to find a way to let Mrs. Peabody know his name was not Harry Higgins. He would even find a way to keep Ramona from causing him trouble on his route. He would find a way to keep her away from the clubhouse, too.

Henry realized that it was now too late for him to do any work on the clubhouse this afternoon. Tomorrow afternoon the first thing he would do was make a sign saying, "No girls allowed."

The only thing wrong with this idea was that Ramona could not read.

CHAPTER FIVE

Ramona and the Clubhouse

WHENEVER it was not raining, Henry and his friends worked hard on the clubhouse. They measured and sawed and nailed, according to Murph's plan. When Henry was delivering his papers he noticed that one of his customers was having his roof covered with asphalt shingles, and he was able to persuade the workmen to give him enough leftover material to shingle the roof of the clubhouse. He bought two big hinges, so they could have a door that would really open and close.

116

Beezus and Ramona and sometimes Lisa came over almost every day to watch the progress of the building. They stayed until time for the Sheriff Bud program on television, which Ramona never missed.

"I could help," offered Beezus. "I bet I can drive nails."

"No girls allowed," said Murph curtly.

"I could make curtains for the windows," suggested Beezus.

"Who wants curtains?" answered Henry, who would have been willing to let Beezus help, because for a girl she was pretty sensible, but when a boy is working with other boys he sometimes feels he has to act the way they do.

So Beezus sat on the Huggins' back steps and watched, while Ramona amused herself. Ramona never had any trouble keeping herself entertained. She climbed to the top step and began to count, "Ten, nine, eight, seven, six, five, four, three, two, one. *Blast off!*" Then she jumped to the ground.

"I know where I could get an old door mat," suggested Beezus hopefully.

"What's the use of having a clubhouse if you have to wipe your feet like in a regular house?" asked Robert.

It was not possible for Beezus to make a suggestion that would please the boys. "Get lost," said Murph rudely.

"Well, all right for you, smarty!" It was easy to see that Beezus' feelings were hurt. "Mess around with your old boy stuff. See if I care! Come on, Ramona, let's go home. It's almost time for Sheriff Bud."

Ramona finished blasting off and trotted along home with her sister.

Henry was really sorry to see Beezus' feelings hurt, but he did not like to say so in front of the other boys, who were too busy installing the real glass windows to pay any attention to what had just happened.

While the boys worked, Murph began to recite some strange sounds. They were not words, so Henry and Robert had trouble catching exactly what it was he was saying. The syllables, whatever they were, had a catchy sound and rhythm.

"Say that again, Murph." Henry found himself wanting to make the sounds himself.

Once more Murph rattled off the syllables. This time Henry caught a "beep" and a "boom."

"Hey, that sounds keen," said Robert. "Where did you learn that?"

"From my cousin in California," answered Murph. "He learned it from a lifeguard."

"Say it again and slow down," said Henry. "I want to learn it."

Murph laid down his hammer and recited slowly and distinctly.

"Fadatta, fadatta, fadatta,
Beepum, boopum, bah!
Ratta datta boom sh-h
Ahfah deedee bobo."

Henry and Robert laid down their tools, too. "Fadatta . . . fadatta . . . fadatta." They began slowly at first but in a few minutes they had mastered the sounds and could rattle them off as fast as Murph.

"Hey, I have an idea!" Henry was enthusiastic. "We could be a club and use it for our secret password and always say it so fast other kids couldn't learn it."

"Sure," agreed Robert. "All the kids will want to learn it and we won't teach it to them."

"Especially girls." Murph picked up a screw driver and went to work to install the door hinges.

At last the clubhouse was finished. The siding was snug and tight. The hinges worked perfectly, the asphalt shingles were nailed down so securely the roof could not possibly leak. Yes, the boys agreed, it was a good solid house. It was just about as solid as a real house. They thumped the walls appreciatively and stamped their feet on the floor.

And the best part of it was, it was big enough for three boys to sleep in if they didn't move around much, and who could move around in a sleeping bag?

"Yes, sir, solid as the rock of Gibraltar." Murph spoke with pride, for he was the one who had drawn up the plans in the first place.

Then Murph built a shelf and Henry went into the basement and lugged out the stuffed owl which his mother would not let him keep in his room, because she thought it looked as if it had moths. He set the owl on the shelf. It was exactly what the place needed, a really masculine touch.

"Fadatta, fadatta, fadatta," chanted the boys.

"When we all get sleeping bags we can spend the night out here," said Henry.

Robert and Murph, it developed, already had sleeping bags, so Henry dropped the subject. He did not want them sleeping in the clubhouse while he slept in his own bed. Fortunately it was time for him to start his paper route, so there was no more discussion of sleeping in the clubhouse.

Then mysterious things began to happen in the clubhouse. One day after school Henry found the owl's glass eyes turned so that it looked cross-eyed. That's funny, he thought. He straightened the eyes and forgot about them.

But the next day when Henry and Robert entered their clubhouse they were startled to see that the owl, its eyes once again crossed, appeared to be smoking a cigarette. Upon closer examination they found that a small tube of white paper had been fastened to the owl's beak with Scotch tape.

"How do you like that!" Robert ripped off the cigarette in disgust while Henry straightened the eyes once more. "I'll bet old Beezus did this."

That was just what Henry was thinking. He felt

a little disappointed that sensible Beezus would do a thing like this, not that he could really blame her after the way she had been treated. . . .

The boys found a can of paint in Henry's garage and started painting a *No Girls Allowed—This Means You,*" sign, which Robert finished after Henry went to start his paper route.

The next afternoon Henry, Robert, and Murph raced home from school on their bicycles to protect their clubhouse from a possible invasion of Beezus and Ramona. When they opened the door they found the owl's eyes were crossed once more, it was wearing a doll's pink bonnet with a ribbon tied under its chin—if an owl could be said to have a chin—and in its beak it held a crayoned sign that said: *Down with boys!*

"Well, how do you like that!" exclaimed Henry, thinking that Beezus must have come in the morning before school, because they had ridden so fast she could not possibly have reached the clubhouse ahead of them this afternoon.

"The nerve of some people," said Robert. "A doll bonnet on our owl!"

"That's a girl for you." Murph tore down the sign.

"A lock, that's what we need," said Henry.

"A padlock," agreed Murph.

"With a key," said Robert.

Henry dug into his pocket for some of the money he had earned on his route, and the three boys rode off to the hardware store to select a clasp and padlock. When they returned, the owl was holding a sign that said: *Ha ha, you think you are smart.*

Murph screwed the clasp in place, because he was the fastest with tools. While he worked, Henry and Robert decided that because the lock came with only two keys and each member could not have one, they should find two secret hiding places. They talked it over in whispers and after looking around to make sure Beezus was not hiding in the shrubbery, they hid one key under an oilcan in the garage and the other under a flower-pot on the back porch. They vowed always to put the keys back in place, because it would not be fair for any one boy to carry a key when there were not enough keys to go around.

It was with a feeling of a deed well done that the boys snapped shut the padlock when it was time for Henry to start his route. That would keep old Beezus out! She could not possibly get in now. The house was solidly built and the windows taken from the old garage were not the kind that could be opened.

After that the boys had no more trouble. Their next project was painting the house. The front and the north side were to be white, while the

back and the south side were to be green. The
boys did not have enough paint of one color for the
whole house, and anyway, as Murph pointed out,
nobody could see all four sides at the same time.
Henry painted a little each afternoon before starting his route, and Robert and Murph continued to
work after he had gone.

Beezus and Ramona sometimes walked up the
driveway to see what was going on. When the
boys ignored them, they went away, but they did
not go away quietly, because Ramona was always
singing some tune or other that she had learned
from television. Sometimes it was a song about
shampoo, but usually it was a verse about a bread
that builds strong bodies eight different ways.

"I guess we fixed her," the boys congratulated
one another. "You won't catch her bothering us
any more." And when the girls were gone they
chanted their magic words:

"Fadatta, fadatta, fadatta,

Beepum, boopum, bah!

Ratta datta boom sh-h

Ahfah deedee bobo."

All for one and one for all. That was Henry, Robert, and Murph.

Then one cold November afternoon Henry came home from school to find that his mother had left a note telling him she had gone downtown and would not be back until six o'clock. She also told him not to eat any pie. Henry used his finger to wipe up some juice that had oozed through the piecrust. *M-m-m.* Blackberry. Then he made himself a peanut-butter sandwich and with Ribsy trotting after him, went outside, where he removed a key from under the flowerpot, unlocked the clubhouse, and carefully returned the key to its hiding place.

Henry stepped inside the clubhouse and patted

the owl's head. Everything was in order. Ribsy curled up in a corner and prepared to go to sleep.

"Hello." It was Ramona's voice.

Henry turned and saw the little girl sitting on the back steps. She was bundled up, because the day was cold and she too was eating a peanut-butter sandwich.

"Oh . . . hello," he said. "Where's Beezus?"

"Home."

"Why didn't she come with you?" Henry felt that Ramona could cause enough trouble when she was with Beezus. He did not want her around without her older sister to look after her.

"Because you are mean to her," answered Ramona.

Henry felt slightly uncomfortable, because there was truth in what Ramona said. Even so, boys had a right to do boy things without girls around, didn't they? And Beezus didn't have to mess up their clubhouse, did she?

He looked at Ramona sitting on the steps chewing her peanut-butter sandwich. "Why don't you go home?" he asked, seeing no reason for being hospitable to Ramona.

"I don't want to," said Ramona, and went on chewing.

Well, as long as she had a sandwich to keep her busy . . . Henry looked around the clubhouse to see how it could be furnished. An orange crate nailed to the wall would make a good cupboard. He measured the space with his hands. Yes, an orange crate would be just the right size.

Henry was aware that the clubhouse had suddenly grown darker. He turned and saw that the door must have blown shut. Just then he heard a *snap* and he had a terrible feeling. He tried the door. It was locked. Locked from the outside and there was only one person who could have done it—Ramona.

Henry looked out of the window and saw

Ramona sitting on the steps, calmly licking her fingers. "You let me out of here!" he yelled.

Ramona stopped licking long enough to answer. "I don't have a key."

This stopped Henry. Of course she did not have a key. Both keys were carefully hidden and he was not going to tell any girl where they were, either. He could get out some way.

Henry threw his shoulder against the door. Nothing happened. It was a good, solid door. He threw his shoulder against the walls. Still nothing happened. They were good solid walls. Henry rubbed his shoulder and decided that Murph had done a good job of planning the clubhouse. Maybe too good.

Next he jumped up and down as hard as he could. The floor was a good solid floor. The whole clubhouse, Henry concluded, was as solidly built as a jail, and right now that was exactly what it was.

Next Henry considered breaking a window. He looked around, but there was not a hammer or a stick of wood he could use. If he slammed his fist through the glass, he would be sure to cut himself, and even if he did break the glass, the windows were divided into four small panes and he had no way of removing the dividing pieces of wood.

Next Henry tried yelling. "Help! Help!" he shouted at the top of his voice. "Help! Help!" Ribsy stood up and barked. Nothing happened. Nothing at all unless you counted the pleased look on Ramona's face. Where was everybody anyway?

"Huh-huh-huh-help," said Ramona, as if she were thinking very hard. Little puffs of vapor came out of her mouth, because the afternoon was so cold. "Help begins with an *h!*" Plainly Ramona was pleased with herself for making this discovery. Her kindergarten teacher was teaching her class the sounds the letters make.

Henry knew that his mother was downtown.

Robert was getting a haircut, Beezus was home, and he did not know where Murph was. Then he caught a glimpse of Mrs. Grumbie, his next-door neighbor looking out of an upstairs window. "Help!" he yelled, pounding on the door. "Let me out!"

Mrs. Grumbie nodded and waved. She was used to boys playing in Henry's back yard.

There was nothing to do, Henry decided, but try to make himself comfortable until his mother came home. He sat down on the floor and leaned against the wall. Ho-hum. It was going to be a long, cold wait. He felt cross and disgusted. That Ramona . . . that pest . . .

Suddenly Henry leaped to his feet. His route! His paper route. He *had* to get out. He could not stay trapped until six o'clock or he wouldn't get his papers delivered in time. And he knew what his father would say about that. Boy!

The only thing to do, Henry decided, was to tell

Ramona where the key was and to get her to unlock the padlock. That would not be so terrible, now that he stopped to think about it. All he would have to do was find another hiding place after Ramona had gone home.

Henry looked out of the window. Ramona was no longer on the steps. Apparently she had lost interest in Henry when he was silent, because now she was skipping down the driveway. He couldn't let her go. She was his only hope.

"Ramona! Wait!" yelled Henry.

Ramona stopped and looked back.

"Come here," called Henry. "I want to tell you something."

This tempted Ramona. She walked back and stood under the clubhouse window, looking up at Henry.

Henry had a feeling that if he was going to get Ramona to do what he wanted he had better make this good. "Uh . . . Ramona, I am going to let you in on a secret. A big secret."

Ramona, who liked secrets, looked interested.

Henry decided to build it up. "A secret that only *boys* know," he added impressively.

"I don't like boys," Ramona informed him. "Boys are mean."

Henry saw that he had better choose his words with more care. At the same time he had to hurry, because it was almost time to start his route. "Only three people in the whole world know the secret." He watched Ramona's reaction. She seemed to be waiting for him to go on.

Henry lowered his voice as much as he could and still make himself heard through the glass. "I am going to tell you where the key to the clubhouse is—"

"Where?" demanded Ramona.

"Wait a minute," said Henry. "First you have to

promise something." He worked hard to look as if there was something mysterious and exciting about the promise he was about to extract, but it was hard work. He was tired of the game and wanted to get out. Now. "If you promise to unlock the padlock, I will tell you where the key is."

Ramona stared stonily at Henry. "I don't want to."

"But *why?*" Henry was desperate.

"I just don't," Ramona informed him.

Oh-h. Henry groaned. Then he was mad, just plain mad. That Ramona! She was going to make him lose his route, and then he would never get his sleeping bag, and his father would be cross with him, and Mr. Capper would find a bigger boy to take the route. . . . Henry banged his fist against the side of the clubhouse. For some reason that made him feel better. He began to stamp his feet and pound his fists and yell. At least, he thought grimly, this was keeping Ramona interested. And he couldn't let her get away. She was his only hope . . . almost, it seemed, his only contact with civilization. It occurred to him that it must be almost time for the Sheriff Bud program on television, and Ramona never missed Sheriff Bud.

It seemed silly to yell "help!" and "let me out!" when nobody was going to help him or let him out. Henry tried a Tarzan yell. Ramona sat down on the back steps and propped her chin up on her fist.

"Open Sesame!" yelled Henry, just in case it might work. The door remained shut.

Then in desperation Henry tried the club yell, hoping that somehow it would work like a magic spell.

"Fadatta, fadatta, fadatta,
Beepum, boopum, bah!
Ratta datta boom sh-h
Ahfah deedee bobo!"

To his surprise it did work like a magic spell. Ramona got up and came over to the clubhouse window. "Say that again, Henry," she begged.

This time it was Henry's turn to say no. To do so gave him great satisfaction.

"Please, Henry."

Henry saw that he had a bargaining point. A girl who would sing television commercials would naturally like something that sounded really good. "I'll say it again if you get the key and unlock the padlock first."

Ramona thought it over. "Puh-puh-puh-padlock begins with a *p!*" she said triumphantly.

Henry groaned. "I *know* padlock begins with a *p*," he said. "Now will you get the key?" Then he added hastily. "Key begins with a *k*."

"We haven't had *k* yet at school." Ramona seemed suddenly agreeable. "Where is the key?" she asked.

Feeling like a traitor to Robert and Murph,

Henry revealed the secret. "Under the flowerpot on the back porch."

Ramona found the key and Henry could hear her fumbling as she inserted it in the padlock. "Say it," she ordered.

Henry rattled off the club's secret words. "Now unlock it," he begged, and outside he could hear Ramona struggling with the padlock.

"I can't," she said. "I can't make the key turn."

Henry pressed his nose against the window. "Look," he said, "go get Beezus. If you do, I'll teach you both to say fadatta, fadatta, fadatta. And . . . tell her I'm sorry."

I am a traitor, thought Henry, a one-hundred-per-cent traitor. But what else could he do? He had to get his papers delivered somehow. Then he began to worry about Ramona. Maybe she would forget to tell Beezus. Maybe she would remember Sheriff Bud, turn on the television set, and forget all about him.

There was nothing Henry could do but wait. Actually he did not wait very long, but it seemed that way. It seemed to him that he waited and waited and waited. The clubhouse felt colder and damper and more like a dungeon every minute.

At last Henry heard footsteps coming up the driveway. Beezus had come to his rescue—he hoped. Beezus was alone, and Henry guessed that Ramona had stayed home to watch television. "Hi, Beezus," he called through the window. "It's sure nice of you to come and let me out . . . after the way I have . . . uh . . . acted." The last words Henry found difficult to speak, but he felt better when he had said them.

Beezus looked as if she had not made up her mind to let Henry out. "I didn't say I was going to let you out," she reminded him. "You don't want girls around, you know."

Henry had no answer for this. "Aw, come on, Beezus," he pleaded. "I've got to start my route."

Beezus thought it over. "All right, I'll let you out, but only because I know you have to start your route," she agreed, like the sensible girl she was. "But first teach me the secret words."

Henry knew when he was licked. "Oh, all right, if that's the way you feel about it. Fadatta . . . fadatta . . . fadatta."

"Fadatta . . . fadatta . . . fadatta," Beezus repeated gravely.

"Beepum, boopum, bah."

"Beepum, boopum, bah." Fortunately Beezus learned quickly and soon mastered the secret words. She was a girl who kept her part of the bargain. She unlocked the padlock and slipped it out of the clasp. "There," she said.

"Thanks, Beezus," said Henry, as he stepped out to fresh air and freedom. He picked up his bicycle. He had no time to talk if he was going to get his papers folded and delivered.

Beezus did not seem to mind that Henry was in

such a hurry. "Fadatta, fadatta, fadatta," she chanted. "Good-by, Henry. I'm going home to teach the secret words to Ramona like I promised."

Henry threw his leg over his bicycle and pedaled down the driveway. Now the secret words would be all over the neighborhood. Robert and Murph would not like it, but Henry hoped that since they knew Ramona they would understand and not mind too much.

That Ramona! thought Henry. Always causing him trouble on his route. He would have to do something about her, but what anybody could do about Ramona, he did not know. All he knew was that if he was going to keep his paper route and his clubhouse he had better do something, and do it soon.

CHAPTER SIX

Henry Writes a Letter

NATURALLY as soon as Ramona learned the secret words, she recited them every chance she got and soon they were all over the neighborhood. They were all over Glenwood School, too. Everywhere Henry went he heard fadattas and beepum, boopum, bahs. He began to wish he had never heard the silly thing. Quite a few mothers felt this way, too, and asked their children *please* to stop saying that—that *thing*. But the whole school went right on saying fadatta, fadatta, fadatta.

And all because of Ramona. Yes, Henry decided, something was going to have to be done about Ramona, but what he did not know.

"Say, Mom," Henry said one evening, "how can I keep Ramona from being such an awful pest all the time?"

"Just don't pay any attention to her," answered Mrs. Huggins.

"But Mom," protested Henry. "You don't know Ramona."

Mrs. Huggins laughed. "Yes, I do. She is just a lively little girl who gets into mischief sometimes. Ignore her, and she will stop bothering you. She only wants attention."

Henry could not help feeling that his mother did not understand the situation. He had ignored Ramona. That was the whole trouble. He was not paying any attention to her so he had found himself locked in the clubhouse. This was not a little mischief. It was a terrible thing for her to do.

"Surely you are smarter than a five-year-old," remarked Mr. Huggins jokingly.

Henry did not have an answer for his father, who, after all, was safe in his office all day and did not know what a nuisance Ramona could be.

Next Henry consulted Beezus. "Ramona sure causes me a lot of trouble on my route," he remarked one afternoon. "Isn't there some way to get her to stop pestering me?"

Beezus sighed. "I know. I've told Mother, and Mother has told her to behave herself, but you know how Ramona is. She never listens."

"I know," Henry said gloomily. Ramona was a real problem. When Mrs. Quimby persuaded her to stop doing one annoying thing, Ramona promptly thought up something entirely new but equally annoying. If only Henry could find a way to stay ahead of Ramona. . . .

One afternoon Henry arrived at Mr. Capper's garage in plenty of time to fold his papers. He counted his stack of forty-three *Journals* and as long as he was early, he took time to glance through the paper. He looked at the headlines and read the comic section. Then a picture of a smiling lady caught his eye. It was the lady who gave people advice when they wrote to her about their problems.

Because he had a problem, Henry paused to read her column. A girl who signed her letter, "Flat Broke" said that her father did not give her a big enough allowance. Her father did not understand that she needed more money for school lunches, bus fare, and other things. What should she do about it? The smiling lady told her to talk it over with her father and explain to him exactly what her expenses were. The smiling lady was sure he would understand.

Henry thought this over. Maybe he should write

to the lady about Ramona. He could write, I have a problem. A girl in my neighborhood has a little sister who pesters me on my paper route. How can I get her to stop? Then he could sign the letter Disgusted.

Henry tried to think how the lady would answer his letter. Dear Disgusted, she would say, but what would she say next? Probably she would tell him to talk his problem over with Ramona's mother and everything would be all right. Oh no, it wouldn't, thought Henry, just as if he had really read an answer to a letter he had really written. Ramona's mother knew all about his problem and had not been able to solve it. As Beezus said, Ramona never listened very much.

Henry began to fold his papers. There must be somebody Ramona would listen to. And then a picture in an advertisement gave Henry an idea. Santa Claus! Ramona might listen to Santa Claus. Henry grinned to himself. He would really fix

Ramona if he waited until Christmas Eve and climbed up on the Quimbys' roof and yelled down the chimney in a deep bass voice, Ho-ho-ho, Ramona Geraldine Quimby, you stop pestering Henry Huggins on his paper route or I won't leave you any presents. Ho-ho-ho.

"Ho-ho-ho," said Henry out loud, to see how much like Santa Claus he could sound.

Just then Mr. Capper came out of the back door. "Who do you think you are? Santa Claus?" he asked.

"No, sir." Embarrassed, Henry went on folding papers.

Still, Henry was pleased with this picture of himself ho-ho-hoing down the chimney at Ramona, but unfortunately there was just one thing wrong with it. Boys were not allowed to go climbing around on their neighbors' roofs on Christmas Eve or any other time. And anyway, Ramona

might not even listen to Santa Claus. Henry would not be at all surprised.

Henry was zigzagging down the street on his bicycle, throwing papers to the right and to the left, when he saw Beezus and Ramona hurrying along the sidewalk. Ramona was wearing a mustache cut from brown paper and stuck to her upper lip with Scotch tape. Henry recognized this as another attempt to copy one of Sheriff Bud's disguises.

"Hi, Beezus," he said.

Ramona pulled at Beezus' hand. "Come on," she said. "Come on, or we'll be late."

"I can't understand it," remarked Beezus. "She can't even tell time, but she always knows when it's time for the Sheriff Bud program."

"Like Ribsy," said Henry. "He can't tell time either, but he always knows when it's time to meet me after school." He pedaled on down the street, when suddenly a thought struck him. *Sheriff Bud.* If there was anyone Ramona would listen to, it was Sheriff Bud.

Henry was so excited by this inspiration that he threw a paper on the wrong porch and had to go back to get it. Of course she would listen to Sheriff Bud, but how could Henry get Sheriff Bud to tell Ramona to stop pestering him on his paper route? Write him a letter, that's what he would do. Sheriff Bud was always waving around handfuls of letters and wishing listeners happy birthdays and hoping they would get over the measles or something. He was always pretending he could see people in the television audience, too. Henry

had never heard him tell a listener to stop pestering someone, but there was no reason why he
couldn't. It would be worth trying anyway.

As soon as Henry finished his route he went
home and turned on the television set. There was
Sheriff Bud in his ten-gallon hat. This time he was
wearing a false nose. He held a microphone in one
hand, and between commercials was interviewing
a row of children who had microphones hung
around their necks. All the children said hello to
many, many friends out in television land. Henry
thought it was a silly program, although he still
sometimes watched the cartoons that were shown
between the endless commercials.

Ordinarily when Henry wrote a letter he used
the typewriter, because it was more fun than pen
and ink, but today he was in too much of a hurry
to hunt around and poke all those keys. He found
a piece of paper and a pen, and after his address
and the date, began, "Dear Sherrif." That looked

peculiar so he added another *f.* "Dear Sherriff" still looked peculiar so he consulted the dictionary.

Then Henry tore up his letter and started over. "Dear Sheriff Bud," he wrote in his best handwriting. "I need your help. There is this girl who pesters me on my paper route. She always watches your program so could you please tell her to stop pestering me? Her name is Ramona Geraldine Quimby. Thank you." Then he signed his name, addressed an envelope to Sheriff Bud in care of the television station, found a stamp, and went out to mail the letter.

As soon as the mailbox clanked shut, Henry knew his scheme would not work. Sheriff Bud received thousands of letters every week. He was always talking about the thousands of letters he received. He waved great handfuls of them around. Why would he pay any attention to one letter and a pretty smudgy one, at that?

But doubtful as he was, Henry somehow hung

on to a faint hope that Sheriff Bud might really read his letter and help him out. The letter would be delivered the next day but he might not have time to read it before the program went on the air. Maybe the day after . . .

Two days later Henry rang the Quimbys' doorbell about the time the Sheriff Bud program was starting. "Hello, Beezus," he said, when his friend opened the door. "I was wondering—how about a game of checkers before I start my route?"

Beezus looked surprised. She and Henry used to play checkers often, but since he had become a paper carrier and spent so much time working on the clubhouse, he had not found time to play with her. "Why . . . yes, come on in."

As Henry had expected, Ramona was sitting on a hassock in the living room watching Sheriff Bud, who today was wearing sideburns. While Beezus got out the checker set, Henry watched the program.

"And I want all you little folks out in T.V. land to do something for old Sheriff Bud," the Sheriff was saying. "I want you to tell Mother right now, *right this very minute,* to put Crispy Potato Chips, the potato chips positively guaranteed never to bend, on her shopping list. Yes, sirree, this *very minute.*" His smile filled the whole screen.

"Mother!" called Ramona. "Sheriff Bud says—"

"I don't care what Sheriff Bud says," answered Mrs. Quimby from the kitchen. She sounded very cross. "I can make out my grocery list without that man's help."

Beezus set up the checker board on the coffee table and, kneeling, she and Henry began to play. For once Ramona did not bother them, but Henry found it difficult to think about the game and try to follow Sheriff Bud at the same time. They both stopped playing whenever a cartoon came on, but Beezus had no trouble beating him twice in succession.

Once when the sheriff waved a sheaf of letters Henry's hopes rose, but Sheriff Bud only wished a lot of people happy birthday and told how many people had written in to say they liked Nutsies, the candy bar chockfull of energy. Henry wished he had said in his letter that both he and Ramona ate Nutsies all the time. And Crispy Potato Chips, too.

By the time the program had ended Beezus had defeated Henry a third time. Naturally Henry could not let this record stand. "I bet I can beat you tomorrow," he volunteered.

"I bet you can't," said Beezus, "but you can come over and try."

Henry left, and by working fast delivered all his papers on time. The next afternoon he once more presented himself at the Quimbys' front door, this time to show Beezus he really could beat her at checkers. He would forget all about Sheriff Bud. It had been silly of him to think his letter

would be read out of all the thousands the television station received. Beezus had the checkers
waiting on the coffee table and as usual Ramona
was sitting on the hassock watching Sheriff Bud,
who was wearing a pair of large false ears. His
voice filled the living room.

"Ramona, turn that program down!" called Mrs.
Quimby from the kitchen.

Ramona did not budge.

This time Henry was determined to ignore even
the cartoons. Beezus made the first move with a
red checker and Henry moved his black checker.
Beezus jumped him, he jumped her, and the game
was on.

"And now, kiddies out there in T.V. land, if
Mother doesn't have a cupboard full of—" Sheriff
Bud was saying.

Mrs. Quimby appeared in the living room.
"Ramona, turn that thing off. I am sick and tired
of listening to that man tell me what to buy."

"No!" screamed Ramona. "No! I don't want to turn it off."

"Then turn it *down*," said Mrs. Quimby, and went back into the kitchen. This time Ramona lowered the sound of the television set slightly.

"Your move," Beezus reminded Henry.

Henry studied the board. If he moved there, Beezus could jump him. If he moved there, he could jump her if she moved her man in the right direction.

"And now for today's mail," announced Sheriff Bud.

Henry could not help glancing at the television screen. Sheriff Bud was holding the usual handful of letters, but this time he was pointing straight ahead at someone in the television audience. "Ramona Geraldine Quimby, I see you out there," he said. "I see you out in T.V. land."

Henry and Beezus dropped their checkers. Mrs. Quimby stepped out of the kitchen. Ramona clasped her hands together and her eyes grew round. "He sees me," she said in awe.

"Ramona Geraldine Quimby," said Sheriff Bud, "I want you to do something that will make old Sheriff Bud very, very happy."

"Whatever it is, I'm not going to buy it." Mrs. Quimby sounded indignant.

Ramona leaned forward, her eyes wide, her mouth open.

Henry's eyes were just about as wide and his mouth was open, too.

Sheriff Bud sounded as if he and Ramona were alone. "Ramona, it will make old Sheriff Bud very, very happy if you stop pestering"—he stopped

and squinted at a letter in his hand—"Henry Huggins on his paper route. Do you promise?"

"Yes." Ramona barely whispered.

"Good," said Sheriff Bud. "We've got to get those papers delivered. If you stop pestering Henry on his route, you will make me just about as happy as it would if you told Mother you wanted Crispy Potato Chips for lunch every day. And now—"

But no one was listening to the television set.

"Henry!" shrieked Beezus. "Did you hear that?"

"I sure did." Henry was feeling a little awed himself. It had seemed as if Sheriff Bud really could see Ramona. He could not, of course, but . . .

"Honestly!" Mrs. Quimby snapped off the television set. "That man will do anything to squeeze in more commercials. Crispy Potato Chips! Really!"

Only Ramona was silent. She did not even object to her mother's turning off the television set.

She turned to Henry with her eyes wide with awe. "Do you really know Sheriff Bud?" she asked.

"Well . . . I guess you might say he is a friend of mine," said Henry and added, to himself, Now.

Then Mrs. Quimby spoke to her youngest daughter. "Ramona, have you been pestering Henry on his paper route again?"

Ramona looked as if she were about to cry. "I—I won't do it any more," she said.

"That's a good girl," said Mrs. Quimby. "Delivering papers is an important job and you mustn't get in Henry's way."

"I bet I know how Sheriff Bud knew about it," said Beezus with a smile. "Your move, Henry."

Henry grinned as he advanced his checker. Beezus promptly jumped and captured two of his men. Oh, well, what did he care? It was only a game. His paper route was real.

Henry grimaced at Ramona who smiled back almost shyly. Henry moved another checker, which Beezus captured. He did not care. His paper route was safe from Ramona. If she pestered him again, all he had to do was to say, "Remember Sheriff Bud," and his troubles would be over. It was as easy as that. He had finally hit upon a good idea that had nothing wrong with it. Not one single thing.

"I won!" Beezus was triumphant.

"I'll beat you in the next game," said Henry, and this time he was sure he would.

CHAPTER SEVEN

Henry's Little Shadow

AFTERWARDS Henry realized that he should have known something would go wrong with his plan to keep Ramona from pestering him. Now, because he was a friend of Sheriff Bud, Henry had become such a hero to Ramona that she wanted to follow him wherever he went. Next, Mrs. Quimby said that she was disgusted with the Sheriff Bud program and Ramona was not to watch it any more. Not ever. This left Ramona plenty of time for tagging after Henry.

The worst part of it was there was nothing Henry could do about Ramona's tagging along, because she behaved herself. She stood quietly on Mr. Capper's driveway while Henry folded his papers. Henry began to wish she would pester him so he could yell at her to go away. Fortunately, none of the other paper carriers thought much about her, because many small children in the neighborhood admired the big boys who delivered the papers. Henry was always glad to spring on his bicycle and ride away from her. If he had delivered his papers on foot she would have tagged after him.

Then one day at school Beezus said, "Henry, I don't think you are going to like what Ramona is going to get for Christmas."

"What is she getting?" asked Henry.

Beezus looked worried. "I'm not supposed to tell. I just thought I better warn you is all."

Henry did not know what to make of this message. He did not see how a doll or whatever it was that a girl in kindergarten was going to get for Christmas could bother him. As for himself, he hoped he would get a sleeping bag, because he had not saved his paper-route money as fast as he had expected. He had spent quite a bit on nails and a padlock for the clubhouse, and when he counted the money he had collected for his paper route he found he was short a couple of dollars and realized he must have made some mistakes in giving change. This cut into his profits, and after he had done his Christmas shopping he was still several dollars short of a sleeping bag.

Henry was not disappointed on Christmas morning when he opened a big package and found, not a sleeping bag, but a microscope. He could have a lot of fun with a microscope. It was so cold his mother would not let him sleep outdoors anyway, and next month he would have enough money to buy the sleeping bag.

It was not until Christmas afternoon, when Henry was folding his papers, that Henry found out what Beezus meant. He looked up and saw Ramona standing there on the driveway in her snow suit. Henry dropped the paper he was folding when he saw that over her shoulders she was wearing a cloth bag, a small copy of the one *Journal* carriers wore. It even had *READ THE*

JOURNAL embroidered on it in red yarn. Embroidered! It was terrible. In each half of her bag Ramona carried some old rolled-up newspapers. She also carried a battered Teddy bear in the front half. She was smiling proudly.

Naturally the other carriers practically laughed themselves sick at the sight of Henry's admirer. Red with embarrassment, Henry tried to pretend he did not see Ramona. He bent over and folded papers as fast as he could, so he could get out of there.

"Henry, see what Santa Claus brought me," said Ramona, ignoring the laughter. "Now I can be a paper boy like you."

The other boys whooped.

"Why don't you go home?" Henry asked crossly.

"I want to watch," said Ramona politely.

Henry could see that in spite of the boys' laughter Ramona was proud of her very own *Journal* bag, and there was nothing he could do about it, because she had kept her promise to Sheriff Bud and was being good. Henry could see that another of his good ideas had turned out wrong. Even when Ramona was good she was a problem.

Then Beezus, wearing a brand-new Christmas car coat with a hood, came hurrying up the driveway. "Come on home, Ramona," she said, then turned to Henry. "I tried to warn you. A *Journal* bag was the only thing she wanted for Christmas and so Mother had to make her one. She had a terrible time. She couldn't find a pattern."

Henry slung his bag of *Journals* over his shoulders. "Thanks anyway," he said ruefully, as he threw his leg over his bicycle and rode away from Ramona and the laughter of the other boys.

The next morning, when Henry woke up, he discovered that snow was beginning to fall, a few light flakes at first and then more and larger flakes. What luck! Snow during Christmas vacation. He looked out of his bedroom window and saw that there was already an inch of snow on the roof of the clubhouse. After breakfast Henry dragged his Flexible Flyer out of the basement to have it ready, in case there was enough snow for coasting.

All morning snow fell. By noon it was easy to roll up a snow man. The police blocked off a hill not far from Henry's house and all the boys and girls went coasting. Henry slid so much and got into so many snow fights he had to go home and put his clothes through his mother's clothes dryer before he could go out again.

Cars that did not have snow tires slipped on the icy pavement and skidded into the curbs. Some people who were fortunate enough to have their chains with them thump-thumped down the streets as the snow packed down into ice. By three o'clock Mr. Huggins came driving slowly up the street and skidded gently into a drift at the foot of the driveway. He said the stores downtown were closed and many people could not get across the bridges, because the streets were blocked by skidding cars. Mrs. Huggins looked into the refrigerator and the cupboards to see how much food she had on hand, because she could not go to market and there was no telling when the milkman could get through.

The whole city was in a wonderful state of confusion, and Henry enjoyed every minute of it. He hoped it would be days, even weeks, before the snow thawed. Then the mailman, a muffler tied over his ears and his hat on top of that, came puffing up the steps hours late. The sight of him reminded Henry that he too had work to do, and it was not going to be easy in this weather. Snow or no snow, the *Journal* had to be delivered.

Henry dried his woolen gloves in the dryer for the third time that day before he started out, this time on foot. At Mr. Capper's garage he had a long cold wait before the truck that brought the papers

was able to get through. FOOT OF SNOW
BLANKETS CITY was the headline that day.

In spite of the cold Ramona also waited in her
snow suit with her little *Journal* bag over her
shoulders. She kept busy by making a snowman
on the driveway. "Fadatta, fadatta, fadatta," she
said to herself as she worked. When the snowman
was finished she tried her *Journal* bag on it. Henry
hoped she would leave it there but she did not.
She put it over her own shoulders again.

When Henry had managed to fold his papers
with fingers numbed by the cold, he discovered
that this time Ramona could tag after him, because he had to cover his route on foot. And follow
him through the snow she did, about ten feet
behind him, even though walking was not easy.
In some places the snow had drifted, in others it
was packed down into ice. Henry walked as fast as
he could, but Ramona struggled along after him.

A man who was trying to shovel snow in front of his house grinned at Henry and said, "I see you have a little shadow."

Henry was mighty glad to see Beezus clumping through the snow in her boots. "Come on home, Ramona," she coaxed. "It's getting colder."

"No," said Ramona. "I want to go with Henry." She trudged along in her boots and there was nothing for Beezus to do but follow along and keep an eye on her.

Henry threw the first paper, which landed with a *plop* in the snow that had drifted on his customer's front steps. Softly a few flakes of snow fell on the paper. This isn't going to work, thought Henry. The papers would get buried on this side of the street, where the snow was drifting. Nobody would be able to find them. He struggled up the front walk, his heavy *Journal* bag banging against his legs, and picked the paper out of the drift. Then he rang the doorbell and handed the paper to his customer, who thanked him and said with a smile, "I see you have a little shadow."

"Yeah," said Henry, without enthusiasm.

Henry soon saw that it was too much work to wade through drifts with his *Journal* bag bumping against his legs. "Beezus, do me a favor, will you?" he asked. "Go get my sled for me."

"It will take quite a while if I have to take Ramona with me," said Beezus. "I could go faster without her."

Henry realized this was true. Ramona's legs were short and the snow was almost to the top of her boots. He did need that sled, though. "O.K., she can tag along with me," he said, knowing she would, whether he wanted her to or not.

Silently Ramona floundered along after him, and Henry grudgingly admitted to himself that she was not pestering him. She had a perfect right to be on the sidewalk, didn't she? If only she were not wearing that ridiculous *Journal* bag. And if only everyone he met would not say, "I see you have a little shadow."

Once Ramona said companionably, "There is an easy house number. One zero zero one." She was proud of her new ability to read numbers. Henry did not answer her.

It was not long until Beezus came, dragging Henry's sled behind her. He was mighty glad to lift the papers from his shoulders and set them on the sled.

"Come on, Ramona," coaxed Beezus. "You can be a paper boy some other day."

"No, I can't," said Ramona, in a small voice. "Henry always rides his bicycle, and I can't keep up with him." So on they trudged.

The next house on the snowdrift side of the street was the house of Mrs. Peabody. Henry took a paper from his sled, waded up to the front door and rang the doorbell.

"Why, it's Harry Higgins!" exclaimed Mrs. Peabody, opening the door just a crack so the cold would not come in. "My, but you are a thoughtful boy to bring the paper right to the front door!"

"His name isn't Harry Higgins!" Ramona shouted. "His name is Henry Huggins!"

Mrs. Peabody looked startled and opened the door a bit wider. "Is it really?" she asked Henry.

"Well . . . yes," admitted Henry, "but that's all right." Just the same he was grateful to Ramona for straightening Mrs. Peabody out. He felt almost kindly toward the little girl in spite of that terrible *Journal* bag.

"My, I am sorry," said Mrs. Peabody. "To think that I have been calling you Harry Higgins all this time when your name is really Henry Huggins. I don't see how I could have made such a mistake."

"Aw, I knew who you meant." Henry was embarrassed.

Ramona began to cry.

"Come on, let's go home," said Beezus impatiently.

Ramona cried harder. "I—I'm too t-tired," she sobbed.

"Why, the poor little thing," said Mrs. Peabody. "She's all worn out. If I could get my car out of the garage I would drive her home myself."

Henry looked at Ramona, standing there sobbing in the snow. Her face was red with cold and blotched with tears. With her boots buried in snow she looked even smaller than she really was. She rubbed her eyes with her cold, soggy mitten, and sniffed pitifully.

Henry's feelings were all mixed up. He remembered how she had locked him in the clubhouse and what a pest she had been. At the same time he was grateful to her, because she had told Mrs. Peabody his real name. Doggone it, thought Henry. Doggone it all anyway. Why did this have to go and happen? He felt sorry for Ramona— actually felt sorry for her. This was really the last straw. He did not want to feel sorry for Ramona in that stupid old *Journal* bag of hers. He tried hard not to feel sorry for her but he could not help himself.

"Come on, Ramona," he said, even though he didn't want to. "Get on the sled and I'll pull you home."

"I'll help," said Beezus gratefully. She lifted her little sister onto the sled in front of Henry's papers. "Now hang on."

Henry and Beezus took the rope and began to pull the sled. By this time the streets were almost empty of cars, and they could run, slipping and sliding, on the snow that had been packed down into ice.

Ramona stopped crying. "Mush!" she yelled between sniffs. "Mush!"

"Aw, keep quiet," said Henry rudely. He was in no mood to play sled dog for Ramona. He did not feel *that* sorry for her.

"Oh, thank you, Henry," said Beezus, when they had deposited Ramona on her front steps. "I don't know how I would ever have got her home without your help."

"That's O.K.," said Henry gruffly, and retraced his steps to start his route once more. And all because of Ramona. It seemed to Henry that he had never had a worse time delivering papers, not even when there was an extra-thick Sunday edition. Half his papers had to be delivered to the door or at least stuffed into the mailbox. He was too warm inside his car coat, but an icy wind began to blow through his trousers, chilling his legs. His boots were heavy and his gloves were wet again. He was tired, cross, and hungry. By the time Henry had delivered his last paper and dragged his sled home again, it was dark and snow was falling through patches of light cast by the street lamps.

"Henry, I was beginning to worry about you," said Mrs. Huggins, when he had stamped the snow off his boots and entered the kitchen.

"It takes longer to deliver papers in the snow," Mr. Huggins pointed out.

"It sure does, Dad," agreed Henry. "It sure does." And he thought, especially when someone like Ramona lives on the route.

The next day the snow had stopped and the sun shone on a sparkling world. The city began to recover. Snowplows cleared the main streets and by late afternoon most of Henry's neighbors had shoveled their walks. Henry was rested but so was Ramona. As soon as he started his paper route, there she was again wearing her little *Journal* bag. Henry wished all the snow was cleared away, so he could ride his bicycle again. Ramona, still very good, tagged along, and all the people who were now shoveling their driveways stopped working and smiled and said, "I see you have a little shadow." There was nothing Henry could do about it. A line of the poem he had once had to speak in school kept running through his head.

"I have a little shadow that goes in and out with
     me,
And what can be the use of him is more than
     I can see."

Boy, whoever wrote that poem knew what he was talking about!

The third day just enough snow had fallen to freeze on the cleared sidewalks and make them too slippery for Henry to ride his bicycle. Because delivering papers was still difficult Henry and the other boys gathered early to fold and count the papers. Henry was almost ready to start his route when Mr. Capper came around to check on the boys. He grinned at Henry. "Well, Henry," he said, "I see you got your name in the paper."

"Who, me?" asked Henry in surprise.

"Yes, Henry Huggins," said Mr. Capper, opening a paper. "Right here on the editorial page."

Henry could not understand what Mr. Capper was talking about. What would his name be doing on the editorial page or any place else in the paper? It must be some other Henry Huggins.

Mr. Capper began to read. "Dear Editor."

Henry understood that much. Someone had written a letter to the newspaper.

"Dear Editor," Mr. Capper read. "I wish to call attention to the fine work a boy named Henry Huggins is doing delivering the *Journal* in our neighborhood."

"Hey, that's me!" exclaimed Henry.

"I told you," said Mr. Capper, and continued reading for all the boys to hear. "Henry is always prompt and courteous, but it was yesterday during the heavy snow that I was particularly impressed with his work. Delivering papers that day was not easy, but Henry went out of his way to ring my doorbell and hand me my paper so that it would not get buried in a snowdrift. Not only that, he took time out from his route to give a little girl who was cold and tired a ride home on his sled. The *Journal* should be proud of this fine young citizen. Sincerely yours, Bessie Peabody."

At first Henry was speechless and then he felt as if he was suddenly growing about four inches taller.

All the other carriers looked at Henry with respect.

"Boy, I wish somebody would write a letter like that about me!" said Scooter.

"I've been delivering papers three years and nobody ever wrote a letter about me," said Joe.

"Me neither," said all the other boys.

"And Henry is our youngest carrier," Mr. Capper reminded them. He gave Henry a friendly slap on the shoulder. "Keep up the good work, Henry. I am proud of you."

Henry felt himself grow another inch. Mr. Capper was proud of him! He had said so in front of all the other boys.

On his way down the driveway Henry passed Ramona with her little *Journal* bag over her shoulders. She slipped on an icy spot and sat down hard. Before she could start to howl Henry boosted her to her feet, because he suddenly realized that if it weren't for Ramona, Mrs. Peabody would have written a letter to the *Journal* praising Harry Higgins, and Mr. Capper would have thought it was about a carrier in some other neighborhood.

Henry knew he had had a very close call. "Be

careful and don't fall again," he cautioned Ramona. "You might get hurt." Then he started delivering papers, with Ramona following ten feet behind him. Today this did not bother him. Mr. Capper was proud of him, so he did not care who tagged after him. Besides, he was too busy thinking what his father would say when he read Mrs. Peabody's letter in his evening paper.

Henry decided not to say anything to his father. He would let him discover the letter for himself. His father would be reading along and all of a sudden he would see Henry's name in the paper. He would probably be so surprised he would just about jump out of his chair. . . .

That evening it seemed to Henry that his father never would get around to reading the paper. First he dawdled over his dessert and asked for a second cup of coffee.

"Why are you so restless tonight?" Mr. Huggins asked Henry.

"Me? I'm not restless," said Henry, wishing his father would hurry up and drink that coffee.

"I'll carry your dishes into the kitchen, Dad," Henry offered.

Mr. Huggins looked surprised. He got up from the table and remarked, "Maybe I'll build a fire in the fireplace, it's such a cold night."

"That's funny, Dad," said Henry. "I was just thinking it was awfully warm in here."

Mr. Huggins turned on the television set.

That was too much for Henry. He couldn't wait any longer. "Say, Dad, did you read tonight's paper?" he asked.

"I glanced at the headlines. Why?"

"Well—I just wondered if you happened to read the editorial page," said Henry.

"Not yet." Mr. Huggins looked curiously at his son. "Why are you so interested?"

"I got my name in the paper." Henry could not keep the pride out of his voice.

"On the editorial page?" Mr. Huggins sounded disbelieving as he reached for the evening paper. He folded it back to the editorial page.

"There." Henry pointed at the letter.

"What is it?" asked Mrs. Huggins, coming in from the kitchen. She leaned over her husband's shoulder to read. "Why, Henry!" she exclaimed. "Wasn't that a nice thing for Mrs. Peabody to do for you!"

"Henry, I am proud of you!" said Mr. Huggins. "I don't care how much snow there is. I'm going right out and buy half a dozen papers so we can send copies of this to your relatives."

"Gee, thanks, Dad," said Henry modestly. He had waited a long time to hear his father say he was proud of him.

"I'll admit that when you took on the route and then got mixed up in building a clubhouse, I didn't think you could handle it, but you've done a good job," said Mr. Huggins.

Henry was pleased and at the same time a little embarrassed by this praise from his father.

Mr. Huggins went to the hall closet and put on his overcoat and hat. "By the way," he remarked, "how much more money do you need for that sleeping bag?"

"About five dollars," Henry admitted.

Mr. Huggins took out his wallet, opened it and handed Henry a five-dollar bill. "There you are. Tomorrow you go to the sporting-goods store and buy that sleeping bag."

"Thanks, Dad." Henry accepted the bill. "You mean I can sleep out in the clubhouse when there is snow?"

Mrs. Huggins spoke up. "You may not. Do you think I want you catching your death of cold?"

"But the sleeping bag is filled with down," Henry pointed out. "It's nice and warm."

"I don't care," said Mrs. Huggins. "You can't sleep out until we have some warm dry weather."

"O.K., Mom." Henry was agreeable, because he had not really expected his mother to let him sleep outdoors in the snow. He would have the sleeping bag and that was what counted. That, and knowing his father and Mr. Capper were proud of him and realized he could handle a paper route.

"Coming with me, Henry?" asked Mr. Huggins.

"Sure, Dad." Henry pulled his coat out of the closet. Good old Mrs. Peabody, he thought to himself as he put on his cap and pulled the ear flaps down over his ears. I knew she would be the best customer on my route. He picked up the paper to admire his name in print once more, and as he looked at it he could not help thinking, Good old Ramona.

Enter the World of Beverly Cleary

Beverly Cleary was born in McMinnville, Oregon, and until she was old enough to attend school she lived on a farm in Yamhill, a town so small it had no library. Her mother arranged to have books sent to their tiny town from the state library and acted as a librarian in a room over a bank. It was there that Mrs. Cleary learned to love books.

Generations of children have grown up with Ramona Quimby, Henry Huggins, Ralph S. Mouse, and all of their friends, families, and assorted pets. Beverly Cleary continues to capture the hearts and imaginations of children of all ages throughout the world.

Dear Mr. Henshaw

In this Newbery Award-winning book, a correspondence with his favorite author helps sixth-grader Leigh Botts deal with some tough problems—a new school, missing his dog Bandit, a lunch thief, and especially his parents' divorce.

Strider

In the sequel to the Newbery winner *Dear Mr. Henshaw,* Leigh Botts is down in the dumps. His parents have divorced and his dog has run away, and it doesn't look as if things could get any worse. But Leigh's life takes a turn for the better when he adopts a stray dog named Strider.

Beezus and Ramona

Beezus tries very hard to be patient with her little sister, but four-year-old Ramona has a habit of doing the most unpredictable, annoying, embarrassing things in the world. Sometimes Beezus doesn't like Ramona much, and that makes her feel very guilty. Sisters are supposed to love each other, but pesky little Ramona doesn't seem very lovable to Beezus right now.

Ramona the Pest

Ramona is off to kindergarten, and it is the greatest day of her life. She loves her teacher, Miss Binney, and she likes a little boy named Davy so much she wants to kiss him. So why does Ramona get in so much trouble? And how does Ramona manage to disrupt the whole class during rest time? Anyone who knows Ramona knows that she never *tries* to be a pest.

Ramona the Brave

Now that she's six and entering the first grade, Ramona is determined to be brave, but it's not always easy, with a scary new all-by-herself bedroom, her mother's new job, and a new teacher who just doesn't understand how hard Ramona is trying to grow up.

Ramona and Her Father

In this Newbery Honor Book, the whole family is grumpy when Mr. Quimby loses his job. Ramona keeps trying to cheer up her family, but every new idea seems to cause more trouble. Her sister and parents, even her teacher, seem to have lost their patience with Ramona. But when her father tells her he wouldn't trade her for a million dollars, Ramona knows everything will be okay.

Ramona and Her Mother

When Ramona's mother takes on a full-time job, there's
trouble in the Quimby household. Seven-and-a-half-year-
old Ramona feels unloved and starts twitching her nose
like a rabbit, until her teacher becomes concerned.

Ramona Quimby, Age 8

Ramona feels quite grown up taking the bus by herself,
helping big sister Beezus make dinner, and trying hard to
be nice to pesky Willa Jean after school. Turning eight
years old and entering the third grade can do that to a
girl. So how can her teacher call her a nuisance? Being a
member of the Quimby family in the third grade is harder
than Ramona expected.

Ramona Forever

From the moment Howie Kemp's mysterious "rich"
Uncle Hobart arrives from Saudi Arabia, life becomes more
and more confusing. What's so special about Uncle Hobart,
who only teases Ramona? And why are Ramona's mother

and Aunt Bea keeping secrets? Life for Ramona is full of beginnings, discoveries, and surprises. But through all of the happiness and change, and some small moments of sadness, she's always wonderful Ramona—forever!

Ramona's World

Ramona is sure this will be "the best year of her life, so far." She can show off her calluses from swinging on the rings in the park. The boy she calls Yard Ape sits across the aisle from her in school. Her teacher, Mrs. Meacham, praises her writing. Best of all, she has Daisy, her new best friend. But little does Ramona know the challenges her fourth-grade year holds in store!

Henry Huggins

Henry Huggins feels that nothing very interesting ever happens to him. But from the moment a stray dog in the drugstore begs for a taste of his ice cream cone and downs it in one gulp, everything is different. Henry names the dog Ribsy and decides to keep him. And that's only the beginning of Henry's exciting new life!

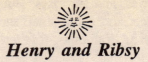

Henry and Ribsy

Henry Huggins is trying his hardest to keep Ribsy out of trouble for a whole month. But Ribsy doesn't make it easy for Henry. What can one boy do with a dog who steals a policeman's lunch and an ice cream cone from Ramona Quimby?

Henry and Beezus

All Henry Huggins can think about is owning a bicycle, especially since that big show-off Scooter McCarthy has one. Selling bubble gum to all the kids at school brings Henry plenty of trouble but very little money for his bike fund. Can a girl really help Henry earn the money for a bicycle? Henry's friend Beezus helps him turn the most humiliating situation of his life into a real business success.

Henry and the Clubhouse

Henry Huggins has a lot of good ideas when he first begins his paper route, especially the idea to build a clubhouse. Henry and his friends don't want any girls hanging

out at their new clubhouse. But a silly old sign that says
NO GIRLS ALLOWED can't stop Beezus and Ramona
Quimby.

Henry and the Paper Route

Henry Huggins couldn't wait to turn eleven years old
so he could have a paper route like his friend Scooter. He
was sure he could prove that he was responsible enough
to handle the job. But Henry is sidetracked by four lively
kittens, one boy with a robot, and Ramona Quimby, the
ever-present pest of Klickitat Street.

Ribsy

Poor Ribsy! Somehow he's gotten himself hopelessly
lost in a huge shopping mall parking lot. Even worse, he
ends up in the wrong family's car. Ribsy doesn't want to
live in a house where three girls give him a bubble bath.
All he wants to do is go home and be Henry Huggins's
dog again. Instead, he's about to begin the liveliest adventure of his life!

The Mouse and the Motorcycle

Ralph only wanted to ride the mouse-sized motorcycle someone had left on the table in the hotel room where Ralph lived. Instead, both Ralph and the motorcycle take a terrible fall into the wastepaper basket, where they are trapped until Keith, the owner of the motorcycle, rescues them. Keith teaches Ralph to ride the motorcycle, and the two of them soon find out that adventures can be both fun and dangerous!

Runaway Ralph

Ralph has made up his mind—he is going to run away. Envisioning fun, freedom, and delicious crumbs from peanut-butter-and-jelly sandwiches, he hops on his red bike and zooms away to the summer camp down the road. Once he arrives, he runs headlong into a strict watchdog, a mouse-hungry cat, and even more fur-raising escapades. Suddenly home doesn't seem like a bad place to be.

Ralph S. Mouse

When Ralph's home at the Mountain View Inn is overrun by rowdy mice who want to use his red motorcycle, he packs up his prized machine and moves to a new home—inside Irwin J. Sneed Elementary School!

Ellen Tebbits

Ellen Tebbits believes she would die of embarrassment if any of the girls at school were to learn her secret. Then she meets Austine Allen, a new girl in class who is hiding the very same secret. They become best friends immediately, until Ellen slaps Austine in the middle of a crowded school lunchroom!

Otis Spofford

There is nothing Otis Spofford likes better than stirring up a little excitement. Otis also loves to tease Ellen Tebbits—probably because Ellen is so neat and clean, and she never fails to become angry. One day Otis's teasing goes a little too far, and now he is worried—because Ellen isn't just angry . . . she's planning something.

Emily's Runaway Imagination

Adventure is pretty scarce in Pitchfork, Oregon, so Emily keeps herself amused bleaching Dad's old plow horse and feeding the hogs an occasional treat. Then she decides that Pitchfork needs a library—and making it happen is the perfect challenge for a girl with a runaway imagination.

Muggie Maggie

When Maggie Schultz arbitrarily decides cursive writing is not for her, her rebellion gets her into trouble. Then Maggie becomes the message monitor, but she can't figure out what the teacher's notes say. Suddenly, Maggie finds cursive interesting. How can she read people's letters if she can't read cursive?

Socks

It was Socks's lucky day when he went to live with the Brickers. He got all of the attention he wanted. But that was before the Brickers came home with a new baby. Suddenly a crying little bundle is getting all of the attention, and Socks feels as if he's been replaced. What Socks doesn't know is that the baby is getting bigger every day and soon he will be joining Socks in all kinds of fun and mischief!

Mitch and Amy

Mitch and Amy are always squabbling about something. They think being twins is fun, but that's about the only thing they have in common—until the school bully starts picking on Mitch and Amy, too. Now the twins agree about one thing, and they can't waste any more time fighting with each other.

Fifteen

It seems too good to be true. The most popular boy in school has asked Jane out—and she's never even dated before. Stan is tall and good-looking, friendly and hard-working—everything Jane ever dreamed of. But is she ready for this? With warmth, perceptiveness, and humor, Beverly Cleary chronicles the joys and worries of a girl's first crush.

Jean and Johnny

It should be the happiest moment of Jean's life—instead of the most embarrassing. Why couldn't she have been ready when the best-looking, most popular boy in school asked her to dance? Instead she is stepping all over his feet and is completely tongue-tied. Despite her family's warning about chasing the handsome Johnny Chessler, Jean has to learn from experience the perils of a one-sided romance.

The Luckiest Girl

Shelley's spending the winter in California, and she feels as if she's living in a fantasyland. Now the star of the school basketball team is smiling at her, and all of the other girls are green with envy. Shelley feels like the luckiest girl in the world. She's about to discover the magic of falling in love—and a whole lot more!

Sister of the Bride

Barbara can hardly believe her older sister is getting married. With all of the excitement, Barbara can't help dreaming of the day she will be the bride. But as the big day draws near and her sister turns suddenly apprehensive, the sister of the bride finds herself having second thoughts about running into love.

A Girl from Yamhill

In the first volume of her autobiography, Beverly Cleary shares the fascinating story of her life. She recalls her early years as a child growing up on a rural farm and later on her beloved Klickitat Street in Portland, Oregon, the setting for many of her stories.

My Own Two Feet

The girl from Yamhill grows up. In the second volume of her autobiography, Beverly Cleary shares with her readers the origins of her early career. Cleary brings to life her memories of leaving home, her beginnings as a writer, and the wonderful moment when she sold her first book, *Henry Huggins*.